THE ATONEMENT IN
NEW TESTAMENT TEACHING

THE ATONEMENT IN
NEW TESTAMENT TEACHING

BY

VINCENT TAYLOR
Ph.D., D.D. (Lond.), Hon. D.D. (Leeds)

Principal and Ferens Tutor of New Testament Language and
Literature at Wesley College, Headingley, Leeds

WIPF & STOCK · Eugene, Oregon

Wipf and Stock Publishers
199 W 8th Ave, Suite 3
Eugene, OR 97401

The Atonement in New Testament T eaching
By Taylor, Vincent
Copyright©1963 Epworth Press
ISBN 13: 978-1-60608-726-8
Publication date 5/5/2009
Previously published by Epworth Press, 1963

CONTENTS

Part One

THE ATONEMENT IN PRIMITIVE PREACHING AND BELIEF

Part Two

THE ATONEMENT IN NEW TESTAMENT THOUGHT

Part Three

THE DOCTRINE OF THE ATONEMENT IN THE LIGHT OF THE NEW TESTAMENT

PREFACE TO THE SECOND EDITION

THE issue of a Second Edition of my book, *The Atonement in New Testament Teaching*, gives me a welcome opportunity to acknowledge the kindness of reviewers and of readers who have found this investigation useful. For the most part this Edition does not differ materially from the First. I have given the most careful consideration to such criticisms and suggestions as have come my way, but I have not found reason to modify the argument in substance. I should explain, however, that I am now disposed to give greater weight to the view described on p. 214, which discusses the relation of the Crucifixion as an event in history to the Eternal Sacrifice. There is great force in the submission that, as the work of the Son of God, the Atonement is not to be limited to that which happened to human eyes on Calvary; although, as it seems to me, the greatest care must be taken to avoid the obvious dangers of docetism. In British ears at least this is the peril of Brunner's claim that the historical manifestation of the Son of God is the *incognito* of His divinity. Brunner, however, would warmly repudiate such an interpretation, and his argument in his great work, *The Mediator* (1934), merits the closest attention. 'It would be absurd', he writes, 'to say: in the year 30 the Atonement of the world took place. But we can say: this event, which those who know history tell us probably took place about the year 30, is the same as that which we know through faith as the Divine Act of Atonement' (*op. cit.*, 504 *f.*).

I desire to express my gratitude to my friend, Mr. John Eades, for his valuable help in adjusting the Index of New Testament Passages to the pages of the new edition.

VINCENT TAYLOR

PREFACE TO THE FIRST EDITION

In this Fernley-Hartley Lecture I have carried a stage farther the investigation begun in my book, *Jesus and His Sacrifice*, which was published in 1937; and for this reason it is necessary for me to explain how the two works are related to each other.

In *Jesus and His Sacrifice* I examined the Passion sayings in themselves and against the background of the Old Testament ideas relating to the Kingdom of God, the Messianic Hope, the Son of Man, the Son, the Suffering Servant, and Sacrifice. On the basis of this study I discussed the immediate implications of the Passion sayings and the more ultimate questions which are raised by them. Finally, with greater daring, I faced the question: In what form may the doctrine of the Atonement be stated when the theological implications of the sayings are worked out? I claimed that this question is not only interesting and important in itself, but is also necessary to the investigation, since the problem of Gospel Origins is injuriously isolated unless it is related to the end as well as to the beginnings. At the same time, however, I was careful to observe that, 'in order to justify a theory of the Atonement, a much broader basis is necessary than that which is afforded by the sayings of Jesus', and that, in what followed, I did not pretend that the sayings demanded the theory presented. My claim was that the views set forth were in harmony with the investigation which I had made.

It was apparent that a more extended inquiry on a broader basis was necessary; and, accordingly, I welcomed the opportunity presented by the invitation of the Trustees of the Fernley-Hartley Trust to deliver the annual Lecture at the Methodist Conference of 1940, especially as it came to me with the request that I should consider as my subject the doctrine of the Atonement on the lines of the concluding section in *Jesus and His Sacrifice*. I felt it right to consult Messrs. Macmillan & Co., the publishers of that work, with reference to this suggestion, and desire here gratefully to acknowledge their courtesy in agreeing to the proposal, although the Lecture is to be published by The Epworth Press. I think, also, I ought to add that Messrs. Macmillan have now published a third work, entitled *Forgiveness and Reconciliation: A Study of New Testament Theology*, in which I approach the doctrine of the

Atonement from another standpoint, namely, that of the Christian experience itself, and in which I discuss, in the light of New Testament teaching, Forgiveness, Justification, Reconciliation, Fellowship, Sanctification, the Atonement, and the Gospel.

In the present book I have treated, first, the place of the Atonement in primitive preaching and belief; secondly, the teaching of St. Paul, the writer of the Epistle to the Hebrews, and St. John; thirdly, the immediate implications of the New Testament teaching as a whole; and, finally, the ultimate problems which arise, and the doctrine of the Atonement which seems to me to be most in harmony with that teaching.

Particular attention has been devoted to the investigation of primitive Christian belief. The idea that the great New Testament writers, especially St. Paul, are the originators of the doctrine of the Atonement, is entirely false. Each depended in a marked degree upon that which he drew from the common faith of the Church, and I have sought to ascertain, as far as is possible, the elements which each writer received and the points to which he gives a distinctive emphasis. I have not thought it necessary to discuss the identities of the authors of the Epistle to the Hebrews and of the Johannine Writings. The second of these problems I have discussed elsewhere in *The Gospels: A Short Introduction*, and in the present work I have referred to the author, without prejudice, as St. John. I have also used the traditional name for the unknown author of the First Gospel.

The discussion of the sacrificial theory set out in this work I shall await with considerable interest. The merit of this theory appears to me to be the extent to which it enables us to unify the various elements of New Testament teaching, the close connexion which it provides between the representative ministry of Christ and the appropriation by the believer of the blessings of His work, and the degree to which it serves the needs of thought, of preaching, of worship and the devotional life, and of practical service in the Christian way of life. The objections to it seem to me to be based upon obsolete conceptions of sacrifice and a legacy of fear received from the rejection of certain theories of the Atonement, especially the theory of Penal Substitution, which modern Christianity has no option but to discard.

In the Preface to *Jesus and His Sacrifice* I spoke of the approach of an Armageddon in which the immense claims of Christianity must finally be tried in the fires of conflict. Armageddon is now upon us and, in my submission, a more virile and positive theology is one of the greatest needs of the Church to-day. The present work is offered as a small contribution to this end, with a full recognition of its imperfections and of the necessity for criticism and further investigation. We are living at the close of an era during which a failure to recognize the serious character of the problem of sin, and an easy optimism, not to say a feeble sentimentalism, in our presentation of the love of God, have reduced theology and preaching to a perilously low ebb; and unless our apprehension and statement of Christian doctrine can regain life and vigour, the ministry of the Church, so vitally needed by the world to-day, is likely to remain in eclipse for at least a generation. The words of Anselm: *Nondum considerasti, quanti ponderis sit peccatum* ('Not yet hast thou considered how great is the weight of sin'), ought to haunt the imagination of the modern theologian, and equally the warning, not found in *Cur Deus Homo?*: 'Not yet hast thou considered how strong is the love of God.'

In conclusion, I desire to make one or two explanations, and to express my gratitude to those to whom it is due.

The few abbreviations I have used will in most cases explain themselves. By *Theol. Wort.* I mean the great work, *Theologisches Wörterbuch*, edited by Gerhard Kittel, the suspension of which, midway in Volume IV, is an unavoidable consequence of the war. In most cases other references are fully given, but occasionally, in quoting well-known commentaries, I have been content simply to give the page number after the author's name. I must also explain that I have followed the example of the English edition of Huck's *Synopse* in using the sign S for Codex Sinaiticus.

I here take the opportunity of expressing my deep sense of obligation to three friends who have been kind enough to read portions of the typescript and to give me valuable criticisms and suggestions, to Dr. W. F. Howard of Handsworth College, Birmingham, to Dr. R. Newton Flew of Wesley House, Cambridge, and to my colleague, Dr. H. Roberts of Wesley College, Headingley. I am also grateful to three other colleagues, Dr. H. Watkin-Jones, the Rev. N. H. Snaith, and the Rev. T. C. Baird, and to the Revs. E. J. Turner and W. Foy, for help in reading the proof-sheets; and to several other students, including the Revs. H. Evans, W. Lillie, N. Richardson, A. Tuley, R. P. Woods and D. E. Wright, for help given in furnishing me with a copy of a considerable part of the typescript.

PART ONE

THE ATONEMENT IN PRIMITIVE PREACHING AND BELIEF

INTRODUCTION

In beginning our investigation, it is necessary to define clearly the object we have in view. Our purpose in Part I is to ascertain, as fully as we can, the common faith of the first Christian communities in relation to the suffering and death of Christ. How did the first Christians explain the death to themselves, and how did they interpret it to others? What were the distinctive ideas which they emphasized, and to what extent can we trace their influence in various parts of the Church? Many of the statements of St. Paul, the author of the Epistle to the Hebrews, and the Fourth Evangelist are so personal as to call for separate treatment; and these will be examined in Part II. Each of these writers, however, shared in the common faith of the Church; and to appreciate the importance and value of their distinctive teaching it is necessary to ask what elements entered into this common faith. We need not suppose that throughout the primitive Church the same beliefs were everywhere emphasized in the same way; on the contrary, it is rather to be expected that at some centres certain aspects were appreciated more than others, and in consequence, received greater emphasis, just as in later times and indeed down to the present day. Variety rather than uniformity, and simplicity of statement rather than elaborate argument, are likely to have been characteristic of the earliest period.

Our knowledge of early preaching and belief obviously cannot be gained directly. Indirectly, however, this knowledge can be obtained from a careful study of the Synoptic Gospels, the Acts of the Apostles, 1 Peter, and the Apocalypse, and certain passages in the Pauline Epistles, the Epistle to the Hebrews, and the Johannine Writings. The period with which we are specially concerned is the three decades from A.D. 30 to 60. All the writings mentioned above, with the exception of the earlier Pauline Epistles, fall outside this period, but each in different ways is a witness to what was taught and believed in the Christian communities at this time. The Synoptic Gospels, written from A.D. 65 to 85, rest on

earlier sources, which reflect the interests and beliefs of the first
generation of believers as well as those of the Evangelists and the
generation in which they wrote, and much the same is true also
of the Acts of the Apostles. 1 Peter, which is not earlier than
A.D. 67, and, in the opinion of many, fifteen or twenty years later,
contains many primitive ideas, and although we cannot always
distinguish exactly between the beliefs which the author shared
with his readers and those on which he leaves his personal impress,
it is a valuable witness to early belief. The Apocalypse, written
about A.D. 95, cannot be neglected in spite of its late date, since it
reflects beliefs which must long have been current in the Roman
province of Asia.

In addition to the writings already mentioned, the Epistle of
St. James, the Epistle of St. Jude, Second Peter, and the Pastoral
Epistles must also be examined. Some of these writings contribute
nothing of a positive kind to the discussion, but their silence raises
questions which must be considered. The Pastorals and Second
Peter are too late in date to be of direct value, but we must ask
how far they contain distant echoes of primitive belief, and, in the
case of the Pastorals, what information they yield regarding the
faith of the Church at the end of the first century.

One point of special importance must be mentioned which
concerns all the writings we shall examine in Part I. Questions of
authorship, while of very great moment in their proper place, are
of secondary importance for the kind of inquiry we propose to
make. What we desire to know is how ordinary unknown Christians in the first days of the faith thought of the death of their Lord;
and, with this object in view, it makes very little difference who is
the author of a particular writing, provided we can date it with
reasonable accuracy, and provided we know that it was a work of
accepted standing in the early Church. In the case of the Pauline
Epistles the situation is otherwise, because here we are dealing
with a writer of marked individuality and creative power. It is
also a real loss that we cannot identify the author of the Epistle to
the Hebrews and the unknown writer of the Fourth Gospel and
the Johannine Epistles. One must not undervalue the importance
of the long critical battle which British scholarship in particular
has waged with a high degree of success for the Lukan authorship
of the Third Gospel and the Acts and to a less extent for the
Petrine authorship of 1 Peter; but it is none the less true that negative conclusions would still leave these writings as priceless records

of primitive belief. So far as the Pastoral Epistles are concerned, in respect of which it must be recognized that the struggle has now turned definitely against the theory of Pauline authorship, the conclusion that they are the work of an admirer of St. Paul actually furthers our knowledge of the development of the organization and belief of the Church. A constant embarrassment so long as we must champion the theory of Pauline authorship, they shed a welcome light upon the dark years out of which they emerge. All the writings we shall examine are mirrors in which we can discern the thoughts and beliefs of men, in some cases not influenced at all, and in other cases influenced to an astonishingly slight extent, by the greatest of New Testament teachers. In its own place, side by side with the inestimable value of the work of these teachers, this fact has a significance and a value which can hardly be exaggerated.

(a) The Synoptic Gospels

The Synoptic Gospels throw light upon the death of Christ in two ways, first, by disclosing in the sayings of Jesus the way in which He Himself thought of His death, and, secondly, by revealing, in the material selected and the form in which it is given, the significance found in it by the first generations of primitive Christianity. Radical critics tend to reduce the evidence to the second of these categories; we can learn much from the Gospels about the beliefs of the communities, but little or nothing of the views of the historical Jesus. Such an estimate of the evidence is arbitrary and unscientific. It betrays an unnecessary scepticism as regards the historical value of the sayings which, in many cases, come from different sources and support one another; it also leaves an unbridged gap between the beliefs of early Christianity and the teaching of Jesus. Further, it fails to do justice to the restraint of the sayings, their comparative freedom from later theological colouring, and to the fact that, fragmentary as they appear in the records, they indicate a uniform and singularly fresh and original interpretation of His Messianic suffering.

Elsewhere I have discussed fully the question of the attitude of Jesus to His death, and, in consequence, what is here offered is not more than a brief summary of the results there presented.[1]

Jesus undoubtedly believed that His sufferings were not due to chance or human violence alone, but were events lying deep in

Jesus and His Sacrifice (3rd Ed., 1943), pp. 254-98.

the Providence of God. His death would fulfil the end determined in the divine counsels, and in this purpose His will and that of the Father were at one. 'How is it written of the Son of man,' He asked, 'that he should suffer many things and be set at nought?' (Mark ix. 12 *b*; cf. Mark viii. 31, ix. 31, x. 33 *f*., xii. 10 *f*., xiv. 21; Luke xvii. 25; John xii. 23, 27, xvii. 1). If in Gethsemane He prayed that the cup might be removed from Him, He also said, 'Howbeit, not what I will, but what thou wilt' (Mark xiv. 36; cf. John x. 18, xviii. 11).

Further, Jesus interpreted His suffering, death, and resurrection positively, as active elements in His Messianic vocation. His Passion was not only something to be endured; it was an achievement to which His life was dedicated, closely connected with the Kingdom or Rule of God. 'The Son of man', He taught, 'is delivered up into the hands of men, and they shall kill him; and when he is killed, after three days he shall rise again' (Mark ix. 31). 'I have a baptism to be baptized with,' He said, 'and how am I straitened till it be accomplished!' (Luke xii. 50; cf. Mark x. 38; John xvii. 19). This conviction was the result of His re-interpretation of the doctrine of the Son of Man in terms suggested by the picture of the Suffering Servant in Isaiah lii. 13–liii (Luke xxii. 37; cf. Mark x. 45). In making this identification, Jesus radically changed the idea of the Messianic office and determined the character of His personal vocation. His divinely appointed task was that of the Son of Man who should victoriously challenge the powers of evil, and should suffer and die, representatively and vicariously, for men. ' This is your hour,' He said to those who effected His arrest, 'and the power of darkness' (Luke xxii. 53 *b*). 'The Son of man', He declared, 'came . . . to give himself a ransom for many' (Mark x. 45), and at the Supper He spoke of His blood as 'shed for many' (Mark xiv. 24). When He described it as 'my blood of the covenant' (Mark xiv. 24; cf. 1 Corinthians xi. 25: 'the new covenant in my blood'), He was clearly thinking of a covenant relationship between God and men established by His death. His outpoured life would be the medium of a renewed fellowship with God.

The fulfilment of this purpose involved a close personal relationship between Himself and sinners and a poignant experience of the consequences of human sin. An experience of this kind was an inevitable element in His destiny as the Suffering Son of Man, and it is implied in His words, 'My soul is exceeding sorrowful even unto death' (Mark xiv. 34) in Gethsemane, and in the cry of desolation from the Cross: 'My God, my God, why hast thou forsaken me?' (Mark xv. 34). In view of the sacrificial significance of the words concerning His 'blood of the covenant' (Mark xiv. 24), and His unique conception of Messianic Sonship, it is reasonable to believe that He interpreted His death, or, to speak more exactly, His surrendered life, as a sacrificial offering in the power of which men might participate by personal self-committal to Himself, by fellowship in the Supper which He appointed, and by sacrificial service in daily life (cf. Mark viii. 34, x. 39). Unique as His thought of Messianic suffering was, He none the less regarded it as a redemptive activity which, in their own measure, men were to reproduce in their lives.

In this account of the Messianic experience of Jesus an element of constructive interpretation is as obvious as it is necessary. It is unsatisfactory to leave His sayings as *membra disjecta*; they must be treated as a whole, and examined in the light of His attitude to the Kingdom of God, the Messianic Hope of Israel, the Son of Man, the Servant of Yahweh, and the idea of Sacrifice. The bond which unites His thoughts and makes them a consistent whole is the sacrificial principle implicit in the Old Testament sacrifices and transmuted in the idea of the Suffering Servant. In the thought of Jesus there is no slavish dependence upon the ritual of the Old Testament sacrificial system, or the separate ideas associated with individual sacrifices, as, for example, the sin-offering, but a keen and original appreciation of the underlying motives of sacrifice, and a readiness to use these conceptions as the moulds for His new and distinctive thoughts. The greatness and the originality of His thinking lie in His unique combination of sacrificial ideas with those of Messiahship and of the Divine Rule of God, into a new and virile conception of redemptive service for men separated by sin from true fellowship with God.

If this account does justice to the thoughts of Jesus concerning His death, it is not to be expected that the fulness of their meaning would at once be apparent to the first generation of His followers. It is, however, a tribute to the fidelity with which the tradition of His words was preserved that, from the sayings, an appreciation of His attitude is possible. What the primitive communities handed down is not this, or indeed any, construction, but the separate items of tradition on which it is based. Only rarely do the Evangelists stand aside, as it were, from the picture and comment thereon, as, for example, when Mark says: 'And he began to teach them, that the Son of man must suffer many things . . .' (Mark viii. 31), or when the Fourth Evangelist comments on the words of Caiaphas: 'Now this he said, not of himself: but being high priest that year, he prophesied that Jesus should die for the nation; and not for the nation only, but that he might also gather together into one the children of God that are scattered abroad' (John xi. 51 f.). Had there been any attempt to impose a doctrinal interpretation upon the material, the results would be visible, not only in a significant phrase here and there in the sayings,[1] but in the form and arrangement of the whole. As it is, the Form-critics[2] point out how rarely Jesus is represented as speaking in the Passion narrative, and sayings which are suspected of doctrinal colouring can be shown to be harmonious with the religious standpoint of Jesus.[3] Doctrine is certainly to be found in the sayings, but it is implicit in the tradition, not imposed upon it.[4]

What, then, are the ideas which the religious interests of the primitive communities preserved? The answer is not in doubt: they are those we have seen integrated and combined in the thought of Jesus. These ideas include: (1) the necessity of Christ's death; (2) its Messianic character; (3) its vicarious nature; (4) its representative aspect; (5) its sacrificial significance; (6) its close association with the ideas of resurrection and exaltation. Its necessity is taught in the numerous sayings to which attention has already been drawn, which insist that the Son of Man 'must suffer'; its Messianic character is implicit in the use of the title 'Son of Man'; its vicarious nature is seen in the declaration that it is 'for many'; its representative aspect in the fact that it is the act of the Son of Man for men; its sacrificial significance in the use of the terms 'blood' and 'covenant'; its connexion with the thought of exaltation in the declaration that 'after three days he shall rise again'. These are the thoughts which were precious to the first communities, which answered their questions and met their religious needs, and which, for these reasons, have been handed down in isolated sayings, Pronouncement stories, and the Passion narratives of St. Mark and St. Luke. Scattered and relatively

---

[1] E.g. the addition, 'unto remission of sins', in Matthew xxvi. 28.

[2] Cf. K. L. Schmidt, *Der Rahmen der Geschichte Jesu*, 305.

[3] Mark x. 45 and xiv. 22, 24 are cases in point. Cf. *Jesus and His Sacrifice*, pp. 99–105, 114–39.

[4] Cf. Sir E. Hoskyns and N. Davey, *The Riddle of the New Testament*, pp. 156–61.

uncombined, they are like the remains of a mosaic pavement which point to an original design; or rather, since we are dealing with living tradition, they resemble individual limbs and organs which suggest a body of which they are separate members. The true story of New Testament origins is not that of doctrinal additions added stage by stage to the tradition of a religious movement of an unreflective character, but that of a society which is steeped in doctrine from the beginning as the result of the original impulse given to it by the life and teaching of its Founder, a society which after His death preserves His thoughts in fragments, emphasizing now this, now that, aspect of His teaching, almost losing some of them for a time, and then in the hands of its later constructive thinkers recovering them, interpreting them, and combining them in ways which set the current for subsequent theological developments down to modern times. This is the kind of development which belongs to an organic process, not one of accretion and corruption, but one of growth and integration. The Synoptic tradition marks a stage in this process, in which the separate ideas noted above are emphasized. In the Acts and the earlier Epistles we shall meet with the same thoughts with interesting but natural developments in certain cases.

(b) The Acts of the Apostles

Although a relatively late writing, the Acts of the Apostles is of the greatest importance because it is based on early sources, some of which were very probably written in Aramaic and were connected with such early centres of Christianity as Jerusalem, Cæsarea, and Antioch. Streeter correctly indicated the value of the book when he wrote: 'What Acts really represents—modified a little by later experience and touched only here and there with a phrase caught up from Paul—is *pre-Pauline Gentile Christianity*.'[1] This estimate of its teaching means that we can use it with confidence as a witness to the earliest Apostolic preaching with reference to the death and resurrection of Jesus. It is true, of course, that it contains no theory of the Atonement, and that its teaching appears somewhat bare and colourless when compared with the relatively more developed ideas of the Pauline Epistles, the Epistle to the Hebrews, and the Johannine Writings. This fact, however, is not one to be received with regret; for it will be

---

[1] *The Four Gospels*, pp. 556. The italics are Streeter's.

found that the views which are expressed in the Acts, and still more the implications of much that is almost naïvely stated, stand in close lineal connexion both with the teaching of Jesus and the theology of the Epistles.

Instead of attempting to summarize the evidence of isolated texts, it will be best to examine the three most distinctive sections, Acts ii. 22–36, iii. 13–26, xiii. 23–41, and to associate with these other important passages which fall outside these limits.

Acts ii. 22–36. This section is given by St. Luke as part of the sermon of St. Peter on the day of Pentecost, but, without entering into any critical discussions of this delineation, it is treated here simply as an example of the ideas current in the earliest preaching. The simplicity of the description of the person of Jesus is in itself a proof that later dogmatic interests have not seriously coloured the record. Jesus is described as 'a man approved of God unto you by mighty works and wonders and signs, which God did by him in the midst of you' (ii. 22). With this may be compared the similar description in x. 38: 'who went about doing good, and healing all that were oppressed of the devil.' His death, it is suggested, was not simply a judicial murder, for He was 'delivered up by the determinate counsel and foreknowledge of God' (ii. 23). This suggestion of divine purpose, it should be noted, is one that is frequently emphasized in these chapters.

Why Jesus was 'delivered up' is not explained, but it is made abundantly clear that the humiliation accomplished in death is only a stage in a wider intention. God raised Him up 'having loosed the pangs of death: because it was not possible that he should be holden of it' (ii. 24). This emphasis on the Resurrection and the Exaltation of Jesus is characteristic of the preaching (cf. also ii. 32, iii. 15, iv. 10, x. 40, etc.). Whatever the work wrought in death may be, it is associated with the present activity of Jesus 'at the right hand of God', and especially with the out-pouring of the Spirit (ii. 33). Through death He has passed to a position of superhuman dignity: 'God hath made him both Lord and Christ' (ii. 36). Already in this discourse it is clear that the dominating conception is that of the Servant, humiliated in death and exalted by God in the fulfilment of his supreme service for men. This claim is valid even though the Servant has not yet been mentioned.

Acts iii. 13–26. Here again we have a second witness to the earliest preaching. In this section the reference to the Servant is explicit.[1] 'The God of Abraham, and of Isaac, and of Jacob, the God of our fathers, hath glorified his Servant Jesus' (iii. 13; cf. iii. 26, iv. 27, 30). Jesus, it is held, has fulfilled 'the things which God foreshowed by the mouth of all the prophets, that his Christ should suffer' (iii. 18). He is the prophet of whom Moses spoke (iii. 22; cf. vii. 37), and He must be given the hearing and obedience of men. All these ideas are broad and general in character, but the exhortations with which they are accompanied imply a close connexion between the suffering and service of Jesus and the facts of human sin. Otherwise, it is inexplicable that such passages as those indicated above should be immediately followed by the exhortation: 'Repent ye therefore, and turn again, that your sins may be blotted out, that so there may come seasons of refreshing from the presence of the Lord' (iii. 19; cf. ii. 38). It is not because of some prophetic word which Jesus has spoken that men are to repent, but because of what He is and does. His work, according to the preaching, still awaits completion; in the heavenly session He awaits 'the times of restoration of all things' (iii. 21). Meantime, His followers are the heirs of Israel's hope; they are 'the sons of the prophets, and of the covenant which God made with your fathers' (iii. 25). To them God has sent His Servant, to bless them and to turn away every one from their iniquities (iii. 26).

Acts xiii. 23–41. Similar ideas are present in this section. Here, however, Jesus is described as 'Saviour'. 'Of this man's seed [David's] hath God according to promise brought unto Israel a Saviour, Jesus' (xiii. 23), and to Jews and to God-fearers 'is the word of this salvation sent forth' (xiii. 26). Once more it is insisted that 'God raised him from the dead' (xiii. 30; cf. 33), and He is identified with the Messianic Son described in Psalm ii. 7: 'Thou

---

[1] In the able and scholarly essay on 'The Titles of Jesus in Acts' in *The Beginnings of Christianity*, i, v, pp. 354–75, H. J. Cadbury suggests that it is doubtful whether the term 'Servant' as applied to Jesus in Acts iii. 13, 26, iv. 27, 30, is reminiscent of the figure in Second Isaiah, or whether it is 'suggestive of the language in which the notable figures of sacred history are described' (p. 369). The point, he says, cannot be settled with certainty, and he warns us against 'the too easy assumption of dependence on the Second Isaiah's '*Ebed-Yahweh*' (*ibid.*). Certainly the word παῖς is used in the Old Testament of Moses, Jacob, Abraham, Job, Israel, David, and Zerubbabel, but the subject-matter of Acts iii and iv renders it difficult to think that it is used of Jesus in this archaic sense, while the references to 'delivering up' (iii. 13), 'raising' (iii. 26), and 'glorifying' (iii. 13) strongly suggest Isaiah liii. There is also a sacrificial reference in the use of the word 'anoint' (iv. 27), and perhaps also in the use of 'holy' (iv. 27, 30), even if these expressions are not found in Isaiah liii. Blessing also is associated with the gift of the Servant Jesus, and deliverance from iniquities (iii. 26). There can be little doubt that the usual interpretation is correct.

art my Son, this day have I begotten thee' (xiii. 33). 'Through this man', it is said, 'is proclaimed unto you remission of sins: and by him every one that believeth is justified from all things from which ye could not be justified by the law of Moses' (xiii. 39). Probably here we have an echo of Pauline teaching, the idea being, as Lake suggests:[1] 'Forgiveness for everything—which the Law never offered.'

From these sections, and other passages in the Acts, it is clear that the earliest preaching is closely related to the teaching of Jesus. The first preachers emphasized, as Jesus Himself had taught, that His life, death, and resurrection followed the path of providential purpose, and gave expression to a divine plan. As Jesus spoke of Himself as 'the stone which the builders rejected' (Mark xii. 10 *f.*; cf. Psalm cviii. 22 *f.*), so the first preachers affirmed: 'He is the stone which was set at nought of you the builders, which was made the head of the corner' (iv. 11), and they went on to assert that 'in none other is there salvation: for neither is there any other name under heaven, that is given among men, wherein we must be saved' (iv. 12). Jesus, they declared, had been exalted to be 'a Prince and a Saviour, for to give repentance to Israel, and remission of sins'; and out of their conviction of the truth of these claims they announced: 'We are witnesses of these things; and so is the Holy Spirit, whom God hath given to them that obey him' (v. 31 *f.*). It is not said, however, that Jesus died to make forgiveness possible; the forgiveness rather is the outstanding blessing of the Messianic salvation. It is received 'through him', or 'through his name' by 'every one that believeth on him' (x. 43; cf. xiii. 38).

Notably absent from the witness of the Acts are references to the representative aspect of the work of Christ and to vicarious suffering, except so far as they may be thought to be implicit in the Servant conception; and, although there are several references to 'the breaking of bread' (ii. 42; cf. xx. 7, 11, xxvii. 35), no eucharistic teaching is associated with the death of Christ. It would be rash, however, to press this negative evidence and to infer that these ideas had no place in primitive preaching and belief. Allowance must be made for the limitations of the sources to which St. Luke had access and for the character of his special doctrinal and religious interests. In particular, and as regards the Supper, it is possible, and even probable, that its meaning was

---

[1] *The Beginnings of Christianity*, iv, p. 157.

not from the first apprehended with uniformity throughout the primitive communities.[1] In short, we need to guard against the assumption that the Acts gives us a complete picture of the Apostolic preaching and of the beliefs of the first Christians. The evidence needs to be supplemented by that which we find in I Peter and in certain parts of the Pauline Epistles.

One important passage calls for attention before we pass from the Acts. This is the reference in xx. 28 in St. Paul's address at Miletus to 'the church of God which he purchased with his own blood', or rather, to adopt the rendering favoured by J. H. Moulton, 'the blood of one who was his own'.[2] This striking passage obviously bears a sacrificial meaning; it implies that the Church is the New Israel which God has gained for Himself by the life of Jesus freely surrendered in death.[3] Such an idea stands out so boldly against the background of the Acts, and is so closely in harmony with Pauline teaching[4] that it is reasonable to infer that the passage reproduces St. Paul's actual words to the Ephesian elders. But if the thought is Pauline, it is not exclusively Pauline; it is probably an element in the common Christian belief of the time, stressed doubtless in some circles more than in others, which St. Paul shared with many preachers and teachers.[5] Isolated as the passage is in the Acts, it is none the less a witness to primitive thought and belief.

(c) Passages in the Pauline Epistles, the Epistle to the Hebrews, and the Johannine Writings

In investigating New Testament origins, it is totally mistaken to think of 'Paulinism' as a closed system. St. Paul shared the most

---

[1] For an interesting account of a development in which the 'Lord's Supper' is held to be the whole fellowship meal covering those aspects of it which later were differentiated as *Agape* and Eucharist, see G. H. C. Macgregor, *Eucharistic Origins*, 136 *ff*. This view should be distinguished from that of Lietzmann in *Messe und Herrenmahl*, who marks off the Jerusalem type represented by Luke, the *Didache*, and the Egyptian Church from the Hellenistic and Pauline type represented by I Corinthians, Mark, and Matthew. See Detached Note, pp. 161–6.

[2] *Prolegomena*, p. 90. Cf. Lake, *The Beginnings of Christianity*, iv, p. 262; also Cadbury's Note, v, p. 372.

[3] The underlying idea may well be that of the deliverance of Israel from Egypt. Cf. R. J. Knowling, *The Expositor's Greek Testament*, ii, p. 437. For περιεποιήσατο, Lake prefers the rendering 'rescued', and writes: 'The original meaning is bound up with the primitive belief that Christians are the People of God, of which ἐκκλησία is another name. God had saved them by the blood of his Chosen One. Possibly there is an allusion to the blood of the Passover' (*op. cit.*, iv, pp. 261).

[4] Cf. Eph. v. 25–7.

[5] See the later discussion of the teaching of I Peter.

vital elements in his Christian thinking with the Church at large; otherwise, it would have been quite impossible for him to say, as he does in the Epistle to the Galatians with reference to the leaders of the Church at Jerusalem, 'I laid before them the gospel which I preach among the Gentiles' (ii. 2), and to claim that they imparted nothing to him (ii. 6) and gave to Barnabas and himself 'the right hands of fellowship' (ii. 9). With complete justice we may use the Pauline Epistles themselves in order to discover the character of pre-Pauline Christianity.[1] To a considerable extent the same also is true of the Epistle to the Hebrews, the Fourth Gospel, and 1 John, in spite of the distinctive teaching found in these writings. Each rests upon and reflects the common faith of the primitive Church.

Many of St. Paul's references to the death of Christ bear the stamp of his personality and of his distinctive thought to such a degree that they cannot be cited as evidence for the common Christian belief; they represent his contribution to the unfolding of its meaning, and as such must be considered later. Among the passages which may justly be cited as indicating thoughts which he shared with others, and which may be accepted as indications of primitive Christian belief, are 1 Corinthians xv. 3, 1 Thessalonians v. 9 f., Galatians i. 4, phrases in 2 Corinthians v. 14, Romans iv. 25, v. 8, the tradition regarding the Supper in 1 Corinthians xi. 23-5, and perhaps also 1 Corinthians vi. 20, vii. 23. In any list of this kind 1 Corinthians xv. 3, 'For I delivered unto you first of all that which also I received, how that Christ died for our sins according to the scriptures', must be included. The words 'I delivered unto you' and 'I received' are naturally used of the imparting and of the reception of tradition. Various Old Testament passages, including Psalm xvi. 8-11, Isaiah liii. 5, 2, Kings xx. 5, Jonah i. 17 and Hosea vi. 2, have been suggested in explanation of the phrase 'according to the scriptures',[2] but it may well be that it is used broadly like the phrase 'the things which God foreshowed by the mouth of all the prophets' in Acts iii. 18. The central statement, 'Christ died for our sins', reads almost like an excerpt from a primitive creed, and it appears elsewhere in such variant forms as 'Christ died for us' (Romans v. 8), 'one died for all' (2 Corinthians v. 14), and 'Jesus our Lord . . . who was

---

[1] Note the use of this principle in J. Weiss's *History of Primitive Christianity.*

[2] An interesting discussion of this phrase is given by W. Bussmann in *Synoptische Studien*, iii, pp. 180-91.

delivered up for our trespasses' (Romans iv. 25). Earlier preaching as well as a written message seems implied by such a passage as 1 Thessalonians v. 9 *f.*: 'For God appointed us not unto wrath, but unto the obtaining of salvation through our Lord Jesus Christ, who died for us, that, whether we wake or sleep, we should live together with him'; and the same is true of Galatians i. 4: '[Our Lord Jesus Christ], who gave himself for our sins, that he might deliver us out of this present evil world, according to the will of our God and Father.' The eschatological note in these passages reveals their primitive character; they represent the things said by the first preachers as they thought of the death of Christ in relation to the End-time. 1 Corinthians vi. 20, 'Ye were bought with a price' (cf. vii. 23), probably re-echoes the saying of Jesus: 'The Son of man came ... to give himself a ransom for many' (Mark x. 45), and is a reminiscence of mission preaching rather than a newly minted phrase. The narrative of 1 Corinthians xi. 23–5 is direct evidence of the wide currency of the saying, 'This is my body', and of the association of the idea of the covenant with the out-poured blood of Christ, a point which is not affected by differences of opinion upon the question whether the more original form of this saying is Mark xiv. 24, 'This is my blood of the covenant, which is shed for many', or 1 Corinthians xi. 25, 'This cup is the new covenant in my blood'.[1] The statement of 1 Corinthians xi. 26, 'For as often as ye eat this bread, and drink the cup, ye proclaim [καταγγέλλετε] the Lord's death till he come', probably refers to the recital of the words of Jesus regarding His death at each celebration of the Supper,[2] and is thus an indication of the close connexion between the rite and the Passion in the mind of the early Church. As J. Denney has truly said, 'the sacraments, but especially the sacrament of the Supper, are the stronghold of the New Testament doctrine concerning the death of Christ'.[3]

As in the case of the Pauline Epistles, statements in the Epistle to the Hebrews and the Johannine Writings can be used to illus-

---

[1] For reasons given in *Jesus and His Sacrifice*, pp. 131–3, I think priority should be given to the Markan form. In agreement with J. Behm, *Theol. Wort.*, ii, p. 136, R. N. Flew regards the Pauline form as the more primitive, *Jesus and His Church*, 99 *f.*

[2] Cf. J. Denney: 'In all probability καταγγέλλετε ("publish") implies that the Sacrament was accompanied by words in which its significance was expressed; it was not only a picture in which the death of Christ was represented and its worth to the Church declared; there was an articulate expression of what it was, and of what the Church owed to it' (*The Death of Christ*, p. 136). See also J. Schniewind, *Theol. Wort.*, i, p. 70.

[3] *The Death of Christ*, p. 278. See also pp. 84 *f.*

trate primitive beliefs, and in Part II this relationship will be
examined in detail. In these writings, however, primitive beliefs
are fused with new ideas to a greater extent than in St. Paul's
Epistles and are therefore less accessible for our immediate.
purpose. One primitive idea, however, is prominent in them all,
and may therefore be considered at this point. The references to
'the blood of Christ' or 'his blood', which we have already found in
Mark xiv. 24, Matthew xxvi. 28, and Acts xx. 28, and which we
shall meet again in 1 Peter i. 2, 19, and frequently in the Apocalypse,[1] appear also in St. Paul's Epistles, in Romans iii. 25, v. 9,
1 Corinthians x. 16, xi. 25, 27, Ephesians i. 7, ii. 13, Colossians 1.
20; in Hebrews ix. 12, 14, x. 19, xii. 24, xiii. 12, 20; in John vi.
53–6 (cf. xix. 34), and 1 John i. 7, v. 6, 8. There can be little
doubt that, in using these phrases, St. Paul, the author of Hebrews,
and St. John are simply making use of the vocabulary of the
earliest preaching and worship, and it is therefore important to
inquire what these terms meant to the first Christians.

In a recent discussion, Johannes Behm[2] has described the phrase
'blood of Christ' as like 'Cross', 'only a more vivid expression for
the death of Christ in its redemptive significance'.[3] It may be
doubted whether this explanation sufficiently accounts for a
term which is used so frequently, and which by its associations is
linked, as 'Cross' is not, with the ideas of the Old Testament
sacrificial system. Behm denies that the ideas of the cultus (*kultische
Opfergedanken*) were connected with the phrase, and interprets it as
a symbolic clothing of the idea of self-giving, of complete obedience
over against God, which Jesus manifested in His death upon the
Cross.[4] This opinion, it may be suspected, marks the revulsion
of the modern man from the thought of blood sacrifices and
attaches too little importance to the ancient significance of blood
as the symbol of life freely offered for men. It is quite true, as
Behm points out, that in later Judaism the older ideas appear
faded and spiritualized, as the symbols of personal and ethical
activities; but it does not follow that the same process must have
been followed in the New Testament period, only accelerated, so
that 'the blood of Christ' becomes a mere figure of speech. In
primitive Christianity the tendency is likely to have been the
opposite of this. Without losing the spiritual emphasis in Jewish

---

[1] i. 5, vii. 14, xii. 11, xix. 13.
[2] See the article on αἷμα in *Theol. Wort.*, i, pp. 171–5.
[3] *Op. cit.*, i, p. 173.   [4] *Op. cit.*, i, p. 174.

teaching, the tendency of the followers of Jesus, with the thought of His death ever before them, would be to discover deeper meanings imperfectly expressed in the Old Testament cultus, but perfectly fulfilled in His redemptive work. While the ancient system provided them with figures of speech, appropriate raiment for new religious beliefs, we cannot with conviction suppose that it furnished them with no more than this. In using these metaphors, primitive Christianity must have discovered important points of contact between the new facts and the old ideas. Self-giving and complete obedience to God may certainly be included in the meaning of 'the blood of Christ', but the list of derivative ideas is hopelessly attenuated unless it also includes the thought of life through death and of an offering through which men may draw nigh to God. The Epistle to the Hebrews is itself the proof that the development described actually took place in early Christianity. The use of the terms 'the blood of Christ', 'his blood', and the like, by the first communities, shows, however, that the author of that Epistle was not making a totally new departure when he developed the argument of his immortal work. He was elucidating, and carrying further, common thoughts of ordinary men throughout the Christian world of his day.

(d) The First Epistle of St. Peter

How far 1 Peter can be used as a witness to primitive preaching and belief is a question which cannot be treated summarily. Whoever he was, the author has left the impress of his mind upon his Epistle; he is a pastor anxious to strengthen his readers against the 'fiery trial' of impending persecution (iv. 12). He tends also to stress the royal and priestly character of the Christian Society (ii. 5, 9 f.) and to dwell upon the sacrificial character of Christ's death (i. 2, 19, ii. 24, iii. 18). It cannot be said, however, that he has an original and constructive mind, and that he is comparable in this sense to St. Paul, the author of Hebrews, and the Fourth Evangelist. He stands more closely related to the faith shared in common by himself and his readers; he is a voice from the Church of his day.

But what day? This question is more important than the allied question of authorship. Indeed, Petrine authorship is practically impossible if the Epistle is later than A.D. 67.[1]

[1] Ramsay, it is true, in *The Church in the Roman Empire*, 279 *ff.* while supporting the Petrine authorship, dates the Epistle A.D. 80, but his arguments have not been found convincing.

The arguments for a later date are, I think, very far from being conclusive. B. H. Streeter's interesting suggestion, that the Epistle is made up of two writings, a sermon and a letter, by the same writer about the year A.D. 90, is offered by him 'with full consciousness of its precarious character',[1] and his further conjecture, that the author is Aristion of Smyrna, is described as a 'scientific guess'.[2] It is very doubtful if one can say more in their favour, and the same is probably true of all theories which date the Epistle towards the end of the first century. Arguments from the state of the external evidence, which cannot be described as weak, do not carry us far, since the enigmatic silence of the Muratorian Fragment can be variously estimated.[3] The relation between the Epistle and other New Testament writings is more instructive. The writer appears to have known Romans and Ephesians, but his knowledge of Hebrews is uncertain, and there is more to be said for the view that James is dependent on 1 Peter than for the opposite opinion. Further, the dependence on Romans is more easily explained if the writer is a contemporary of St. Paul, since its influence upon him is neither deep nor far-reaching. J. W. C. Wand has pointed out that, of the eight passages usually cited as parallels to passages in Romans,[4] two are Old Testament prophecies (ii. 6–8, ii. 10), two give lists of common Christian duties (ii. 13–7, iii. 8, 9, 11), a fifth is semi-liturgical (ii. 5), a sixth depends rather on thought than words (iv. 7–11), and the remaining two are doubtful (i. 14, 22).[5] There is enough agreement to imply a knowledge of Romans, but not to suggest that the writer had 'studied' St. Paul's Epistles or was in any sense his 'pupil'.[6] The argument from the excellence of the Greek bears upon the question of authorship rather than date, and is adequately met by the view that Silvanus was not only St. Peter's amanuensis, but shared to an appreciable degree in the composition of the letter.[7] The strongest objection to the early date is based on the references to persecution in iv. 12–16, and

---

[1] *The Primitive Church*, p. 122.   [2] *Op. cit.*, p. 130.

[3] Cf. Moffatt, *Introduction to the Literature of the New Testament*, p. 337.

[4] See the list in Sanday and Headlam, *I.C.C., Romans*, pp. lxxiv–vi.

[5] *The General Epistles of St. Peter and St. Jude* (Westminster Commentaries), p. 19.

[6] Cf. E. F. Scott, *The Literature of the New Testament*, p. 220.

[7] Cf. J. H. Moulton, *Grammar*, ii, pp. 25 *f.* See v. 12: 'By Silvanus, our faithful brother, as I account him, I have written unto you.' Protest should be made against the cavalier manner in which this argument is often treated. See the comments of J. W. C. Wand, *op. cit.*, pp. 29 *f.*, and the invaluable report of the Hellenistic Seminar of Manchester University (H. G. Meecham, *Expository Times*, xlviii, pp. 22–4).

especially to the possibility of suffering for the name 'Christian',[1] but there is no need to date the letter during the reign of Trajan (A.D. 98–117) or of Domitian (A.D. 81–96) on this account, especially in view of the favourable attitude to the State implied in ii. 13–17 and the strong and detailed references to persecution in Mark xiii. 9–13 which are not later than c. A.D. 65. The objection that the Neronic persecution did not extend to the Empire is pointless, since actual martyrdom is not implied by the Epistle, while iv. 12 implies the sudden emergence of a new peril, the results of which are not yet known. The situation is exactly that which might be contemplated by one who saw the beginnings of Nero's persecution at Rome.[2]

We need not hesitate, therefore, to use 1 Peter as indicating the common mind of the Roman Church in respect of the death of Christ in the second generation of primitive Christianity.[3] No doubt we must allow for the author's personal emphasis, but, in view of the absence of anything which might be described as a constructive representation of the doctrine, we may reasonably assume that the ideas which he expresses are those which he shared with others in the circles in which he moved.

What, then, are the primitive Christian ideas revealed by 1 Peter?

It may be of some interest to compare the ideas we have already found in the Synoptic tradition with those present in 1 Peter. The necessity of Christ's death is not emphasized in this Epistle, although the thought of a divine purpose is implicit in the description of Christ, immediately after a reference to His blood, in the words: 'who was foreknown indeed before the foundation of the world, but was manifested at the end of the times for your sake' (i. 20). Its Messianic character also is not stressed, although Hort[4] renders τὰ εἰς Χριστὸν παθήματα 'the sufferings destined for Messiah' (i. 11). The writer's interest is rather in the thought of

---

[1] Cf. iv. 16: 'But if a man suffer as a Christian, let him not be ashamed, but let him glorify God in this name.'

[2] This is the view held, among others, by Wand, op. cit., pp. 16 f.; McNeile, Introduction to the New Testament, p. 212; Peake, A Critical Introduction to the New Testament, pp. 94 f.; Moffatt, Introduction to the Literature of the New Testament, p. 339; Hort, The First Epistle of St. Peter, pp. 1–5; Bigg, I.C.C., St. Peter and St. Jude (A.D. 58–64), p. 87.

[3] J. Weiss, who dates the Epistle A.D. 81–90, speaks of it as giving 'only a faded picture of conditions in the primitive community' (The History of Primitive Christianity, p. 805). Even as such, the evidence of 1 Peter would be valuable, but, obviously, its value is much greater if, as we have argued above, its date is c. A.D. 67.

[4] The First Epistle of St. Peter, p. 54. Cf. i. 19; op. cit., p. 78.

Christ as the Suffering Servant, for, although he does not use the term, the ideas of Isaiah liii are plainly visible in the description of Christ as one 'who did no sin, neither was guile found in his mouth: who when he was reviled, reviled not again; when he suffered, threatened not; but committed himself to him that judgeth righteously' (ii. 23); and also, though not exclusively, in the words: 'who his own self bare our sins in his body' (ii. 24; cf. Isaiah liii. 12). The vicarious aspect of Christ's death, implied in Mark x. 45 and xiv. 24, is expressed by the phrases 'for your sake' (i. 20), 'for you' (ii. 21), and 'our sins' (ii. 24); its representative character is also indicated by these expressions and is quite unambiguously described in the words: 'who his own self bare our sins in his body upon the tree' (ii. 24), and in the statement that He 'suffered for sins once, the righteous for the unrighteous' (iii. 18). Beyond question a 'sin-bearer' fulfils a representative function, whatever the precise nature of the action may be.

Over and above these contacts with Mark is the agreement in the sacrificial interpretation of the death of Christ which is so distinctive of 1 Peter. In i. 18 f., with a possible dependence on Mark x. 45,[1] the readers of the Epistle are reminded that they were 'redeemed [ἐλυτρώθητε], not with corruptible things, with silver or gold, from your vain manner of life handed down from your fathers; but with precious blood, as of a lamb without blemish and without spot, even the blood of Christ'.[2] If the word 'redeemed' stood alone, it might be sufficient to interpret the passage of a costly deliverance from an evil manner of life;[3] but the reference to 'precious blood', which is further described as that of 'a lamb without blemish and without spot', implies a background of sacrificial thought. Almost certainly the Passover Lamb is in mind,[4] for although in the narrative of Exodus xii the blood is a sign to the destroyer, in later Jewish thought it was

---

[1] Cf. Hort, op. cit., p. 78; Denney, The Death of Christ, p. 92. Windisch says that, while the idea is kindred to that of St. Paul, it need not be dependent on his teaching or writings, H.Z.N.T., Die katholischen Briefe, p. 57. Cf. Werner, Der Einfluss paulinischer Theologie im Markus-evangelium, pp. 60 ff.

[2] The phrase 'of Christ' depends either on 'blood' (R.V.) or is in apposition with 'lamb' or, again, with the following participle, forms a genitive absolute. Cf. Wand, op. cit., p. 56.

[3] λυτροῦσθαι is used in the Septuagint of the redemption of possessions (Leviticus xxv. 25–8), of deliverance from enemies (Psalm cvii. 2), from sin (Psalm cxxx. 8), from death (Hosea xiii. 14), and especially of the deliverance of Israel from Egypt (Exodus vi. 6; Deuteronomy vii. 8, etc.), and of the exiles from Babylon (Isaiah xli. 14, xliii. 1, 14). Cf. Westcott, The Epistle to the Hebrews, pp. 295 f.; Hort, op. cit., p. 75.

[4] Cf. Windisch, op. cit., p. 57; Wand, op. cit., p. 56; Hort, op. cit., p. 79.

interpreted as 'covenant-blood'.[1] Confirmation of this estimate of i. 18 *f.* is supplied by the phrase, 'unto obedience and sprinkling of the blood of Jesus Christ', in i. 2. Here the association of the ideas of 'obedience' and 'sprinkling' points irresistibly to the narrative of Exodus xxiv. 1–8, where the people, on promising to obey, are sprinkled with the blood of the covenant sacrifice.[2] Both i. 2 and i. 18 *f.*, therefore, are in fundamental agreement with Mark xiv. 24, where the phrase, 'my blood of the covenant', must also be interpreted in the light of Exodus xxiv. 8.[3] The Petrine passages, together with Mark xiv. 24, show that at Rome the death of Jesus was interpreted as establishing a covenant relationship with God, in virtue of His dedicated and freely surrendered life for men.

It must not be supposed that 1 Peter limits the interpretation of Christ's death to the significance of any one sacrifice. The phrase 'for sins' in iii. 18 suggests that the sin-offering is in mind; but there is nothing in the Epistle to indicate that any exclusive significance is attached to this particular sacrifice. A contrast, indeed, may be suggested by the word 'once' in the statement: 'Christ also suffered for sins once, the righteous for the unrighteous'; but the main thought is that Christ has fulfilled a representative and sacrificial act related to sins. How little primitive Christian thought is limited by the suggestiveness of individual Levitical rites is revealed by ii. 24, 'who his own self bare our sins in his body upon the tree', where the language inevitably recalls that of Isaiah liii. 12, 'he bare the sin of many', while the thought is actually much closer to the narrative of the scapegoat in Leviticus xvi.[4] In this combination of ideas the passage recalls John i. 29: 'Behold, the Lamb of God, which taketh away the sin of the world!'[5] In the opinion of many commentators,[6] the Cross is conceived in 1 Peter ii. 24 as an altar, but it may be doubted if this idea appears anywhere in the New Testament,[7] and the thought

---

[1] Cf. J. Jeremias, *Die Abendmahlsworte Jesu*, pp. 80 *f.*; Hort, *op. cit.*, p. 79.
[2] Cf. Windisch, *op. cit.*, p. 52; Wand, *op. cit.*, pp. 39 *f.*; Hort, *op. cit.*, pp. 23–5; Denney, *op. cit.*, p. 90.
[3] Cf. *Jesus and His Sacrifice*, pp. 136 *f.*
[4] Windisch points out that for the author it is less a question of forgiveness than of the putting aside of sin. He suggests that the words, 'who his own self . . . in his body', stand in contrast to the act of the high priest who consigns the sins of the people to the scapegoat (Leviticus xvi. 21 *f.*)—*op. cit.*, p. 65.
[5] Cf. *Jesus and His Sacrifice*, pp. 225–8.
[6] Alford, *The Greek Testament*, iv, p. 355; Bigg, *op. cit.*, pp. 147 *f.*; Wand, *op. cit.*, p. 83.
[7] Not even in Hebrews xiii. 10. See later, pp. 105–10.

of sin as slain by the offering of a sinless victim is entirely foreign to Old Testament conceptions of sacrifice.[1] The meaning, suggested by such passages as Numbers xiv. 33, Leviticus v. 17, and Exodus xxviii. 43, is that Christ bore in His person the consequences of human sin up to, or as far as,[2] the Cross, and that His death is the offering of Himself for men. The real difficulty of the passage, as Bigg has observed, 'lies in the number of allusions which St. Peter has crowded into one short phrase',[3] and which, we may add, he has not worked out to the extent visible in the writings of St. Paul and the Epistle to the Hebrews. What we see in 1 Peter is the ferment of primitive Christian thought rather than the reflections of an individual teacher. In order to express the meaning of Christ's death, it draws upon underlying ideas of the sacrificial system, rather than the special associations of any one rite, and combines them with other ideas, such as those of imitation and of sin-bearing, which have no place in that system. In this respect it resembles the thought and teaching of Jesus Himself, except that it is popular and derivative rather than original and creative.

In addition to the characteristics already described reference must also be made to the emphasis laid upon the sufferings of Christ. The writer prefers to say that He 'suffered' rather than that He 'died'. He describes himself as 'a witness of the sufferings of Christ' (v. 1), and speaks of his readers as 'partakers of Christ's sufferings' (iv. 13). 'Christ also suffered for you' (ii. 21), and 'for sins' (iii. 18), he reminds them; and he exhorts them to arm themselves with the same mind, 'forasmuch as Christ suffered in the flesh' (iv. 1). He has left them an 'example' (ὑπογραμμόν), that, in this respect, they should 'follow his steps' (ii. 21). No doubt this teaching represents a special interest of the writer, due to the fact that many of his readers were slaves exposed to oppression. None the less, in these exhortations he is reflecting a primitive Christian tendency. The first Christians were profoundly impressed by the patience and innocence of Jesus, as the Passion narratives so clearly show. Many passages in the Epistles reveal the same interest. The Thessalonians are reminded that they became imitators of the Lord, 'having received the word in much affliction' (1 Thessalonians i. 6), and St. Paul prays that their hearts may be

---

[1] 'That which is slain at the altar is always regarded as a gift acceptable to God: the slaying is only the method in which it is irrevocably made His; and nothing is more perverse than the attempt to present sin in this light' (Denney, *op. cit.*, p. 96).

[2] Cf. R.V., marg.: 'carried up . . . to the tree'.   [3] *Op. cit.*, p. 148.

directed 'into the love of God, and into the patience of Christ' (2 Thessalonians iii. 5). In Philippians ii. 5 the sublime passage on the humiliation and exaltation of Christ is preceded by the exhortation: 'Have this mind in you, which was also in Christ Jesus'; and in Hebrews xii. 2 the injunction to run with patience the appointed race is followed by the picture of Jesus, 'who for the joy that was set before him endured the cross, despising shame, and hath sat down at the right hand of the throne of God'. There can be no doubt, then, that when the author of 1 Peter speaks of the 'example' of Christ's suffering, he is expressing a thought highly prized among the first followers of Jesus; and 1 Clement xvi[1] shows its vitality in the period which followed. The emphasis is ethical. In 1 Peter iv. 13 the idea of being 'partakers' of Christ's sufferings is not mystical, but concrete and practical: it has no analogy to the Pauline idea of dying with Christ. The readers are to be patient as He was. There is no suggestion of opposition or resistance to their oppressors. The saying in Luke xxi. 19, 'In your endurance ye shall win your souls', is entirely in harmony with this teaching.

The purpose of Christ's suffering is defined in terms which are both ethical and religious. Christ suffered for sins, 'that he might bring us to God' (iii. 18). The verb προσάγω here used has the suggestion of dignity, and while it is too much to say that it describes the action of the high priest in entering within the veil, or the presentation by Moses of Aaron and his sons (Exodus xxix), it certainly calls to mind the act of a mediator who brings or 'conducts' men to God.[2] In ii. 24 the purpose of the sin-bearing of Christ is 'that we, having died unto sins, might live unto righteousness', and to this statement the pregnant words are added: 'by whose stripes ye were healed'. Here again we receive the impression of great ideas current in primitive Christianity which have not yet been worked out. Windisch is entirely justified in saying that the ideas remind us of St. Paul, but are none the less originally formed, so that once more theological or even literary dependence

---

[1] 'The sceptre of the majesty of God, even our Lord Jesus Christ, came not in the pomp of arrogance or of pride, though He might have done so, but in lowliness of mind.' Isaiah liii is then quoted in full and Psalm xxii. 6–8. Clement then continues: 'Ye see, dearly beloved, what is the pattern that hath been given to us; for, if the Lord was thus lowly of mind, what should we do, who through Him have been brought under the yoke of His grace?' Cf. also Ignatius, *Ep. Eph.*, x, 3.

[2] The interpretation favoured by Wand, p. 100, of an official conducting of courtiers before the King, does not suit the tone of the passage as a whole. See the comments of Denney on the passage, *op. cit.*, pp. 101–4.

upon him cannot be proved.[1] The word translated 'having died' (ἀπογενόμενοι) means 'having ceased' or 'departed from'.[2] There is thus only an apparent parallel to the Pauline idea of dying to sin, but full agreement in the positive claim that the end in view in the suffering of Christ is life lived in obedience to righteousness and complete healing through His redemptive ministry. The basic idea of the Petrine passage, and, in particular, the words, 'by whose stripes ye were healed', is the thought of a divine representative. Primitive Christianity already held this thought, apart altogether from the teaching of St. 'Paul, even as, in varying forms, it has retained it down to the present day. In 1 Peter, however, it lies, as it were, in solution, waiting to be developed; all that we can see are faint shapes slowly emerging and destined to be the symbols of subsequent Christian thinking.

From what has been said above, it will be seen how important 1 Peter is as a witness to primitive Christian belief concerning the death of Christ. Its importance is even greater if, as Windisch has suggested, i. 18–21, ii. 21–5, and iii. 18–22 are early Christian hymns, for these are the passages in which the soteriological teaching of the Epistle is found. Windisch[3] maintains that they are *Christuslieder*, loosely attached to their present context, and marked by a definite poetic structure. The last of the three is a baptismal hymn (*Taufhymnus*), perhaps originally sung, as Wand[4] suggests, at the celebration of that sacrament. This suggestion deserves closer study, for, if the claim of Windisch is sound, the testimony of these passages to primitive belief is not seriously affected by the acceptance of the later date for the composition of the Epistle. If, however, as we have argued, the date is *c.* A.D. 67, these hymns may come from the fifties and, in view of their associations with worship, may incorporate communal beliefs which are earlier still. In any case, their doctrinal ideas are not simply those of an individual writer, however eminent, but those of a primitive community.

In passing from this section, it will be useful to note some of the ideas which are either wanting in 1 Peter or receive only a rudimentary expression:

(1) First among these is the small extent to which the resurrection is related to the atoning work of Christ, despite its prominence

[1] *Op. cit.*, p. 66.
[2] Cf. Moulton and Milligan, *The Vocabulary of the Greek Testament*, p. 59.
[3] *Op. cit.*, pp. 65, 70. Cf. Wand, *op. cit.*, pp. 81, 99 *f.*
[4] *Op. cit.*, p. 100.

in Petrine thought (cf. i. 3, 21, iii. 21).[1] Only in i. 21 does it appear in a soteriological passage; and here it is appended to, rather than integrated with, the statement about redemption, in a reference to the faith of the readers in God: 'who through him [Christ] are believers in God, which raised him from the dead, and gave him glory; so that your faith and hope might be in God'. The suggestion may be hazarded that it is the acceptance of the myth of the descent into Hades[2] which has interposed a gap in the writer's thought between the death of Christ and His resurrection. Some support is given to this suggestion by the fact that, after speaking of the suffering of Christ in iii. 18 a, he fills the place we should expect to be occupied by a reference to the resurrection with the words: 'quickened in the spirit', which prepare the way for the reference to the descent. Only after the later allusion to baptism comes the reference to the resurrection and the session on high in the words: 'through the resurrection of Jesus Christ; who is on the right hand of God, having gone into heaven; angels and authorities and powers being made subject to him' (iii. 21 f.).

(2) A second notable omission is the absence of eucharistic teaching in 1 Peter, which is all the more surprising because of its sacrificial emphasis and the evidence, furnished by the form of Mark xiv. 22–5, that the importance of the Supper was highly esteemed in Rome. One sees from this Markan passage, not to speak of the Apostolic practice of communicating the tradition implied by 1 Corinthians xi. 23–5,[3] how mischievous the argument *ex silentio* can be. The true significance of the silence of 1 Peter, and of many other New Testament writings, is that the meaning of the Supper could not be fully appreciated in the primitive Church until a larger understanding of the Sacrifice of Christ had been reached in early Christianity.

(3) Perhaps the most important element wanting in 1 Peter is teaching about faith in relation to Christ as Redeemer and Saviour. The one reference to faith is in i. 21 in the words, 'believers in God', and 'so that your faith and hope might be in God'. The explanation must be as before: that it is only when the theological implications of Christ's atoning work are carried to a

---

[1] See also the allusions to the Resurrection in the speeches of Peter in the Acts.

[2] In view of the weighty objections of A. S. Peake, *Commentary*, p. 911, it is difficult to accept the brilliant suggestion of J. Rendel Harris, *Expositor*, vi, 4, pp. 346 ff., that the name Ἐνώχ has dropped out of the text of iii. 19 after ἐν ᾧ καί. Cf. Windisch, *op. cit.*, p. 71.

[3] 'For I received of the Lord that which also I delivered unto you. . . .'

point transcending that reached in 1 Peter, that faith mounts from confidence and trust in God to faith union with Christ in whom we have our redemption. Only as His work is more fully understood can faith in His person embrace the realities of His saving activity. Our estimate of what He is and does determines the quality and range of our faith.

Enough, perhaps, has been said to reveal the rich deposit of primitive Christian thought embedded in 1 Peter. What we have in this Epistle is not diluted Paulinism, but pre-Pauline Christianity with its loosely associated thoughts, beliefs, and reflections, all awaiting the integrating touch of inspired teachers like St. Paul, St. John, and the writer of the Epistle to the Hebrews, and the subsequent discussions of doctors of the Church. It is difficult to agree with the opinion that St. Paul's 'friends and followers caught his tones but missed his meaning',[1] as applicable to 1 Peter. The truth is rather that the Apostle caught the meaning of his friends and supplied the lost chords of a broken harmony.

(e) The Apocalypse

It might seem strange and unwarranted to cite, as a witness to primitive Christian belief about the death of Christ, a writing which in the opinion of most critical scholars comes from the last decade of the first century.[2] None the less, this use of the Apocalypse of John can be made, and for excellent reasons. In the first place, the writer makes use of earlier sources, Hebrew and Greek, which he appears to employ with few changes beyond those necessary to adapt them to the world-situation of his day. Again, his *forte* is not that of a theologian; he is not concerned to commend or expound the faith, but rather to enhearten the persecuted Christians of the Roman province of Asia and to call them to patient and unyielding endurance in loyalty to Christ against the impious claims of Cæsar. Convinced of the coming downfall of Antichrist and the final triumph of Christ's kingdom, and expecting universal martyrdom[3] (cf. vi. 11 b, xiii. 15 b), the writer was not likely to modify the Christian tradition relating to the Cross under the influence of Greek philosophy and religious

---

[1] See the findings of the Hellenistic Seminar of Manchester University on 1 Peter, *Expository Times*, xlviii, p. 24.

[2] Cf. R. H. Charles, *I.C.C., Revelation*, i, pp. xci–vii.

[3] Cf. Charles, *op. cit.*, i, pp. 177, 361.

teaching; and, in point of fact, there is no evidence that he has done so. Finally, much of the teaching contained in the Apocalypse with reference to the death of Christ is enshrined in great Christian hymns, which either existed before the author wrote or gathered up into themselves the religious convictions of the Asian churches. This is a point of much importance, for as a rule hymns are repositories of accepted belief rather than media for the dissemination of new views. For these reasons, then, we may use the Apocalypse with confidence as indicating the traditional teaching of early Christianity in Asia. If further assurance were needed, it would be given by the opinion of Hastings Rashdall regarding the author. 'He is simply full', he writes, 'of that earlier and simpler doctrine of the atonement which was certainly pre-Pauline, and which was generally taught in churches little or not at all influenced by St. Paul.'[1] His further observation that the Apocalypse 'is almost as un-Pauline as the Epistle of St. James'[2] is an exaggeration. It will be found that the teaching of this writing, limited and simple as it is, contains elements of great importance for the study of the doctrine of the Atonement.

Among the many songs of the Apocalypse are three which hymn the praises of Christ as the Lamb of God slain for men and yet living and triumphant over death:[3]

Worthy art thou to take the book,
And to open the seals thereof;
For thou wast slain,
And hast redeemed unto God with thy blood
Men of every tribe, and tongue, and people, and nation,
And hast made them unto our God a kingdom and priests,
And they reign upon the earth (v. 9 f.).

Worthy is the Lamb that hath been slain
To receive the power, and riches, and wisdom,
And might, and honour, and glory, and blessing (v. 12).

Unto him that sitteth upon the throne, and unto the Lamb,
Be the blessing, and the honour, and the glory,
And the power, for ever and ever (v. 13).

These songs may have been composed by the seer himself, for the style and the diction are his.[4] Dibelius, however, who has recently drawn attention to the New Testament evidence for the use of hymns in the early communities, thinks that they were

---

[1] *The Idea of Atonement in Christian Theology*, p. 172.   [2] *Op. cit.*, p. 173.
[3] The translations are those of R. H. Charles, *op. cit.*, ii, pp. 400 f.
[4] Cf. Charles, *op. cit.*, i, pp. 135 f.

perhaps not composed by him in the first instance, but only quoted by him.[1] In either case they express ideas which had long been current. The theme of these songs is significant. Just as the earliest piece of continuous narrative in the Gospel tradition was the Story of the Passion, so the earliest examples of Christian hymnody included songs of the Crucified.

What, then, are the doctrinal ideas expressed in these songs and in the Apocalypse generally? In order to answer this question, we must consider v. 6, which introduces the figure of the Lamb and other passages in which He is mentioned, including i. 5 *f.*, vii. 14, xii. 11, xiii. 8, xiv. 4, and xix. 7.

In v. 6 the seer describes the Lamb which he beholds standing between the throne and the four living creatures and the four and twenty elders: 'And I saw . . . a Lamb standing, as though it had been slain [ὡς ἐσφαγμένον], having seven horns, and seven eyes, which are the seven spirits of God sent out into all the earth.' The Lamb is undoubtedly the Exalted Christ who has already been described in the majestic vision of i. 11–16. This designation, which is used twenty-eight times of Christ in the Apocalypse and once of Antichrist (xiii. 11), is drawn from Isaiah liii. 7 [ἐπὶ σφαγὴν ἤχθη] as the phrase ὡς ἐσφαγμένον clearly shows.[2] The most striking feature in the representation is that the Lamb is alive, bearing the marks of sacrifice, but triumphant over death. The seven horns indicate kingly power and dignity, and the seven eyes omniscience. Obviously the picture is not meant for the imagination, but for the understanding; it is intended to suggest the thought of One who through sacrifice has become King and Lord.[3] The words which precede v. 6 make this especially clear. As he weeps, the seer is bidden to behold 'the Lion that is of the tribe of Judah, the Root of David'. 'And I saw', he writes, 'a Lamb standing, as though it had been slain.' No better indication could be given that the ideas of the King Messiah and the Suffering Servant have been combined. In this combination the thought of primitive Christianity has followed that of Jesus Himself; but with

---

[1] *A Fresh Approach to the New Testament and Early Christian Literature*, pp. 246–54.

[2] Cf. Charles, *op. cit.*, i, p. 141; H. B. Swete, *The Apocalypse of St. John*, p. 76; J. Jeremias, *Theol. Wort.*, i, pp. 344 *f.* Swete suggests that the use of ἀρνίον in the Apocalypse, instead of ἀμνός, may be due to the use of a non-Septuagintal version of Isaiah, or to Jeremiah xi. 19. Jeremias traces the application of the term 'Lamb' to Christ, to two sources, Isaiah liii. 7 and the Passover lamb (*op. cit.*, i, 343).

[3] 'There is no contradiction between the ideas, however it may be with their symbols; for this absolute self-sacrifice which has already been undergone, as our author indicates, has become the avenue to supreme power and omniscience' (Charles, *op. cit.*, i, p. 143).

this difference, that whereas Jesus interpreted the Son of Man in terms of the Servant, early Christian thought conceived the Servant in the power and dignity of the Lion of Judah. The reason, of course, is that Jesus looked forward to the Cross, whereas the seer and his contemporaries looked back upon it and saw that its suffering and shame had been transformed into victory and honour.

These ideas are developed further in the songs which follow. 'Worthy art thou,' sing the elders and the four living creatures, 'for thou wast slain [ἐσφάγης], and hast redeemed [ἠγόρασας τῷ θεῷ] with thy blood [ἐν τῷ αἵματί σου] men of every tribe, and tongue, and people, and nation' (v. 9). The use of sacrificial imagery here is manifest, but we are guilty of undue modernism if we treat the ideas as mere symbolism and nothing more. 'With thy blood' suggests at least the idea of great cost,[1] but it certainly means more than 'by thy violent death'; it indicates a real analogy, which is none the less transcended between the offering of the blood of the sacrificial lamb and the self-offering of Christ. And we must not weaken this idea by speaking of a sublime expression of the spirit of self-sacrifice. A personal act, racial in character, is implied by the description of its consequences: it has redeemed men, or purchased[2] them for God, presumably from sin and from hostile powers. In doing this, it has broken the bands of nationality: the redeemed are 'men of every tribe, and tongue, and people, and nation'. Finally, it has brought into being a new community, 'a kingdom and priests', the members of which even now, in spite of bitter persecution, 'reign upon the earth'. The greatness of the deed of Christ is further emphasized by the praises addressed to Him in the remaining songs of chapter v. The Lamb that hath been slain is worthy to receive 'the power, and riches, and wisdom, and might, and honour, and glory, and blessing' (v. 12). Not only so; His praises are conjoined with those of God Himself. 'And now the climax of the world's adoration has come, and the worship offered to God in iv, and that to the Lamb in v. 1-12, are united in one great closing doxology, in which all created things throughout the entire universe acclaim together God and the Lamb, with praise and honour and glory and power

---

[1] Cf. Charles, i, p. 147; Swete, p. 80; Hort, *The First Epistle of St. Peter*, p. 79, with reference to the blood of the Paschal lamb considered as a ransom.

[2] For other examples of this use of ἀγοράζω see 1 Corinthians vi. 20, vii. 23, 2 Peter ii. 1, and for ἐξαγοράζω see Galatians iii. 13, iv. 5.

for ever and ever'.[1] A Christology so advanced as this in its implications, in which the Lamb and 'him that sitteth upon the throne' are the object of common worship, shows that in the estimation of primitive Christianity Christ was thought of as having accomplished a unique service for mankind. Its closer definition is not attempted in the Apocalypse, but that it is conceived as sacrificial in character cannot be doubted.

This impression is deepened by the opening doxology (i. 5 f.) which follows the seer's greeting to the seven churches of Asia. Here again the structure is rhythmic and the spirit of the words is that of worship:

> Unto him that loveth us and loosed us from our sins by his blood,
> And hath made us[2] to be a kingdom, priests unto his God and Father—
> Unto him be the glory and the dominion for ever and ever.
> Amen.

Here at the outset appear the same thoughts already noted in the three songs of chapter v, the reference to the blood of Christ, the communal aspect of His redemptive ministry, the ascription of unceasing praise to One who in the preceding words is described as 'the faithful witness, the first-born of the dead, and the ruler of the kings of the earth'. New thoughts, however, appear in this doxology which do not find expression elsewhere in the Apocalypse. The reference to love in close association with redemption in the words 'unto him that loveth us' is the first, and indeed the only, allusion of the kind in the records of primitive Christian thought; and here the words refer to the abiding love of Christ, not the love of God. There is, in fact, no evidence at all[3] that the first Christians thought of the death of Christ as the revelation of the love of God apart from the definite affirmations of St. Paul and St. John in Romans v. 8 and John iii. 16 respectively. These Apostolic statements must have made an immediate appeal to the minds of Christian readers, but all the available evidence suggests that other aspects of the death of Christ, vicarious, mediatorial, and sacrificial, held a more prominent place in their thoughts. In the passage before us there appears to be a contrast between the thought of the abiding love of Christ and that of the

---

[1] R. H. Charles, *op. cit.*, i, p. 151.

[2] The literal rendering, 'and he made us', is rightly explained by Charles as a Hebraism, *op. cit.*, i, pp. 14 f., ii, p. 387. Cf. Howard, Moulton's *Grammar*, ii, p. 429.

[3] Not in the Synoptic Gospels, the Acts, 1 Peter, the Apocalypse, nor in any writing which may be held to reflect the thoughts of the primitive communities.

finished act of redemption.[1] The contrast, however, is temporal; but in the order of thought, it is natural to ground the redemptive act in the fact of the abiding love.[2] This step is inevitably suggested, although it is not actually taken within the passage itself.

The reference to the act of loosing[3] from sins has no parallel elsewhere in the Apocalypse. Apparently it is one of deliverance or redemption from the servitude of sin. The phrase does not describe a process of gradual liberation, with a consequent growth in holiness, but a decisive victory out of which these results spring.[4] This redemption is won by the blood of Christ. Many commentators hold that the preposition 'by' (ἐν) denotes price: 'at the cost of'[5] (cf. v. 9), but it can equally well be instrumental: 'by means of', in which case the phrase refers to the sacrifice of Christ.[6] Between these alternatives it is difficult to decide. In itself, this fact indicates the kind of doctrinal situation which confronts us in the Apocalypse. Different ideas are combined. The confusion, if confusion it be, is due to a ferment of thought in the mind of primitive Christianity, as it faces the astounding fact of a slain yet triumphant and exalted Lord. In order to express the meaning of His Passion and exaltation, commercial, legal, and sacrificial ideas are freely combined. In i. 5 f, as in v. 9 f, sacrificial ideas are present, but not in a pure form, as in the circumstances of the case they could not be. Evident in the figure of the Lamb and in the use of the term 'blood', they are visible also in the reference to a priestly community established by the deed of Christ; for the thought of redemption[7] is at once followed by the claim that He has consummated 'a kingdom, priests unto his God

[1] Swete speaks of 'the contrast between the abiding ἀγάπη and the completed act of redemption' (*op. cit.*, p. 7).

[2] Cf. Swete's paraphrase, 'To Him that loves us and—the crucial instance of His love—loosed us from our sins at the cost of His blood' (*op. cit.*, p. 7).

[3] In view of the strong support of the MSS. S A C, λύσαντι ('loosed') must be preferred to the weakly attested λούσαντι ('washed'). Cf. Charles, i, p. 15, ii, p. 237; Swete, p. 7. Hort thinks that λούσαντι may be 'due to failure to understand the Hebraic use of ἐν to denote a price . . . and a natural misapplication of vii. 24' ('and have washed their robes, and made them white in the blood of the Lamb') (WH² *Notes*, p. 136).

[4] Cf. Denney, *The Death of Christ*, p. 243. This view is suggested by the aorist λύσαντι. Only with the greatest caution can we press the significance of tenses in the Apocalypse. Nevertheless, there appears to be a careful discrimination in the tense forms of ἀγαπῶντι and λύσαντι in i. 5, ἐσφαγμένοι in v. 6 and xiii. 7, and ἐσφάγης and ἠγόρασας in v. 9.

[5] Cf. Charles, i, p. 16; Swete, p. 8.

[6] Cf. Alford, *The Greek Testament*, iv, p. 550.

[7] Cf. the parallel idea in v. 9: 'and hast redeemed unto God with thy blood. . . .

and Father', while the unique character of His deed is expressed in 'the glory and dominion' ascribed to Him 'for ever and ever'. The testimony of the Apocalypse is its tribute to this soveriegn act of Christ; the combined commercial and sacrificial ideas are the media by which it is liturgically expressed.

The remaining passages in the Apocalypse to be considered present the exegete with difficult problems. In vii. 14 the triumphant martyrs who have come out of 'the great tribulation' are said to have 'washed their robes, and made them white in the blood of the Lamb'. With great force and learning, R. H. Charles has argued that, in accordance with the ideas of apocalyptic tradition, the 'robes' are the heavenly bodies with which they have been endowed while on earth. These spiritual bodies are a divine gift (vi. 11), but they can be either defiled (iii. 4) or washed 'in the blood of the Lamb' (vii. 14; cf. xxii. 14). For the study of this suggestion, reference must be made to Charles's discussion.[1] The main interest of the passage for our purpose is the phrase 'in the blood of the Lamb'. It is at once evident that this expression does not always indicate price. Here it must refer to the sacrifice of Christ Himself, to the virtue of His surrendered life for men which possesses purifying power.[2] It is because of this cleansing that the martyrs stand before the throne of God and 'serve him day and night in his temple' (vii. 15). Behind this symbolism is plainly present the idea of the ethical and spiritual power inherent in Christ's sacrifice.

The passage, xii. 11, is of importance because the victory of the saints over Satan and his angels is ascribed, not only to their personal testimony and unflinching loyalty, but also to 'the blood of the Lamb': 'And they overcame him because of the blood of the Lamb.' Here it is implied that the defeat of Satan is implicit in the sacrifice of Christ.[3] An act of transcendent importance is plainly in mind, which dooms the powers of evil to certain destruction. Mythological in form as this section of the Apocalypse is, it reflects a deep conviction of primitive Christianity, and was destined to influence Christian theology for a thousand years, while even to-day its spiritual message brings comfort to Christian hearts overborne by the apparent omnipotence of evil.

Yet another passage of the greatest interest is xiii. 8, which

---

[1] *Op. cit.*, i, pp. 82 *f.*, 176, 184–8, 213 *f.*

[2] Cf. 1 John i. 7: 'The blood of Jesus his Son cleanseth us from all sin.'

[3] 'The Blood of the Lamb is here, as in vii. 14, the Sacrifice of the Cross, which is regarded as the primary cause of the martyrs' victory' (Swete, p. 153).

speaks of those whose names 'were not written in the book of life of the Lamb that hath been slain from the foundation of the world'. The belief that Christ's sacrifice is eternal in its significance is great enough to stand apart from the support of this passage, and it is extremely doubtful whether xiii. 8 expresses the idea. Commentators are strangely divided in their views, and popular interpretations are largely the product of wishful exegesis. The problem is whether 'from the foundation of the world' must be construed with the phrase 'the Lamb that hath been slain' or with the word 'written'. Charles[1] supports the former suggestion, which has in its favour the order of the Greek words; Swete[2] and Denney[3] take the latter view, on the ground that in xvii. 8 the names in the book of life are expressly said to have been written 'from the foundation of the world'. This is a strong argument; and when, moreover, we consider the apocalyptic character of the Apocalypse, and the popular nature of its theology, it does not seem probable that the idea of the eternity of Christ's sacrifice should be the truth asserted in xiii. 8. The idea of a catalogue of the redeemed in the Lamb's 'book of life' (xxi. 27) is a belief which could not be permanent in the thought of the Church, but it is entirely in keeping with the predestinarian character of apocalyptic teaching. Its value is that it is the one indication in the Apocalypse of the idea of a divine purpose fulfilled in the redeeming work of Christ.

The last passage to be considered is xiv. 4: 'These are they which follow the Lamb whithersoever he goeth.' Some commentators see in these words an echo of the sayings of Jesus about following Himself (Mark ii. 14, x. 21; Luke ix. 59; John i. 43, xxi. 19. Cf. 1 Peter ii. 21). Charles,[4] indeed, says that the words 'can hardly fail to be an echo of our Lord's', and Swete[5] takes a similar view. Whatever may be the justice of this opinion, the passage shows that the Christians of Asia Minor recognized the need of fidelity to Christ even to the point of martyrdom itself. In xiv. 4 the seer is reminding them of this obligation, as also in xii. 11, 'they loved not their lives even unto death', and directly in

---

[1] *Op. cit.*, i, p. 354. ' The principle of sacrifice and redemption is older than the world: it belongs to the essence of the Godhead' (*ibid.*).

[2] *Op. cit.*, p. 164.

[3] *Op. cit.*, p. 249. Cf. H. T. Andrews, Peake's *Commentary*, p. 937.

[4] *Op. cit.*, ii, p. 10.

[5] *Op. cit.*, pp. 176 f.

ii. 10, in the letter to the Church in Smyrna: 'Be thou faithful unto death, and I will give thee the crown of life.'

We have now passed in review the principal passages in the Apocalypse which relate to the death of Christ. If we are right in the contention that they reveal primitive Christian beliefs, we must now add that they disclose those beliefs in cross section. Some primitive convictions are represented only faintly, or not at all; others stand out with startling distinctiveness. The necessity of Christ's death is nowhere asserted, and appears only remotely in the reference to the Lamb's book of life in which are written the names of the redeemed since the foundation of the world (xiii. 8, xxi. 27). Its Messianic character is implicit in the identification of the Lion of the tribe of Judah, the Root of David, with the slain Lamb, but is not otherwise emphasized. Its vicarious nature and its representative aspect are not expressly indicated; it is presented neither as a dying for sins nor as an offering for men; and only as ultimate implications of the work of Christ and its effects upon men can these ideas be said to belong to its teaching. In contrast with these aspects, attested elsewhere in the records of primitive Christian belief, two characteristics are especially marked. First, its sacrificial significance is unmistakable, but in combination with other ideas of release and purchase which suggest the mart and the counting-house as well as the altar. Secondly, its abiding significance, as the work of a Living Lord, victorious over death, the recipient of the worship of heaven and earth, is everywhere stressed. The deed of Christ, which ransoms men from sin, cleanses them from its defilement, makes them members of an elect community, assures them of the certain overthrow of evil, and gives to them an unfailing example of endurance and of fidelity to God—such is the seer's constant theme, the centre of his personal belief and the heart of the religion of his readers. In such writing as this it would be absurd to press the significance of its silences in respect of any of the points enumerated above. We must esteem it for what it contains, not in the light of its omissions. The only two points which raise serious questions are its silence about the Eucharist and faith. The total absence of eucharistic teaching is due in part, as E. F. Scott[1] has observed, to the fact that the seer is intent upon the idea of fulfilment; but the parallel absence of teaching regarding faith-union suggests, as in the case of 1 Peter, that the deeper reason is the relative simplicity of his

[1] *The Book of Revelation*, p. 141.

soteriology. Only as the sacrifice of Christ is more richly conceived, as a work of personal moment for sinful man and of decisive significance for the world to which he belongs, is the need felt for faith-union with the Redeemer and for a share in the rite in which His Presence and saving power are assured.

(f) The Epistles of St. James, St. Jude, Second Peter, and the Pastoral Epistles

We have now reached the limits within which evidence can be found for the faith of the primitive communities, apart from echoes of earlier teaching in the later New Testament writings.

The Epistle of St. James contains no reference direct or indirect to the death of Christ. As such, it is a standing warning against the perils of the argument from silence. Rashdall based upon its silence the astounding suggestion that it may represent 'the teaching of that Jewish section of the Church which did not even receive the doctrine that Christ died for our sins according to the Scriptures';[1] and maintained that, by any one who accepts its teaching, 'St. Paul's doctrine of salvation by faith can only be accepted in a sense which makes it equally permissible to speak of salvation by works'.[2] The doctrine of a faith which works by love, he claimed, 'must involve the admission that much of the teaching of the Epistle to the Romans requires a good deal of correction, or at least of non-literal interpretation and toning-down, before it can be harmonized with that simple teaching of Jesus Himself which is the direct and immediate source of the Christianity revealed by the Epistle of St. James'.[3]

The idea of 'the simple teaching of Jesus', consisting in the principle of self-sacrifice, is a modernist myth, and the claim that this teaching is preserved in the Epistle of St. James springs from a failure to appreciate the true character of the writing. Exactly the same must be said of such disparaging estimates of its worth as the famous opinion of Luther, who saw in it an 'epistle of straw'. The truth is that the writing is not an epistle at all, but a homily,[4] or rather a series of homilies, on various practical ethical themes,

---

[1] *The Idea of Atonement in Christian Theology*, p. 169.
[2] *Op. cit.*, p. 171.   [3] *Op. cit.*, p. 171.
[4] Dibelius classifies it under the heading of 'Hortatory Christian Literature.' Cf. *A Fresh Approach to the New Testament and Early Christian Literature*, pp. 226 ff. On Luther's opinion see the important article of P. S. Watson, *Expository Times*, lii, p. 313.

composed by an unknown James who modestly describes himself as 'a servant of God and of the Lord Jesus Christ' (i. 1), and who, not unnaturally, in the second or third century was identified with James the brother of Jesus. To expect in such a writing information regarding primitive belief about the death of Christ is as unreasonable as it would be to seek it in the document Q. Knowledge of St. Paul's teaching concerning justification by faith is certainly presupposed in ii. 14–26, but the section is either a polemic against perversions of Pauline teaching, or, as G. Schrenk[1] suggests, is a reaction to the tradition of the synagogue which emphasizes the active character of true faith.

The Epistle of St. Jude is a fiery tract[2] rather than an epistle which limits itself so exclusively to its attack upon a particular form of libertarian false teaching that it contributes nothing useful for our purpose. The robust character of the religion revealed in its closing benediction (24 f.) 'makes us feel how much we might have gained if we could have been granted that other writing which Jude was "giving all diligence to write" concerning "our common salvation" when he was constrained to break off and write the existing Epistle'.[3] In any case, while not pseudonymous, the Epistle is late, belonging probably to the first quarter of the second century, unless the phrase 'the brother of James' can be accepted as original. J. W. C. Wand[4] supports the authorship of Jude, the brother of James, and dates the Epistle before A.D. 80, but the tone of 17, which refers to 'the apostles of our Lord Jesus Christ', and the character of the false teaching which is opposed, make it very difficult to accept this view.

Second Peter is probably based on St. Jude, and in consequence, and in view of its late and meagre attestation,[5] cannot be dated earlier than c. A.D. 150. Nevertheless, and in spite of this date, ii. 1, 'denying even the Master that bought [ἀγοράσαντα] them', is of much interest, as a late echo of a primitive Christian belief.[6] As elsewhere, in passages where this metaphor is used, there is no

---

[1] *Theol. Wort.*, ii, p. 223.   [2] Cf. Dibelius, *op. cit.*, p. 205.

[3] Quoted from my article on 'The Message of the Epistles: Second Peter and Jude', *Expository Times*, xlv, p. 440, in which I have discussed the opinions somewhat summarily stated above.

[4] *The General Epistles of St. Peter and St. Jude* (Westminster Commentaries), pp. 189 f.

[5] It is first mentioned by Origen, who says that its authority was a disputed question.

[6] Although the idea is used by St. Paul (1 Corinthians vi. 20, vii. 23), it is one which he shared with the common faith of the Church (cf. Apocalypse v. 9, xiv. 3 f.; cf. 1 Peter i. 18; Mark x. 45).

suggestion of a person from whom men are bought; the figure expresses the cost of the deliverance from sin wrought by Christ.

The loss of the theory of the Pauline authorship of the Pastoral Epistles[1] is more than compensated for by the light which these letters throw upon the organization, thought, and life of the Church in the period *c.* A.D. 100. The references to the death of Christ in 1 Timothy i. 15, ii. 5 *f.*, vi. 13, Titus ii. 14, iii. 4–7, are naturally based upon Pauline teaching, and perhaps also, in the case of 1 Timothy ii. 5 *f.*, upon the Epistle to the Hebrews and Mark x. 45. At the same time this dependence is not exclusive, and there are distant echoes of early beliefs, derived in some cases from hymns and credal confessions. 1 Timothy vi. 13, 'I charge thee in the sight of God, who quickeneth all things, and of Christ Jesus, who before Pontius Pilate witnessed the good confession', shows how the later Church treasured the historical tradition upon which the doctrine of the atonement rests.[2] With reference to 1 Timothy i. 15: 'Faithful is the saying, and worthy of all acceptation, that Christ Jesus came into the world to save sinners', E. F. Scott has made the interesting suggestion that probably the words are 'taken from some early liturgy, or from hymns in which the Christian confession was embodied'.[3] The introductory phrase, in the opinion of W. Lock, 'implies a knowledge of Synoptic and Johannine language (*cf.* Luke v. 32; John xii. 47), and is a witness to their essential unity, but does not imply direct quotation from either'.[4]

More important than the passages quoted above is 1 Timothy ii. 5 *f.*: 'For there is one God, one mediator also between God and men, himself man, Christ Jesus, who gave himself a ransom for all.' Here again the tone suggests a Church confession, as Moffatt's rendering[5] indicates, but Scott[6] prefers to think that the writer is commenting on the familiar words of Scripture, and Lock[7] says

---

[1] Cf. P. N. Harrison, *The Problem of the Pastoral Epistles*; E. F. Scott, *The Pastoral Epistles* (*Moffatt N.T. Commentary*); and, for the defence of the Pauline authorship, W. Lock, *I.C.C., The Pastoral Epistles*; J. H. Bernard, *The Pastoral Epistles* (Cambridge Greek Testament); R. Falconer, *The Pastoral Epistles*.

[2] 'There may be a semi-quotation of some Baptismal form' (W. Lock, *op. cit.*, p. 71).

[3] *Op. cit.*, p. 13. [4] *Op. cit.*, p. 15.

[5] Moffatt uses quotation marks and translates as follows: 'And "one intermediary between God and men, the man Christ Jesus who gave Himself as a ransom for all."' It has long been recognized that 1 Timothy iii. 16 is a fragment from an early Christian hymn. Dibelius, *op. cit.*, p. 247, speaks of it as 'a fragment in three couplets arranged not historically but purely rhetorically, and on this account possessing poetic character'. This passage, however, does not refer to the death of Christ.

[6] *Op. cit.*, p. 21. [7] *Op. cit.*, p. 28.

that the words spring naturally out of the context. The word 'mediator' calls to mind Hebrews ix. 15 (cf. also Galatians iii. 19 with reference, however, to the Law), but it may have been independently used by the writer. Almost certainly the passage depends on Mark x. 45.[1] The reflexive 'himself' replaces 'his life' in that saying; 'for all' is a correct interpretation of 'for many'; and ἀντίλυτρον ('ransom') is a more elegant synonym for λύτρον.[2] The logion has been further expanded by the introduction of the phrase 'himself man' or 'the man Christ Jesus' probably in reaction to docetic teaching which denied the true humanity of Christ. Following upon the reference to the 'one mediator between God and men', the phrase shows that the character of Christ's representative ministry, as involving a true human experience, has been the subject of reflection on the part of the writer or some earlier thinker. The passage, therefore, not only reproduces early tradition, but also illustrates the process of interpretation which naturally and inevitably followed.

A similar expansion of Mark x. 45 appears in Titus ii. 14: 'who gave himself for us, that he might redeem us from all iniquity, and purify unto himself a people for his own possession, zealous of good works'. These passages reveal the great influence exerted by the saying of Jesus in early Christian thought. The writer has interpreted His self-giving as an act of redemption from sin, involving the idea of a costly ransom, and with this he has combined the thought of a purifying act in virtue of which the community of God is established among men, obedient to His will and ready to obey His commands, 'a people for his own possession, zealous of good works'. The combination of ideas in this short passage is remarkable. The language recalls that of several Old Testament passages, including Psalm cxxx. 8: 'He shall redeem Israel from all his iniquities'; Ezekiel xxxvii. 23: 'I will save them from all their iniquities[3] . . . and I will cleanse them, and they shall be my people, and I will be their God'; Exodus xix. 5: 'Ye shall be to me a peculiar people'.[4] The writer of the Pastorals does not merely quote these passages, or apply them to Christ in an artificial manner. He uses them rather as supplying inevitable language forms by which he can express his belief in an act of Christ which is

---

[1] 'The Son of man came . . . to give himself a ransom for many.'

[2] So F. Büchsel, *Theol. Wort.*, iv, p. 351. Büchsel thinks that J. H. Moulton goes too far in describing 1 Timothy ii. 6 as a quotation of Mark x. 45. Cf. *Prolegomena*, p. 105. See also Lock, p. 28; Scott, p. 22.

[3] LXX.   [4] LXX. Cf. Deuteronomy vii. 6, xiv. 2, xxvi. 18.

priestly and sacrificial in character, closely allied to the sprinkling of the people of Israel at Sinai with the blood of the covenant-sacrifice (Exodus xxiv. 8).[1] In this passage, then, we have something more than an echo of primitive belief. Ideas current within the early communities have been brought together and presented as a uniform conception which closely resembles that which we have seen reason to attribute to Jesus Himself. The description of the faith by which Jesus went to His Cross, present in fragments in the earliest Christian records, is here in process of re-integration. One cannot but feel that if the writer of the Pastorals had known greater leisure from the pressure of practical affairs, he might have taken a place among the leaders of New Testament thought. Far from slavishly repeating the ideas of his hero, St. Paul, he can go back to the words of Jesus Himself and interpret them in the light of the traditional teaching of the early Church. A theologian by instinct, he responded to the imperious claims of the pastoral office and dedicated to organization gifts by which he might have won esteem.[2]

The remaining passage for notice is Titus iii. 4–7: 'But when the kindness of God our Saviour, and his love toward man, appeared, not by works done in righteousness, which we did ourselves, but according to his mercy he saved us, through the washing of regeneration and renewing of the Holy Spirit, which he poured out upon us richly, through Jesus Christ our Saviour; that, being justified by his grace, we might be made heirs according to the hope of eternal life.' Although there are no direct statements in this passage about the character of Christ's death, its assumptions are of great interest and of importance for the story of the development of doctrine. As in ii. 11, 'For the grace of God hath appeared, bringing salvation to all men', salvation comes as an 'epiphany'; it 'appeared', and it is to be traced to the 'goodness' and to the 'humanity' (φιλανθρωπία)[3] of God 'our Saviour'. Too late as a witness to the earliest Christian beliefs, this evidence supports the claim that St. Paul's teaching about the Cross as the proof of the love of God crystallized Christian convictions; for Titus iii. 4 is not an echo of Romans v. 8, but a belief less powerfully, but independently, expressed. It bases salvation, not upon the 'love' (ἀγάπη) of God, but His goodness, humanity and

---

[1] Cf. Lock, op. cit., p. 146; Büchsel, op. cit., iv, p. 353.

[2] Denney's sally, 'St. Paul was inspired, but the author of these epistles is sometimes only orthodox' (The Death of Christ, p. 203), is more brilliant than just.

[3] See Moulton and Milligan, The Vocabulary of the Greek Testament, pp. 668 f.

mercy. The reference to 'the washing of regeneration and renewing of the Holy Spirit'[1] reveals a tendency to think of baptism as efficacious in itself, and the want of any mention of faith, coupled with the conventional allusions to justification, shows how imperfectly the deepest elements of Pauline teaching have been apprehended. The end of salvation, it should be noted, is expressed positively, though with respect to the future rather than the present, in the words: 'that . . . we might be heirs according to the hope of eternal life'. As a whole, the passage reminds us of the statements of the Apostolic Fathers and the Apologists of the second century rather than the creative utterances of the great New Testament teachers. E. F. Scott is well justified when he writes: 'So in these Epistles the ideas of Paul lose their distinctive character, and are made elements in a religion which is mainly statutory and ethical. Paulinism, while still struggling to maintain itself, is giving place to the official theology of the later Catholic Church'.[2] Such opinions, however, should not be taken, and are not intended, to encourage a neglect of the Pastoral Epistles in respect of the theology of the New Testament. There is too much that is traditional rather than Pauline, too much that is anticipatory of later developments, to justify a neglect so costly.

If we summarize the teaching actually present in the Pastorals, the estimate of value suggested above is fully sustained. As the wheel of the first century turns, we see that doctrine retains its historical roots (1 Timothy vi. 13), that the conviction is basal that Christ came to save sinners (1 Timothy i. 15), that He is 'the mediator between God and men' who by the sacrifice of Himself for all men (1 Timothy ii. 5 f.) has redeemed them from iniquity and brought them into a covenant-relationship with God (Titus ii. 14). There is little that is new in these ideas, save greater precision and the use of the term 'mediator'. The new elements in the teaching are the attempt to trace salvation to the goodness and mercy of God Himself and the sacramental emphasis upon the spiritual possibilities of baptism (Titus iii. 4 f.) In view of this teaching concerning baptism, the complete absence of eucharistic doctrine is remarkable until we notice the parallel lack of teaching concerning the faith-relationship between the believer and Christ.

---

[1] Probably both nouns depend on λουτροῦ. Cf. Lock, p. 155; Huther (Meyer's *Commentary*), p. 371; Bernard, p. 178; Scott, p. 175; Oepke, *Theol. Wort.*, iv, p. 306.
[2] *Op. cit.*, p. 177.

When, further, we observe that nothing is said about the truth of a Living and Ascended Lord in contexts where His redemptive ministry is mentioned, the inference is once more suggested[1] that the ideas of faith-union, sacramental communion, and the ministry of a Living Lord go naturally together in a fully co-ordinated Christian experience of salvation, since each is part of a larger whole.

(g) Summary

Before passing to Part II, it will be useful to attempt a summary of the results which have been gained from our investigation of the attitude of the primitive Church to the death of Christ. The ideas which we have found associated with it are many and various. It would be unwarranted to combine them in one comprehensive body of teaching and assume that this complex of ideas represents the mind and thought of the Church everywhere and from the earliest times. As we have recognized from the outset, it is much more probable that some ideas would be emphasized more than others at different centres, that some aspects of the doctrine would remain in abeyance and that others would become prominent only as time passed and the range of experience grew. Our inquiry has shown that this kind of development actually happened, notably with such ideas as faith-union, sacramental communion, and the love of God. The explanation is that the story of the primitive faith of the Church is that of a vital process, sustained by the illumination of the Spirit, and enriched by the experiences and perceptions of individuals within the life of a worshipping society.

If, however, we ought not simply to combine the several ideas, as elements in a relatively stable and universally accepted belief, it is important to note their range and the extent to which they are attested. The ideas in question include the following: the necessity of Christ's death or its place in the divine intention, its Messianic character, its voluntary and vicarious nature, its representative aspect, its relation to sin, its sacrificial significance, its connexion with the Servant-conception, its association with the resurrection or with the thought of a Living and Ascended Lord, the presence of the ideas of a faith-relationship between the believer and the Crucified, the development of eucharistic teaching in connexion with Christ's self-offering, the idea of

---

[1] See earlier, pp. 20 *f.*, 33 *f.*, 42 *f.*

D

sharing His sufferings, the thought of His death as a proof or revelation of the Love of God. All these ideas, to a greater or less degree, we have been able to trace, although in the case of some of them the signs are faint indeed. The extent to which they are present is a question of first importance, and second only in interest to this is the allied question, why some are so clearly present while others appear only in shadows like faint shapes upon a photographic film.

The facts of distribution can be indicated to some extent in a comparative table, in which the New Testament evidence is shown for each of the ideas noted above. No doubt this is a perilous undertaking, in view of the uncertainties of the silences of the records, and the fact that we are dependent for our inference upon single writings which were not written for the purpose of telling us how the death of Christ was interpreted in the circles from which they have come. If, however, we are alive to the character of the evidence, and know how to use it, valuable information can be obtained.

In the table which follows, evidence from the Pauline Epistles, the Epistle to the Hebrews, and the Johannine Writings (apart from the Apocalypse) is omitted. The omission reduces the amount of available evidence, because, as we have seen, all these writings contain elements derived from the common faith of the Church. For our immediate purpose, however, it is best to leave this testimony aside, since, while it is certain that we have definite information about primitive beliefs in passages like 1 Corinthians xv. 5, and in references to the blood of Christ and to deliverance from sin, in other cases it is not possible to draw a sharp line between the tradition which the writers received and the interpretations which they placed upon it. Later it will, of course, be necessary to inquire how these writers treat the ideas mentioned in the table and what further developments of doctrine they introduce.

	Sayings of Jesus.	Acts.	1 Peter.	Apocalypse.	Pastoral Epistles.
1. The idea of the divine purpose.	Sayings.	Acts.	(n. 1.)	(n. 2.)	Past. Epp.
2. Messianic character.	Sayings.	Acts.	(n. 3.)	Apocalypse.	—
3. Vicarious nature.	Sayings.	—	1 Peter.	—	Past. Epp.
4. Representative aspect.	Sayings.		1 Peter.	(n. 4.)	Past. Epp.
5. Relation to sin.	(n. 5.)	Acts.	1 Peter.	Apocalypse.	Past. Epp.

6. Sacrificial significance.	Sayings.	Acts. (n. 6.)	1 Peter.	Apocalypse.	Past. Epp.
7. Servant-conception.	Sayings.	Acts.	1 Peter.	Apocalypse.	—
8. The Resurrection.	Sayings.	Acts.	—	Apocalypse.	—
9. Idea of a faith-relationship.	(n. 7.)	(n. 8.)	—	—	—
10. Presence of eucharistic teaching.	Sayings.	—	—	—	—
			(n. 9.)	(n. 10.)	
11. Suffering with Christ.	Sayings.	—	1 Peter.	Apocalypse.	—
					(n. 12.)
12. Relation to the Love of God.	(n. 11.)	—	—	—	Past. Epp.
13. Moral and spiritual ends.	(n. 13.)	(n. 14.)	1 Peter.	(n. 15.)	Past. Epp.
14. Universality.	(n. 16.)	Acts (n. 17.)	(n. 18.)	Apocalypse.	Past. Epp.

Notes

1. Implied in 1 Peter i. 20.

2. Perhaps implied in the references to the Lamb's 'book of life' (xiii. 8, xvii. 8, xxi. 27).

3. Perhaps implied in 1 Peter i. 11.

4. See p. 42.

5. This is implied by the idea of the New Covenant established by the blood of Christ (Mark xiv. 24) and is brought out by St. Matthew's addition in xxvi. 28: 'unto remission of sins'.

6. Found only in Acts xx. 28 in the speech of St. Paul to the Ephesian elders at Miletus.

7. The roots of the idea are the personal attachment to Himself for which Jesus called, and the command 'Take, eat' (Mark xiv. 22).

8. Acts xvi. 31 is a doubtful example.

9. In a practical rather than a mystical sense.

10. Of martyrdom.

11. Implicit in the relationship in which Jesus stood to the Father, but not the main idea of the purpose of His death.

12. In Titus iii. 4, but with reference to 'the goodness and affection of God' (Moffatt). Cf. Titus ii. 11.

13. Implicit in the teaching of Jesus, especially as regards the Kingdom.

14. Cf. Acts ii. 38, iii. 19–26.

15. Cf. Apocalypse i. 6, v. 10.

16. Implicit in the teaching of Jesus and in Mark x. 45.

17. Cf. Acts x. 43.

18. Assumed in 1 Peter.

Whatever conclusions we may draw from this table, and the danger of hasty inferences cannot be too strongly emphasized, it is undoubtedly of great interest and value. We are certainly entitled to conclude that the first eight ideas in the list and No. 13 represent best the beliefs of primitive Christianity, and that Nos. 9–12, which may well have been present to a greater degree than our sources permit us to trace, depended for their emergence upon a fuller appreciation of the meaning of the death of Christ. Of the first eight, the most strongly attested are Nos. 2, 5, 6, 7, and 8, and the best attested of all are Nos. 5 and 6. From these facts we may conclude that the belief which lay deepest in the mind of primitive Christianity was that Jesus, as the Christ, the Son and Servant of God, had died and risen again to deliver men from sin and to establish, by the sacrifice of Himself, a new covenant-relationship between them and God. No theory, or rationale, of this conviction is given in the records, but the evidence shows that the deed of Christ was widely understood as the fulfilment of the ancient purpose of God, as a vicarious act, and as in some sense representative. The last point we must be content to leave somewhat indeterminate, since the evidence does not allow us to state it with greater precision. We must recognize that the thought of a representative introduces the idea that Christ accomplishes a supreme work for men which they are not able to do for themselves. There is, however, no sign of substitution in this conception, no thought of a work of Christ the benefits of which are received simply on the ground that everything necessary has been done in our stead. Nor, again, is there any trace of the idea of vicarious punishment; primitive Christian thought knew nothing of the belief that Christ was punished for us. At the same time, it was believed that, in dying for men, Christ had entered into, and endured, the consequences of sin. Passages which introduce the thought of a ransom[1] paid at great cost, and statements which say that He 'bore sins'[2] or 'died for sins',[3] as well as the story of the Agony[4] and the Cry of Desolation from the Cross,[5] show that this was an accepted primitive Christian belief. A fuller discussion of this question must necessarily be postponed until we have examined more mature New Testament teaching which bears upon it. Even at the outset, however, it is important to observe these indications of early Christian thought if only to guard against the mistake that, in this matter, St. Paul and other writers were introducing entirely new ideas.

In closing the discussions of Part I, the true character of our conclusions needs to be emphasized. In accordance with the method we have adopted, they cannot be justly described as inferences from the proof-texts. We have preferred to let the authority of the records speak for itself, and no claim for inerrancy has been made. The value of this method is that it discloses the thoughts and beliefs of living communities of believers linked closely by ties of tradition, experience, and worship with the first

[1] Cf. Mark x. 45; 1 Timothy ii. 6; cf. Titus ii. 14.
[2] 1 Peter ii. 24.   [3] 1 Corinthians xv. 3.
[4] Mark xiv. 32–42.   [5] Mark xv. 34.

creative days of Christianity. What we gain is really the first chapter in the history of the doctrine. The importance we attach to primitive Christian beliefs is our own decision, guided by the knowledge and insight we possess. The results themselves are scientific data interpreted by provisional hypotheses. In Part II it will be necessary to examine the form given to primitive beliefs by the great New Testament teachers and the further developments which are distinctive of their teaching.

PART TWO

THE ATONEMENT IN NEW TESTAMENT THOUGHT

INTRODUCTION

It is not our intention in this investigation to suggest that the reflective element was absent in primitive Christianity until we come to the teaching of St. Paul, the author of the Epistle to the Hebrews, and St. John. On the contrary, the presence of thought throughout the New Testament is recognized, with the proviso that outside these writers it is quiescent and conservative, whereas with them it is creative and constructive. St. Paul, the *auctor ad Hebræos*, and St. John deliberately bring thought to bear upon various aspects of the doctrine and express views which have been of decisive moment in the history of subsequent Christian teaching. They are not, however, the originators of the doctrine. Popular as this opinion is, it can only be described as completely mistaken. In varying degrees, each New Testament writer rests upon the common faith of the Church, and each treats, not the doctrine as a whole, but particular aspects which arrested attention and called for treatment in relation to practical religious needs. Many of these needs they perceived in the circumstances and beliefs of their readers; and to others they immediately reacted, even though the problems might not be visible to all, because they saw their importance for the intellectual and spiritual apprehension of the faith.

The distinction between immediate and less obvious needs is important. It explains in part why the special teaching of the writers in question was not immediately influential in the generations which followed. St. Paul, in particular, is not always grappling in his Epistles with the difficulties of his converts; he is often meeting his own difficulties, the problems they had not even perceived, but which presented themselves to his own active mind. It should, therefore, not occasion surprise that his influence on later New Testament writers is superficial, even when there is clear, or reasonably clear, evidence that they had read his Epistles. St. Paul is a pioneer who frequently soars ahead of his generation, greeting from afar kindred souls as yet unborn. In spite of mythological and rabbinical elements in his arguments, he is in many respects the contemporary of such widely separated writers as Irenæus, Augustine, Luther, and theologians of modern times.

I. THE TEACHING OF ST. PAUL

In treating the contribution of St. Paul to the doctrine of the Atonement, several methods are possible. One method would be to examine each individual passage in the order in which it appears in his Epistles; another would be to attempt to trace in historical order the progress of his thought throughout the course of his Gentile Mission; a third would be to gather together under appropriate headings his various statements irrespective of the particular writing in which they appear. Each of these methods has its own value, but, on the whole, it seems best to employ a fourth, in harmony with the nature of the present investigation as far as we have already conducted it. Recognizing that the procedure cannot be carried out with complete exactitude, we have sought to distinguish between ideas which St. Paul drew from the primitive Christian tradition of his day and those which he has himself developed in his writings and to which he has given his own distinctive impress. It is to these elements that we should apply the term 'Paulinism', if we use it at all, and not to all the thoughts which appear in his Epistles. Naturally, we cannot make the distinction we have described complete. Even in taking over traditional teaching St. Paul rarely leaves it as he finds it. He puts his own stamp upon it, now faintly, now unmistakably, and weaves it into the web of his design. It follows, therefore, that we shall be compelled to treat many of his statements both as illustrations of primitive belief and as examples of his special teaching. In these circumstances, the best method will be, first, to see how he presents the ideas mentioned in the list at the end of Part I,[1] and, secondly, to examine closely the ideas which stand out as his distinctive contribution to the doctrine of the Atonement.

One cannot fail to be impressed with the centrality of the death of Christ in his teaching. 'Far be it from me to glory,' he cries, 'save in the cross of our Lord Jesus Christ, through which the world hath been crucified unto me, and I unto the world' (Galatians vi. 14). In Corinth, he tells us, he determined not to know anything 'save Jesus Christ, and him crucified' (1 Corin-

[1] Pp. 50f.

thians ii. 1). He had been sent to preach the Gospel, but 'not in
wisdom of words, lest the cross of Christ should be made void'
(1 Corinthians i. 17). The 'word of the cross' to them that are
perishing is foolishness, but to himself and to all who are 'being
saved' it is God's power (1 Corinthians i. 18). To Jews a
stumbling-block, and to Gentiles foolishness, it is, to those who
are called, 'Christ the power of God, and the wisdom of God'
(1 Corinthians i. 24). Of his antinomian adversaries he tells us
weeping that they are 'enemies of the cross of Christ' (Philippians
iii. 18).

It was inevitable that this supreme interest should find expression in a new terminology. The expression 'the cross of Christ' is
an accepted phrase in our Christian vocabulary, yet, with a single
exception in the Epistle to the Hebrews,[1] St. Paul is the only New
Testament writer who uses it, and it appears, in various forms, ten
times in his Epistles.[2] In it, no doubt, we may hear the horror of
a Jew who was also a Hellenist as he thought of this dreadful form
of execution; but the use of a new term is also the sign of an
increased intellectual concentration upon the climax of the
Gospel story. So, too, in the case of the now familiar phrase 'the
death of Christ' (or 'his death') which he alone uses. The
introduction of a phrase which we have not found as yet in the
vocabulary of primitive Christianity does not mean, in St. Paul's
usage, a narrower conception of Christ's sacrifice; it marks the
thinker's need for additional terms and modes of speech. Besides
these expressions, there are many others which he finds necessary
to clothe his thoughts, such as 'justification', 'reconciliation',
'dying with Christ', and 'rising' with Him. To the despair of the
commentator, he uses a rare word like ἱλαστήριον (Romans iii.
25), and he has hidden one of his richest conceptions in the phrases
'in Christ' and 'in Him'. All these are signs of a virile mind,
which does not disdain emotion in seeking to read the deepest
secret of the Christian faith.

To his task St. Paul brings a mind trained in the best rabbinic
schools of Judasim, steeped in the thought and language of the
Septuagint, influenced, though not deeply instructed, by contact
with Greek philosophy, responsive to contemporary religious
movements, alive to social conditions as he saw them in the course

---

[1] Hebrews xii. 2: 'who for the joy that was set before him endured the cross'.
[2] 1 Corinthians i. 17, 18; Galatians v. 11, vi. 12, 14; Ephesians ii. 16; Philippians
ii. 8, iii. 18; Colossians i. 20, ii. 14.

of his travels by land and sea. To it also he brings a profound religious experience of sin, of spiritual despair, of moral frustration, co-existent with an unquenchable belief in God, in the certainty of His fidelity to His ancient Covenant with Israel and His indestructible will to save men and set them faultless before His throne. It may well lead us to wonder, but it cannot occasion surprise, that such a man should see deeper meaning in the beliefs of the primitive Christian communities, and should also perceive aspects of truth which other had but faintly descried or had not even suspected. Paulinism is not the perversion of primitive Christianity; it is the gleaming product pouring from the crucible of a gifted and consecrated mind which, with prophetic insight, has seen in the existing tradition half-guessed secrets of God's redeeming Love. Proof of this claim will be seen in his treatment of the several ideas we have found latent in the religion and belief of the first communities, and in the new direction he gave to Christian thought in the centuries which followed.

(a) St. Paul's Use of Primitive Christian Tradition

In St. Paul's Epistles there are parallels to all the ideas we have found in the primitive Christian tradition. We shall therefore begin by taking up each of these ideas and noting what his treatment of them actually is.

(1) *The Necessity of the Death of Christ in relation to the Divine Purpose.* We have seen that it was the conviction of Jesus that, as the Son of Man, He 'must suffer', and that with this purpose He completely identified Himself. The earliest preaching, as represented by the Acts, faithfully preserved this note, and it is repeatedly sounded by St. Paul in various ways. It was to the obtaining of salvation, he says, that God 'appointed us' 'through our Lord Jesus Christ' (1 Thessalonians v. 9). Justification and reconciliation are His acts wrought through the redemptive ministry of Christ (Romans iii. 26, v. 8 *f.*, 2 Corinthians v. 18 *f.*). The Cross is His power (1 Corinthians i. 18, 24). It was He who condemned sin in the flesh when He sent His Son as an offering for sin (Romans viii. 3). The Son was sent by Him in 'the fulness of the time' (Galatians iv. 4), and His self-giving and redemptive work are 'according to the will of our God and Father' (Galatians i. 4). From beginning to end, and at every stage in its operation, redemption is in Pauline thought the work of God.

(2) *The Messianic Character of Christ's Death.* While by no means absent in St. Paul's teaching, this aspect is not specially emphasized. He never uses the term 'Son of Man', which indeed, apart from a solitary instance in Acts vii. 56, is not found outside the Gospels. In most cases he uses the word 'Christ' as a personal name;[1] he never speaks of 'Jesus, the Christ', but frequently of 'Jesus' or 'Christ Jesus', and sometimes of 'our Lord Jesus Christ'. These are the names which he commonly uses in his references to the Cross, although twice he speaks of God sending or sparing not 'his own Son' (Romans viii. 3, 32), of His sending forth 'his Son' (Galatians iv. 4), and of our being translated into the kingdom of 'the Son of his love' (Colossians i. 13). His usage is due in part to his instinctive reaction to the circumstances of the Gentile world, to which Jewish Messianism was strange, but even more to his enhanced conception of the Person of Christ which found better expression in names like 'Christ Jesus', 'Christ', 'Son', and 'Lord' than in the title 'the Messiah'. He was far from having parted with his Messianic beliefs, as his reference to Christ as 'born of the seed of David according to the flesh' (Romans i. 3) and his proud claim for his kinsmen, 'of whom is the Messiah as concerning the flesh' (Romans ix. 5), clearly show, not to speak of the eschatological hopes, bound up with his fervent expectation of the *Parousia* of Christ, to which he held with passionate intensity. When, however, he thought and wrote of the atoning ministry of God in Christ, he found that he was dealing with a majestic conception of redeeming love which inevitably broke the mould of Messianic teaching, as Jesus Himself showed when He reinterpreted the doctrine of the Son of Man in terms suggested by the Second Isaiah's delineation of the Suffering Servant of the Lord. Jesus could still continue to speak of 'the Son of Man' because He was addressing Jews, and because He was speaking of a 'mystery' to be revealed to His disciples in the Father's time (cf. Matthew xvi. 17). For St. Paul these conditions did not exist; looking steadfastly upon the fact of 'Christ crucified', he was compelled to find new forms of thought and expression.

(3) *The Vicarious Aspect of the Death of Christ.* This truth, which Jesus expressed when He declared that the Son of Man had come to give Himself a ransom 'for many', and when in the same terms He spoke of the shedding of His covenant blood, is repeatedly mentioned by St. Paul in his Epistles. The common habit of

[1] Cf. J. Weiss, *The History of Primitive Christianity*, p. 457.

supporting this statement by a string of references to passages where it may be found is inadequate, since it does not bring home to the mind either the intensity or the variety of his statements. Here, as always, we must consider what he actually says. And what he says is clear and emphatic. Salvation is through our Lord Jesus Christ who 'died for us' (1 Thessalonians v. 9 f.). He 'died for us' while we were yet sinners (Romans v. 8). He was delivered up 'for us all' (Romans viii. 32), gave Himself up 'for us' (Ephesians v. 2) and for the Church (Ephesians v. 25). All 'died' because 'one died for all' (2 Corinthians v. 14 f.). He became 'a curse for us' (Galatians iii. 13). To St. Paul this truth is a precious reality of which he cannot remind his converts too often. Its personal moment for himself is expressed in imperishable words about crucifixion with Christ when he describes faith as faith in the Son of God, 'who loved me, and gave himself up for me' (Galatians ii. 20). In all these cases, except the first, the preposition used is ὑπέρ, 'on behalf of'; in 1 Thessalonians v. 10, with no appreciable difference of meaning, it is περί, 'on account of'. Nowhere does he use ἀντί, 'instead of'. From this we may certainly infer that he did not look upon the death of Christ as that of a substitute. The alleged substitutionary element in his thought is rather to be discerned in his teaching about the representative aspect of Christ's work, and to this we now turn.

(4) *The Representative Element in Christ's Work.* For all who accept the genuineness of Mark x. 45[1] there can be no doubt that, as the Son of Man, Jesus thought of Himself as representing the many for whom He came to give His life as a ransom. As we have seen, the traceable signs of this idea in primitive belief are few and uncertain. It is present in 1 Timothy ii. 6, which is based on Mark x. 45 rather than Pauline statements, but the passage is too late to be explained as more than a distant echo of earlier teaching; and while the idea of 'sin-bearing' in 1 Peter ii. 24 implies representative action, it may be a thought of the writer more than a reflection of popular belief.[2] All the more important, therefore, are the Pauline passages in which the idea of representative suffering appears, and especially the question whether the

---

[1] Cf. *Jesus and His Sacrifice*, pp. 99 ff. For more recent discussions, see W. F. Howard, *The Expository Times*, l, pp. 107–10; F. Büchsel, *Theol. Wort.*, iv, pp. 343–51.

[2] Pauline origin is improbable in view of the absence of the thought of sin-bearing from St. Paul's Epistles.

Apostle is introducing something novel or is treating more fully a current belief. The presence of the idea is certain. It is implied when he urges his readers to reckon themselves 'dead unto sin', but 'alive unto God in Christ Jesus', immediately after he says of Christ: 'The death that he died, he died unto sin once; but the life that he liveth, he liveth unto God' (Romans vi. 10 f.). It is also implicit when he sets the obedience of Christ over against the trespass of Adam, and speaks of the free gift which came to all men *'through one act of righteousness'*[1] (Romans v. 18); and even more plainly when he says that, whereas the many were constituted sinners through one man's disobedience (Adam's), 'even so *through the obedience of the one* (Christ) shall the many be constituted righteous' (Romans v. 19). The thought is explicit in the statement: 'The love of Christ constraineth us; because we thus judge, that one died for all, *therefore all died*' (2 Corinthians v. 14). It is also unmistakable in the affirmation, epigram though it is, 'Him who knew no sin *he made to be sin on our behalf*' (2 Corinthians v. 21) and in the polemical argument of Galatians iii. 13: 'Christ redeemed us from the curse of the law, having become *a curse for us*.' The impression we gain from these passages is not that of a totally unknown idea, enunciated for the first time, but that of a thought, already familiar in the preaching, which is being pressed home with a new and passionate emphasis.

Many questions are raised by these Pauline statements. What is the 'one act of righteousness' by which the gift of justification unto life came to all men? How is the death of all involved in the death of One? How could the sinless Christ be said to have been 'made sin' or to have become 'a curse' for us? It is evident that St. Paul believed that in some way, and in some representative way, Christ acted for men, and that what happened to Him was of supreme moment for them. To this belief he attached great, indeed decisive, importance, and he made it one of the foundation principles of his teaching. Just for this reason it will be best to reserve this question for further consideration among the ideas which belong to his distinctive teaching. It is a principle, rooted in popular belief, to which he gave an emphasis destined to influence the thought of the Christian Church for generations to come.

(5) *The Relation of the Death of Christ to Sin.* Like the representative aspect of the work of Christ, the relation of the death of Christ

---

[1] Cf. G. Schrenk, *Theol. Wort.*, ii, pp. 225 f.

to sin is a popular belief which in St. Paul's hands becomes a characteristic conception. No saying of Jesus, preserved in the Gospel tradition, connects His death with sin. Nevertheless, it would be a complete delusion to suppose that the association was first made either by St. Paul or by any of the first Christian preachers. When Jesus spoke of giving His life as a ransom for the many, He saw the many as sinners, and when He described His blood as covenant-blood, He was thinking of their reconciliation in spite of sin, to God. This connexion is attested by every record of primitive preaching and belief we have been able to trace. One of the most fundamental beliefs of the first communities is the simple creed: 'Christ died for our sins.' To this fact St. Paul himself is a witness; but, as in most of the questions under review, he not only witnesses to the belief, but expresses it, and develops it, in a variety of ways. From the evidential standpoint his most important statement is that to which we have just referred: 'I delivered unto you first of all that which also I received, how that *Christ died for our sins* according to the Scriptures' (1 Corinthians xv. 3). Other passages of like tenor are Galatians i. 4: 'Our Lord Jesus Christ, who *gave himself for our sins*', and Romans iv. 25: 'who was *delivered up for our trespasses*'. Besides these passages are those which describe the work of Christ as one of redemption (ἀπολύτρωσις). 1 Corinthians vi. 20, 'Ye were bought with a price' (cf. vii. 23), is of this character; and the word itself is used in Ephesians i. 7, 'In whom we have our *redemption* through his blood, the forgiveness of our trespasses', and in Colossians i. 14, 'In whom we have our *redemption*, the forgiveness of our sins'. In these passages forgiveness, or, to speak more accurately, the remission of sins, is not the equivalent of redemption, but is mentioned as its most conspicuous blessing. The primary idea is that of deliverance from sin by reason of the death of Christ. In other contexts ἀπολύτρωσις is used in an eschatological sense,[1] of the 'deliverance' accomplished in the End-time, but in Ephesians i. 7 and Colossians i. 14 the suggestion of a present experience is unmistakable. The same idea appears also in Colossians ii. 13 f. Here St. Paul reminds his readers that God had quickened them together with Christ, 'dealing generously [χαρισάμενος] with us in respect of our trespasses'.[2] Using a commercial metaphor, he

---

[1] E.g. in Romans viii. 23; Ephesians i. 14, iv. 30. See the invaluable article of F. Büchsel on the word in *Theol. Wort.*, iv, pp. 354–9.

[2] One must feel very doubtful about rendering χαρίζεσθαι 'to forgive', a meaning not found outside the New Testament.

speaks of God[1] cancelling the bond standing against us, removing it, and nailing it to the Cross of Christ.

Thus far, the passages we have examined repeat, with increased force and variety of statement, primitive Christian convictions; but other Pauline statements introduce new aspects of the death of Christ in relation to sin. Some of them make use of forensic ideas, others are concerned with questions of moral government, while others again express the idea of a victorious conflict with evil powers. By the use of a legal analogy, sin is conceived as a defendant upon whom sentence has fallen; in sending His Son in the likeness of sinful flesh, and as an offering for sin, God *condemned sin* in the flesh' (Romans viii. 3). Or, again, the problem of righteousness is faced, both in relation to God Himself and as regards that standing in His sight which He gives to sinful men. In order to show His righteousness, St. Paul says, God publicly set forth Christ, as a means of atonement, 'because of the passing over of the sins done aforetime, in the forbearance of God' (Romans iii. 25); and, in the words 'being now justified by his blood' (Romans v. 9; cf. v. 18), he bases His activity in declaring men righteous upon the sacrifice of Christ. The thought of the moral government of the world is in his mind when he associates with the words just quoted the claim: 'Much more then . . . shall we be saved from the Wrath through him' (Romans v. 9). This idea of 'the Wrath' is not infrequently present in his writings. Primarily, an eschatological concept, as in Romans v. 9, and I Thessalonians i. 10,[2] it has also a present significance in his teaching (cf. Romans i. 18).[3] By it he means no passionate or irrational anger, but the judgment which falls upon sin in the moral world over which God rules.[4] The thought of a victorious struggle of God with the powers of evil is expressed in Colossians ii. 15: 'Having despoiled the principalities and the powers, he made a show of them openly, triumphing over them in it.' Our

[1] Probably 'God' is the subject throughout. Cf. T. K. Abbott, *I.C.C.*, *Ephesians and Colossians*, p. 257. Lightfoot holds that there is a change of subject ('Christ') before 'he hath taken it away', *Colossians and Philemon*, p. 187. Cf. E. F. Scott (*Moffatt N.T. Commentary*), p. 46.

[2] 'Jesus, which delivereth us from the wrath to come.'

[3] 'For the wrath of God is revealed from heaven against all ungodliness and unrighteousness of men, who hold down the truth in unrighteousness.'

[4] St. Paul speaks more frequently of 'the Wrath' (Romans iii. 5, v. 9, ix. 22, xii. 19; I Thessalonians i. 10, ii. 16) than of 'the wrath of God' (Romans i. 18; Ephesians v. 6; Colossians iii. 6).

interpretation of this obscure verse must depend on the view we take of 1 Corinthians ii. 8: 'the rulers of this world' and of Galatians iv. 3, 9, Colossians ii. 8, 20, where the word στοιχεῖα probably means 'elemental spirits', widely believed to control the destinies of the universe. 'Our wrestling', says St. Paul, 'is not against flesh and blood, but against the principalities, against the powers, against the world-rulers of this darkness, against the spiritual hosts of wickedness in the heavenly places' (Ephesians vi. 12). It would appear from Colossians ii. 15 that he thought also of the work of Christ as a fight of God Himself with these hostile powers, a death-grapple from which He emerged victorious, stripping His enemies of their apparel and leading them, like a Roman conqueror, in triumph.

The ideas described above lead us far beyond the beliefs of primitive Christianity, and it will be necessary, therefore, to consider them more closely in connexion with St. Paul's distinctive teaching.

(6) *The Sacrificial Significance of the Death of Christ.* St. Paul's emphasis upon the sacrificial aspect of Christ's death does not differ notably from that of the primitive communities. As we have seen, the use of sacrificial analogies is present in all the records which indicate early Christian belief. They are equally visible in St. Paul's Epistles, in his teaching about the Eucharist (cf. 1 Corinthians x. 14–22, xi. 20–34), in his use of the term 'blood' with reference to the death of Christ,[1] and especially in Romans iii. 25, 1 Corinthians v. 7, and Ephesians v. 2. To explain the allusions to 'blood' as synonyms for 'death' is mistaken. One can hardly fail to be conscious of a loss of meaning if instead of 'being justified *by his blood*' (Romans v. 9) we read 'being justified in Christ crucified', or if the words 'nigh *in the blood of Christ*' (Ephesians ii. 13) are replaced by 'through Christ as crucified', or again if '*by his blood*' (Romans iii. 25) is interpreted as 'dying a bloody death'.[2] In each case the thought of the life of Christ, freely surrendered and offered for men, is exchanged for a reference to a tragic, but unexplained, historical event. Nor is it enough to describe these phrases as metaphors destitute of sacral associa-

---

[1] 'His blood' in Romans iii. 25, v. 9; Ephesians i. 7; 'the blood of Christ' in 1 Corinthians x. 16; Ephesians ii. 13; 'the blood of the Lord' in 1 Corinthians xi. 27; 'the blood of his cross' in Colossians i. 20; and 'my blood' in the saying of Jesus recorded in 1 Corinthians xi. 25.

[2] Cf. C. A. Anderson Scott, *Foot-Notes to St. Paul*, pp. 25, 33, 178; *Christianity according to St. Paul*, p. 72.

tions.[1] It was impossible to divest them of these associations when the Cross gave to them a deeper meaning than ever they had possessed before.

In Romans iii. 25, 'by his blood' indicates, not simply the idea of cost, but the sense in which God set forth Christ 'as a means of atonement'; it was because His life was poured out in sacrifice for sinners. In Romans viii. 3, the statement that God sent forth his Son περὶ ἁμαρτίας, in view of the usage of the Septuagint, may be a reference to the sin-offering,[2] but in the absence of an emphasis upon this idea in the Pauline Epistles, it should probably be rendered 'for sin'.[3] Of greater importance is 1 Corinthians v. 7: 'For our passover also hath been *sacrificed*, even Christ', where Christ is thought of as the Passover Lamb and the verb θύω is used. Most important of all is Ephesians v. 2: 'Even as Christ also loved you, and gave himself up for us, *an offering and a sacrifice to God* for an odour of a sweet smell', where the words 'offering' and 'sacrifice' are applied to Christ with reference to God. The fact that St. Paul uses the same metaphor of Christian teachers (2 Corinthians ii. 15) and of the gift of the Philippians to himself (Philippians iv. 18), may certainly warn us against pressing its doctrinal use too far,[4] but it does not warrant us in treating it as a rhetorical flourish. The Apostle who could speak of himself as being poured out as a libation in addition to the sacrifice and service of the faith of the saints at Philippi (Philippians ii. 17), and who, in the genuine note embedded in 2 Timothy, could use the same figure of his approaching death (2 Timothy iv. 6), was transferring to himself language he had first found significant in the Cross of Christ.

The question must naturally arise why St. Paul does not make a fuller use of sacrificial ideas. Upon this matter conjectures alone are possible. In part, it is probably due to the fact that he stands too near to the existing sacrificial system, with its patent deficiencies[5] lying obvious before him, at a time when the synagogue was growing in esteem and importance at the expense of the Temple, and when already the later rabbinical emphasis upon the

---

[1] See earlier, pp. 24 f.

[2] So Sanday and Headlam, *I.C.C., Romans*, p. 193. See also the comment of Denney, *The Expositor's Greek Testament*, ii. p. 645.

[3] The R.V. has 'as an offering for sin', but the marginal reading is 'for sin'.

[4] Cf. J. Armitage Robinson, *St. Paul's Epistle to the Ephesians*, p. 196.

[5] Cf. *Jesus and His Sacrifice*, pp. 55 f.

supreme value of repentance and moral endeavour may have been making itself felt. In this connexion, it is of interest to remember that the writer of the Epistle to the Hebrews, whose use of sacrificial analogies is so much greater, wrote nearly a generation later, when the Temple lay in ruins, and at a distance from Jerusalem, and found his inspiration in the ancient Tabernacle of Israel rather than in the Temple of Herod. Possibly also, although on this matter we have no information at all, we should allow something for the revulsion of the educated and much-travelled man at the horrible accompaniments of sacrifice, a revulsion which to this day prevents theologians otherwise well versed in the science of comparative religion from doing full justice to the underlying ideas of the sacrificial system. Most important of all is the fact that the supreme interest of St. Paul is not in the rationale of the Atonement, but in the ethical and religious problems of righteousness rendered acute by the Christian conviction that sinful men can be received into abiding fellowship by a Holy and a Righteous God. A profound thinker, he is not a constructive theologian anxious to build up a comprehensive theory of the meaning of the death of Christ. Later we shall find that in his teaching there are the outlines of several theories which it is impossible to harmonize, as a presentation of Pauline theology, into a consistent whole.

(7) *The Use of the Servant-Conception.* Closely connected with St. Paul's use of sacrificial ideas is his comparative neglect of the Servant-conception of Isaiah lii. 13–liii. In the records of primitive Christian belief we can trace a diminishing emphasis upon an idea which for Jesus Himself was central and determinative. In the early sermons of the Acts the use of the term 'Servant' is notable (cf. Acts iii. 13, 26, iv. 27, 30); in 1 Peter ii. 22–4 the derived imagery is manifest, but the term is not used; in the Apocalypse it is not possible to assess the relative importance of the Servant-conception as compared with that of the Passover Lamb; in the Pastoral Epistles the idea has disappeared altogether. In St. Paul's Epistles the thought of the Servant undoubtedly lies in the background of Romans iv. 25: 'who was *delivered up* for our trespasses', and of Ephesians v. 2: 'even as Christ . . . *gave himself up* for us' (cf. Galatians ii. 20); and it strongly colours the language and thought of the majestic hymn in Philippians ii. 5–11, and especially the words of verse 7, 'but emptied himself, taking the form of *a servant*', and of verse 9, 'Wherefore also God *highly*

E

exalted him, and gave unto him the name which is above every name'. At the same time, the Apostle never speaks of Jesus as 'the Servant' and never expressly quotes Isaiah liii.[1] Once more we can only enter the realms of conjecture. Is the explanation to be found in the widespread institution of slavery and the fact that slaves were despised as mere chattels, without natural rights and at the disposal of their master's whim? Influenced by the use of παῖς in the Septuagint, 'servant' is our term for the despised figure of Isaiah liii, but the Hebrew word is *'ebed*, δοῦλος, 'slave'. Acts overcame the difficulty by using παῖς; could St. Paul not forget his Hebrew Bible? The one person who could use the picture of the Suffering Slave to describe Messianic suffering was Jesus Himself, for we must look askance at light-hearted suggestions which trace the original application of Isaiah liii to Christ to the fertile imagination of the primitive community. Willing as he was to describe himself as 'the slave of Christ' (Romans i. 1; Galatians i. 10; Philippians i. 1), and ready to use it of other Christians (1 Corinthians vii. 22; Ephesians vi. 6; Philippians i. 1; Colossians iv. 12), he may have shrunk from using it directly of Jesus, and especially in commending Him to the acceptance of the Gentile world. It is noteworthy that in Philippians ii. 7 he says that Christ took 'the *form* of a slave', and he speedily follows this by his triumphant emphasis upon the glory of the exaltation and 'the name which is above every name' (ii. 9). He uses the name 'Lord' even when speaking of Christ's death (Galatians i. 4, vi. 14; 1 Corinthians xi. 25), and his horror at the thought of slavery is revealed in his words: 'Ye were bought with a price; become not slaves of men' (1 Corinthians vii. 23). Whether he fully recognized that sublime picture of sacrificial suffering in Isaiah liii for what it is, we must hesitate to say, and the 'explanation' suggested above can be received only with considerable reserve. When all is said, our final answer to the question why St. Paul did not use the Servant-conception in his theology of the Cross must be that we do not know. What is certain is that, for all its sublimity, his treatment of this theme, and especially its significance as the one true sacrifice for men, suffers because he makes such little use of this master-key supplied by Jesus Himself.

(8) *The Resurrection and the Death of Christ.* The relation of St. Paul to the common faith of the early Church is shown by his

---

[1] Apart from the purely literary allusion in Romans x. 16: 'Lord, who hath believed our report?'

account of his preaching, and the tradition he had received, in 1 Corinthians xv. 3–8, the essence of which was that Christ died for sins, that He was buried, and that He was raised on the third day according to the Scriptures. Immediately the death and the burial are mentioned the reference to the resurrection follows. So too in Romans iv. 25: 'who was delivered up for our trespasses, and was raised for our justification'. To separate the two ideas in this passage, and to suppose that St. Paul meant to associate the one with trespasses and the other with justification, is wholly mistaken. The apparent separation may be due to the prominence of the resurrection in the context (cf. iv. 24). What he means is that Jesus died and rose again because of our trespasses and our justification. As Johannes Weiss observes, the parallelism 'is merely the rhetorical expansion of a *single* thought'.[1] In Romans vi. 10 also a reference to death is at once followed by a reference to life: 'the death that he died . . . the life that he liveth. . . .' So also in 2 Corinthians v. 15, his readers are urged, not to live unto themselves, but 'unto him who for their sakes died and rose again'. Further illustration is unnecessary. Nothing is more certain than that of St. Paul the Crucified is the Living Christ, of whom he longs to know both 'the power of his resurrection' and 'the fellowship of his sufferings' (Philippians iii. 10). A further idea is present when in Romans viii. 34, after speaking of the death and the resurrection in the manner already indicated, St. Paul adds, 'who also maketh intercession for us', a ministry which in viii. 27 he assigns to the Spirit. This aspect of the work of the Living Christ, so prominent in the Epistle to the Hebrews, is not developed elsewhere by St. Paul.

(9) *Faith-union with the Crucified.* In this experience we meet with a conception which extends far beyond anything we can find in the records of primitive belief. It would, however, be the greatest of mistakes to suppose that nothing parallel to it existed outside Pauline circles. Its roots lie in that attitude of utter devotion to the person of Christ which became characteristic of the disciples, and which He Himself invited and fostered in the communion meals of Galilee and at the Last Supper at Jerusalem on the night in which He was betrayed. After His death this relationship was deepened and enriched through manifold experiences of suffering, service, and worship, and especially, as the Epistles of St. Paul imply, in connexion with Baptism and

---

[1] *The History of Primitive Christianity*, p. 104.

the Supper. None the less, it is the teaching and terminology of St. Paul which have stamped the idea of faith-union with Christ as the hall-mark of evangelical Christianity.

The Gospel, he declares, 'is the power of God unto salvation to every one that believeth' (Romans i. 16). The righteousness of God manifested in it is 'through faith in Jesus Christ unto all them that believe' (Romans i. 17, iii. 22). It is reckoned to him 'that worketh not, but believeth on him that justifieth the ungodly' (Romans iv. 5). Far more distinctive of Pauline usage, however, is the extent to which the noun 'faith' is employed. It is used to describe the righteousness of God (Romans i. 17, x. 6; Philippians iii. 9), justification (Romans iii. 26, 28, 30, v. 1; Galatians ii. 16, iii. 8, 24), and the means of access to God (Romans v. 2(?); Ephesians iii. 12). The object of faith is sometimes God and sometimes Christ, but no emphasis can be laid upon this distinction since the ultimate object of faith, even when the noun appears to be used absolutely, is God active to redeem in Christ. In the striking rendering of Anderson Scott,[1] God justifies 'him who founds on faith in Jesus' (τὸν ἐκ πίστεως ᾽Ιησοῦ, Romans iii. 26), and the Jesus whom St. Paul preached was One who had laid down His life for men. It ought to be superfluous to say that this faith transcends belief, for St. Paul has perfectly expressed its vital character in the immortal words of Galatians ii. 20: 'that life which I now live in the flesh I live in faith, the faith which is in the Son of God, who loved me, and gave himself up for me'. In Galatians v. 6 it is described as 'faith working through love'; in Ephesians ii. 8 it is closely associated with grace, in the words: 'By grace have ye been saved through faith'; and in Ephesians iii. 17 it is a mediating experience whereby Christ dwells within the heart ('that Christ may dwell in your hearts through faith'). Words could hardly express a more intimate personal relationship, ethical and spiritual, always based upon, and related to, the amazing work of God in Christ.

In this teaching about faith we pass into regions which are distinctively Pauline in depth and emphasis, however real and true may be the lines of connexion between it and the experience of the primitive Church. All the more evident is this fact, when we add to this teaching St. Paul's yet more characteristic emphasis upon faith-union with Christ in his use of the pregnant phrase 'in Christ', and his words, unparalleled elsewhere in the New

---

[1] *Christianity according to St. Paul*, p. 72.

Testament, about 'dying', 'rising', and 'living' with Christ. It is to St. Paul above all others that the Church owes the idea, absolutely vital to a true apprehension of the doctrine of the Atonement, of fellowship with the Redeemer in the realities of His saving ministry.

(10) *The Eucharist and the Death of Christ*. The relation of St. Paul's teaching to the beliefs of primitive Christianity with regard to the Eucharist is a question of very great complexity. Substantially, he is in close agreement with the tradition recorded in Mark xiv. 22–5, the principal difference being the form in which he gives the saying about the cup (cf. 1 Corinthians xi. 25).[1] But to what extent was this tradition familiar to the earliest communities? It is possible that the special source used by St. Luke (cf. xxii. 14–8), and the references to breaking bread in the Acts (ii. 42; cf. ii. 46, xx. 7, 11, xxvii. 35), may indicate communion-meals which pointed forward to the Parousia rather than eucharistic fellowships associated with the death of Christ. If this is so, a problem of the greatest interest and importance is raised regarding the place of the Eucharist in the earliest period. It is not desirable to discuss this question at this stage, although it will be necessary to return to it later.[2] Meantime, the importance of the testimony of St. Paul in relation to the Eucharist must be considered. The narrative of the Supper which he gives in 1 Corinthians xi. 23–5 indicates his belief that he is handing on a valid tradition which he had already imparted to the Church at Corinth. His words: 'I received of the Lord that which also I delivered unto you', suggest teaching received and given rather than the communication of a divine revelation.[3] Moreover, the teaching to which he refers, as 1 Corinthians xi. 23–5 shows, closely connects the Eucharist with the death of Christ. Of the bread he records that Jesus said, 'This is my body, which is for you', and of the cup: 'This cup is the new covenant in my blood.' St. Paul therefore was using primitive tradition when he related the Eucharist to the death of Christ. It is equally clear, however, from 1 Corinthians x. 1–4, 14–22, xi. 20–34, that he had distinctive teaching to give upon this theme which in some respects went beyond what he had previously taught in Corinth. In reading

---

[1] 'This cup is the new covenant in my blood.' Cf. Mark xiv. 24: 'This is my blood of the covenant, which is shed for many.'

[2] See pp. 161–6.

[3] Cf. *Jesus and His Sacrifice*, pp. 201 *f*.

1 Corinthians x. 16, one cannot but ask: Had the Corinthians realized that the cup of blessing was 'a communion of the blood of Christ', and that the broken bread was 'a communion of the body of Christ'? If they had entered into the meaning of these words, they would have been more scrupulous about eating meat sacrificed to idols, and when they assembled 'to eat the Lord's supper' (1 Corinthians xi. 20), their gatherings would not have presented the disorderly features indicated in St. Paul's indignant words: 'What? have ye not houses to eat and to drink in? or despise ye the church of God, and put them to shame that have not?' (1 Corinthians xi. 22). It is probable that on this, as on other questions related to the death of Christ, St. Paul had special teaching to impart. His assumption that those who eat the sacrifices have 'communion with the altar' (1 Corinthians x. 18), and his declaration, 'Ye cannot drink the cup of the Lord, and the cup of devils: ye cannot partake of the table of the Lord, and of the table of devils' (1 Corinthians x. 21), show that he thought of the Eucharist as providing the opportunity to enter into a vital relationship with Christ Himself as the Crucified Saviour, and to appropriate the blessings made possible by His death. All that he says is ethically conditioned; he by no means forgets the importance of the mind and spirit in which men partake of the Supper; but he undoubtedly views it as an objective means whereby the sacrifice of Christ is brought into a saving relationship with the needs of the believer. Such teaching is of the greatest importance for an understanding of his doctrine concerning the Atonement and it must be considered again in connexion with the other elements which belong to his distinctive theology.[1]

(11) *The Idea of Suffering with Christ.* This idea is present already in the sayings of Jesus, in His words about taking up the cross (Mark viii. 34) and still more clearly in the promise to James and John: 'The cup that I drink ye shall drink; and with the baptism that I am baptized withal shall ye be baptized' (Mark x. 39). In the Acts the idea emerges, though not in a mystical form, in such a passage as v. 41: 'They therefore departed from the presence of the council, rejoicing that they were counted worthy to suffer dishonour for the Name', and more faintly in xiv. 22: 'exhorting them to continue in the faith, and that through many tribulations we must enter into the kingdom of God'. These passages, however, are editorial, and primarily represent the point of view of St. Luke

---

[1] I have treated this question more fully in *Jesus and His Sacrifice*, pp. 201-17.

at the time when he wrote the Acts. None the less, they may well be primitive ideas reflected in his sources. In 1 Peter, we have seen, there is a distinct practical emphasis upon the thought of suffering with Christ. The writer describes himself as 'a witness of the sufferings of Christ' (v. 1) and his readers as 'partakers of Christ's sufferings' (iv. 13). Christ has left them an example that they should 'follow his steps' (ii. 21). In the Apocalypse martyrdom is the pledge of loyalty to Christ, a fidelity which will be rewarded by the gift of 'the crown of life' (ii. 10; cf. xii. 11, xiv. 4).

St. Paul fully recognizes and endorses this aspect of primitive belief. 'As the sufferings of Christ abound to us', he says, 'even so our comfort also aboundeth through Christ' (2 Corinthians i. 5). He is 'always bearing about in the body the dying of Jesus' that the life also of Jesus may be manifested in his mortal flesh (2 Corinthians iv. 10). He longs to know 'the fellowship of his sufferings, becoming conformed unto his death' (Philippians iii. 10), and congratulates the Philippians that it has been granted to them for Christ's sake 'not only to believe on him, but also to suffer in his behalf' (Philippians i. 29). His most striking statement, however, is Colossians i. 24 f.: 'Now I rejoice in my sufferings for your sake, and fill up on my part that which remains over of the afflictions of Christ in my flesh for his body's sake, which is the church; whereof I was made a minister.' In these words there is no suggestion that the work of Christ is incomplete, but it is distinctly suggested that the fidelity of a Christian minister and servant of Christ involves a real participation, within the limitations of his opportunities and powers, in the afflictions He endured in the fulfilment of His redemptive ministry for mankind.

(12) *The Love of God in the Death of Christ.* We have seen that this idea is singularly wanting in any of the records which indicate the beliefs of primitive Christianity ,and what is more surprising still, that in none of the recorded sayings of Jesus does He say that the purpose of His death was to reveal the love of His Heavenly Father.[1] These facts must be connected. It was because in His teaching Jesus dwelt upon other aspects of His redemptive work that the first preachers did not give prominence to this great truth. Once it was proclaimed it was sure to meet with an immediate response since it was entirely in harmony with all that Jesus taught concerning the Father. Its absence from the teaching of Jesus, even if we allow for the fragmentary character of the Gospel

---

[1] John iii. 16 is the inspired comment of the Fourth Evangelist.

tradition, must mean that He did not look upon the revelation of the Father's love as the main purpose of His death; and for this reason its truth was more likely to be expressed by one who had reflected upon the Cross, as an accomplished fact, than by Jesus Himself. The first Christian teacher to proclaim it was, of course, St. Paul in the unforgettable words of Romans v. 8: 'God commendeth his own love toward us, in that, while we were yet sinners, Christ died for us.' Even in this passage, if we have regard to its context, it is to be noticed that the reference to the love of God, although not incidental, is not the main thought. All the emphasis of St. Paul's thought is upon the amazing fact that it was 'while we were yet weak', 'while we were yet sinners', and 'for the ungodly', that Christ died; and it is in this connexion that he speaks of the death as the commendation of the love of God. One may say, however, that everywhere its wonder lies behind his statements. It is visible, for example, in his reference, in Ephesians i. 6, to 'the glory of his grace, which he freely bestowed upon us in the Beloved'; in Romans v. 15, when he speaks of the grace of God, and the gift by the grace of Christ, abounding to the many; in Romans vi. 14, in the words: 'Ye are not under the law, but under grace'; and, indeed, again and again, when he mentions grace, especially in relation to justification (Romans iii. 24, iv. 16, v. 17) and salvation (Ephesians ii. 5, 8). The love of God in the sacrifice of Christ is the undertone of his theology. This thought must always have been implicit in Christian teaching, but in St. Paul's Epistles its notes are unmistakable, so that, whenever theology has forgotten or obscured its greatness, his burning words have brought it back to the mind and experience of the Church.

(13) *The Ethical and Spiritual Purpose of the Death of Christ.* In this matter again St. Paul both endorses and develops the teaching of the primitive Church. The moral and spiritual ends which Jesus hoped to attain by His death are not directly stated in the sayings; but His constant preoccupation with the thought of the Kingdom of God implies that it was the establishing of the Rule of God in the hearts of individuals and the life of mankind that He sought to secure. This thought does not appear to have been prominent in the earliest preaching; none the less, the first preachers did speak of 'the times of restoration of all things' (Acts iii. 21) and of the coming of 'seasons of refreshing from the presence of the Lord' (Acts iii. 19). These passages, however, are probably eschato-

logical and Messianic.[1] The full ethical and religious emphasis is illustrated in 1 Peter ii. 24, 'that we, having died unto sins, might live unto righteousness', and 1 Peter iii. 18, 'Christ also suffered for sins once . . . that he might bring us to God'. In these passages it is difficult to resist the theory of Pauline influence, although the tendency to take this view may simply be due to the wealth of ethical teaching in St. Paul's letters. In any case, it is St. Paul, above all others, who has impressed these positive truths upon the mind of Christianity. To him, more than to any one else, it is due that we think of salvation, not only as deliverance from sin, but as the attainment of righteousness and of peace and of true fellowship with God.

The range of the moral and spiritual ends which according to St. Paul are fulfilled through the death of Christ is astonishingly full. Even if we leave aside all the cases in which Christ is said to have died 'for sins', or to deliver us 'out of this present evil world' (Galatians i. 4) or 'out of the power of darkness' (Colossians i. 13), a mere list of his more positive statements is most impressive. The passage just mentioned is immediately followed by the words: 'and translated us into the kingdom of the Son of his love' (Colossians i. 13), and this transition is characteristic. Among the moral and religious ends which he sees fulfilled are justification (Romans iii. 24, 25 f., iv. 25, v. 9, 16, 18), peace with God (Romans v. 2, Colossians i. 20), reconciliation with God (Romans v. 10 f., 2 Corinthians v. 18 f., Ephesians ii. 16, Colossians i. 20-2), sanctification (Colossians i. 22, Ephesians v. 27), sonship (Galatians iv. 5). His most challenging epigram, 'Him who knew no sin he made to be sin on our behalf', is associated with a statement of ethical purpose in the words: 'that we might become the righteousness of God in him' (2 Corinthians v. 21). Most notable is the stress laid on the idea of life, in 2 Corinthians iv. 10, 'that the life also of Jesus may be manifested in our body', and v. 15, 'that they which live should no longer live unto themselves, but unto him who for their sakes died and rose again'; and equally striking is the claim that Christ died and rose 'that he might be Lord of both the dead and the living' (Romans xiv. 9), 'that, whether we wake or sleep, we should live together with him' (1 Thessalonians v. 10). Well indeed might St. Paul say that to those who are called Christ crucified is 'Christ the power of God, and the wisdom of

---

[1] Cf. K. Lake, *The Beginnings of Christianity*, iv, p. 37 f.; R. J. Knowling, *The Expositor's Greek Testament*, ii., p. 116

God' (I Corinthians i. 24), and that He was made unto us 'wisdom from God, and righteousness and sanctification, and redemption' (I Corinthians i. 30). There are few ethical fruits and spiritual blessings which he does not associate in some way or other with the reconciling work of God in Christ.

(14) *Universality.* The universality of the redemptive work of Christ is a constant Pauline assumption. Implicit in the Gospel from the first, its truth is set forth by him, not only in positive utterances like Romans viii. 32: 'He that spared not his own Son, but delivered him up for us all, how shall he not also with him freely give us all things?', but in all his classical statements of the scope of the Gospel, and notably in Galatians iii. 28: 'There can be neither Jew nor Greek, there can be neither bond nor free, there can be no male and female: for ye are all one man in Christ Jesus' (cf. Romans ii. 10, iii. 9, x. 12; I Corinthians xii. 13; Ephesians ii. 13–22; Colossians iii. 11).

(b) St. Paul's Distinctive Teaching

The claim made at the outset is now seen to be fully justified. Every aspect of the death of Christ known to primitive Christianity is recognized by St. Paul and finds expression in his writings. Some of these aspects, in particular, the Messianic character of Christ's death and the relation in which it stands to the idea of the Suffering Servant, fall into the background; others, including its vicarious nature and its sacrificial significance, are accepted and clearly expressed, without becoming distinctive of his thought; while others again, the representative aspect of the death, its relation to sin, the emphasis upon the Living Christ, a faith-relation to Him, communion with Him, and suffering in His service, the perception of the Cross as the work of God and the proof of His love, and the recognition of the ethical and spiritual results of the work of God in Christ, are so powerfully expressed and developed that they constitute the basic elements in St. Paul's religious thinking. The advantage of the method we have followed is that it throws these elements strongly into relief, while at the same time showing how deeply St. Paul's teaching is rooted in the common faith of the primitive Church. Paulinism is this common faith, developed by a master hand into a distinct type, though not a system, of New Testament thought. To the closer study of this teaching we now turn.

Our purpose will not be adequately served by merely taking over one by one, and illustrating further, the several ideas we have found to be of outstanding importance, for we have seen that many of them are closely related to one another, and can be appreciated fully only when this relationship is taken into account. This is especially true of the work of God in Christ, the means by which its blessings are appropriated, and the consequences which follow from it. Further, we have seen that what appeared to be single ideas in primitive belief become highly complex in St. Paul's treatment. This is notably so of the relation of the death of Christ to sin and to the ethical and spiritual ends which it serves. These aspects, together with the associated ideas mentioned above, bear closely upon the representative ministry which St. Paul believes Jesus to have exercised. No method can be more mistaken than the attempt to treat this difficult theme apart from the operations to which, in Pauline thought, it is the necessary postulate.

The best method will be to consider St. Paul's conception of the work of God in Christ, the ends it is intended to meet as they are related to the Law and to sin, its consequences in justification and reconciliation, the form it takes in the suffering and death of Christ and the character of the ministry that is implied, and, finally, the manner in which its blessings are appropriated by the believer.

(1) *God in Christ.* No thought is more fundamental than this in St. Paul's thinking. It is God who forgives, justifies, reconciles, and sanctifies; it is with Him that man enters into peace, to Him that he has access, and from Him that he receives the gift of sonship. No doubt in the wealth of Pauline teaching some of these operations, as, for example, sanctification and sonship, are assigned to the Spirit, or occasionally reconciliation, and almost always fellowship, to the Son. The necessities of human speech, and the desire to express particular relationships, account for these features; but St. Paul has not the slightest intention of mapping out the work of divine grace or of suggesting the thought of a divided Godhead. It follows, therefore, that any theory of the Atonement which implies an opposition or enmity of the Father towards men which is overcome by the gracious work of Christ, is, and must be, a perversion of Pauline teaching. This principle does not ignore the eternal opposition of God to evil and His judgment upon sin in the moral universe He has created; nor does it exclude a ministry of Christ for men directed Godwards which seeks to meet the ethical

conditions without which fellowship is impossible. What the principles does mean, if we are faithful to St. Paul's thinking, is that this work of Christ must be interpreted as the manifestation of the grace of God, and not as a means whereby His favour is won. Everything is of love, provided we do not sentimentalize the idea, but give to it a depth and a wealth of meaning worthy of the being of God.

St. Paul nowhere describes the ideal relationship between God and man, but from his account of reconciliation it is clear that he understands it to be that of a rich and growing fellowship. In the actual situation in which man finds himself this fellowship is broken and thwarted by sin, and upon his unrighteousness, in St. Paul's view, the judgment of God rests. 'The wrath of God', he holds, 'is revealed from heaven against all ungodliness and unrighteousness of men, who hold down the truth in unrighteousness' (Romans i. 18). Instead of tracing the consequences of sin to an impersonal moral principle, he ascribes them to the will of a personal God who is not mocked by wrong-doing (Galatians vi. 7). Nevertheless, he is very far indeed from thinking of this Wrath as angry passion, the manifestation of vindictive feeling towards men. On the contrary, the will of God is essentially a will to redeem; He longs to reconcile men to Himself, to restore the broken fellowship, and to accept men as His sons, and this end He seeks to accomplish in and through Christ. He must fulfil this purpose, however, in perfect fidelity to His own nature, without denying His righteousness, in conditions which are fully ethical. Such is St. Paul's conviction, and it is a point of view which governs all his thinking. Especially does it determine his conception of the Gospel. Thus, it is characteristic of him that he says that in the Gospel 'a righteousness of God' is revealed, grounded in faith and leading to (greater) faith (Romans i. 17). If we were compelled to say whether this is a righteousness which God makes possible[1] or one which He possesses in Himself, the reference to faith would lead us to choose the former alternative. It is probable, however, that both are in mind, as in Romans iii. 26. For St. Paul it is axiomatic that the work of God in Christ must, on the one hand, be fully in harmony with His essential righteousness, and on the other hand, must give a righteous status, which is no fiction, to the man who enters into fellowship with Himself.

This perception of the nature and the conditions of the work of

[1] It cannot be *given*. To bestow righteousness is a contradiction in terms.

God in Christ is absolutely essential to an intelligent appreciation of St. Paul's teaching concerning the Atonement. From first to last his doctrine of the Cross is conditioned by his doctrine of God.

A further point needs to be made before we pass from this question. St. Paul is nowhere conscious of any opposition between righteousness and love. We can be sure that he would have repudiated warmly any suggestion that love is all and righteousness of secondary account. He would have admitted that love is greater than righteousness, but the only love he would have recognized as such is a love founded upon righteousness. This is a point of view which he could take the more easily because to him righteousness is much more than justice was to the Greek. Thanks to his Old Testament heritage, righteousness to him is a quality and, at the same time, an activity; it is what God is and what He does. Within it there is a warmth which impels Him towards salvation. We may state this truth summarily by saying that for Him love is implicit in righteousness and righteousness explicit in love.

(2) *The Law.* Before going on to consider how the work of God in Christ is related to human need, the form it takes and the ends it has in view, it is necessary to bear in mind his attitude to the Law and to sin, for these questions deeply influence his treatment of the death of Christ both in itself and as regards the blessings which it brings to men.

The temptation to think of St. Paul's attitude to the Law as a question of merely academic interest ought to be resisted in view of modern humanistic tendencies to rest progress and salvation upon human effort. Many of our modern problems are anticipated in his Epistles, and especially the question of man's ability to fulfil the ideal.

Modern Jewish writers[1] in recent years have protested against the manner in which Christians, and St. Paul in particular, have spoken of the Law, or Torah; and that the protest has not gone unheeded is seen in a more sympathetic attitude to the question on the part of Christian scholars[2] which is not without its perils. The truth is that St. Paul's statements reveal remarkable contrasts, and the important question to consider is why he gives expression to his more extreme and unfavourable judgments.

On the one hand, St. Paul speaks of the Law in appreciative

[1] Cf. C. G. Montefiore, *The Synoptic Gospels.*
[2] Cf. J. Parkes, *Jesus, Paul and the Jews,* pp. 118–42.

terms which recall the best tributes of Jewish teachers. He hotly repudiates the suggestion that the Law is sin (Romans vii. 7; cf. iii. 1 f.); it is 'holy', and the commandment is 'holy, and righteous, and good' (Romans vii. 12); it is 'spiritual', and he delights in it 'after the inward man' (Romans vii. 14, 22). The man who loves his neighbour 'hath fulfilled the law' (Romans xiii. 8). Indeed, its essence is love, for 'the whole law is fulfilled in one word, even in this; Thou shalt love thy neighbour as thyself' (Galatians v. 14). He even goes so far as to say that in the sacrifice of Christ the end in view was 'that the ordinance of the law might be fulfilled in us, who walk not after the flesh, but after the spirit' (Romans viii. 4). St. Paul cannot justly be charged with blindness to the sublimity of the Law.

On the other hand, he uses language of the strongest kind about the limitations and temporary character of the Law. It 'came in secretly', or as a kind of 'afterthought',[1] 'that the trespass might abound' (Romans v. 20); it was added 'because of transgressions' (Galatians iii. 19) and it works 'wrath' (Romans iv. 15). It was only a 'slave-attendant' to bring men to Christ and has now finished its task (Galatians iii. 24 f.) Sin is not to have dominion over us, because we are 'not under the law, but under grace' (Romans vi. 14). Christ was sent to redeem men 'under the law' (Galatians iv. 5), and He is 'the end of the law unto righteousness to every one that believeth' (Romans x. 4).

That there is an extravagant note in this language can hardly be denied; but the important question is why it is present. It is the language of intense spiritual disappointment. It is used, not by one who hated the Torah, but by one who felt that he had been cruelly deceived. A Pharisee and 'a son of Pharisees', he had sought after righteousness by the way of obedience to the Law, only to meet with frustration and failure. Delighting in the law of God in his true self, he saw 'a different law' in his members, warring against the law of his mind and bringing him into captivity under the law of sin (Romans vii. 22 f.). It is the wretchedness of this memory which leads him to say that Christ is 'the end of the law', together with his discovery that, what the Law could not do by reason of its weakness, God had done when He sent His Son and condemned sin in the flesh (Romans viii. 3). At the cost of consistency, since he had spoken of the fulfilling of the requirement of the Law by this Coming, he speaks with violence of God

[1] Sanday and Headlam, *I.C.C., Romans*, p. 139.

cancelling it and nailing it, like an obsolete bond, to the Cross of Christ (Colossians ii. 14).

There is, however, often a heritage from that which is rejected. It is his intense interest in the Torah which gives him his deep concern for righteousness, and provides for him the forensic moulds in which much of his thought is cast. It is through his very zeal for the Law that he has learnt the majesty of the ethical demand, the vanity of human effort, and the need for complete dependence upon God. Moreover, his 'legalism', often unjustly condemned from want of knowledge, is not cold and unrelenting like the spirit of Roman Law, but is warmed by the atmosphere of Old Testament thought, as it is in the words of the unknown prophet: 'I bring near my righteousness . . . and my salvation shall not tarry', 'My righteousness is near, my salvation is gone forth' (Isaiah xlvi. 13, li. 5).

(3) *Sin.* Our consideration of St. Paul's attitude to the Law has already revealed the seriousness with which he faced the fact of sin. Sin, as he sees it, is hostility towards God as well as the evil acts in which it finds expression. His description of the Gentile world of his day shows the wide range of action and attitude which he brings under this term: 'being filled with all unrighteousness, wickedness, covetousness, maliciousness; full of envy, murder, strife, deceit, malignity; whisperers, backbiters, haters of God, insolent, haughty, boastful, inventors of evil things, disobedient to parents, without understanding, covenant-breakers, without natural affection, unmerciful' (Romans i. 29–31). Equally instructive are the lists in 2 Corinthians xii. 20, Galatians v. 19–21, Ephesians iv. 25–32, and Colossians iii. 5–9. They touch every side of human nature, its gross sins and carnal lusts, fornication, uncleanness, lasciviousness, drunkenness; sins of the spirit, pride, malice, jealousy, anger, railing; social disorders, in the relationships of men to men, children to parents, man to society, lying, backbiting, corrupt speech, covetousness. At all points these evils are seen in their true nature as sins, that is, in the relation in which they set man over against the righteousness and holiness of God as a creature whose thoughts are base, whose affections are perverted, and whose purposes are evil. At the same time St. Paul is by no means blind to the higher elements in man, as his references in Romans ii. 14 *f.* to Gentiles 'which have no law' and yet 'do by nature the things of the law', showing 'the work of the law written in their hearts', so clearly prove. Influ-

enced perhaps by the teaching of the Stoics, he has the greatest reverence for conscience (Romans ii. 15, xiii. 5; 1 Corinthians x. 28 *f.*; 2 Corinthians iv. 2, v. 11, etc.), and his masterly analysis of Romans vii. 7–25 shows how keenly he is aware of the good desires and intentions which arise within the heart of man.

For our special purpose it is important to consider the different ways in which St. Paul sought to account for the presence of sin in human life, since his speculations about its origins have deeply influenced his teaching about the death of Christ. He does not formulate a definite theory and probably did not possess one, but there are indications in his Epistles of at least three ways in which he sought to explain the fact of sin. (1) The best known of these traces sin to the disobedience of Adam. It appears in the unfinished sentence of Romans v. 12: 'Therefore, as through one man sin entered into the world, and death through sin; and so death passed unto all men, for that all sinned: . . .', and in 1 Corinthians xv. 21 *f.*: 'For since by man came death, by man came also the resurrection of the dead. For as in Adam all die, so also in Christ shall all be made alive.' Similar views are found in Wisdom ii. 23 *f.*, a writing with which St. Paul was probably familiar, and later in 4 Ezra iii. 21 *ff.* Indeed, the belief that Adam's sin involved all his posterity, became a commonplace of rabbinical teaching.[1] Nevertheless, there are signs that St. Paul was not entirely satisfied with this theory. He does not emphasize it unduly, but passes on quickly to speak of the superiority of the 'free gift' received in Christ. Moreover, the words 'for that all sinned' do not establish that close connexion between the disobedience of Adam and the sin of man which the theory strictly requires. The rendering of the Vulgate: 'in whom [*in quo*] all sinned', incorrectly translates the Greek ἐφ' ᾧ, 'because', 'for that'; but it is the argument one would expect after the opening statements. No more than other Jewish teachers[2] has St. Paul made this theory his one explanation of the origin of sin. (2) Less obvious, but probably present in the words: 'I see a different law in my members', is an allusion to the *yeṣer ha-ra'*, 'the evil impulse' or 'inclination' by which man is tempted to his undoing; in the language of St. Paul, it is found 'warring against the law of my mind, and bringing me into captivity under the law of sin which is in my members' (Romans vii. 23). Derived in the first place

---

[1] Cf. G. F. Moore, *Judaism*, i, p. 475.
[2] Cf. G. F. Moore, *op. cit.*, i, pp. 474–96.

from Genesis vi. 5, viii. 21, this idea is reflected in Ecclesiasticus xxxvii. 3 and in 4 Ezra iii. 21, and is frequently discussed by the Rabbis.[1] The evil impulse, it is held, was created by God, who gives to men good inclinations as well as bad, but man's responsibility is constantly affirmed. It is difficult to resist the conclusion that similar ideas lie behind St. Paul's use of the term 'flesh', which he does not regard as evil in itself, but as the sphere in man's nature in which the sinful impulse entrenches itself, causing a state of wretchedness and of moral inability from which he sees no way of deliverance save by the power of God in Christ (cf. Romans vii. 24). (3) Closely allied with the foregoing is yet a third tentative explanation of sin as a personal agency associated with other hostile powers which threaten man's blessedness. Thus in Romans v. 12 'Sin' is almost personified,[2] in much the same way in which 'Death' is spoken of in v. 14 as a tyrant reigning over men. A similar thought is present in Romans vi. 16, where it is said that we are the bond-servants of those we obey 'whether of sin unto death, or of obedience ,unto righteousness'. The flesh lusts against the spirit so that we cannot do the things we would (Galatians v. 17). It was 'the serpent' who beguiled Eve in his craftiness (2 Corinthians xi. 3), 'the rulers of this world' who crucified 'the Lord of glory' (1 Corinthians ii. 6, 8), 'the elemental spirits' to whom his converts had been in bondage (Galatians iv. 9; cf. Colossians ii. 20). In such passages the thought of a hierarchy of evil, which approaches the boundaries of dualism, is suggested; sin with other evil powers attacks man from without and seeks to compass his servitude.

These different conceptions, which are not harmonized in St. Paul's thought, affect the form in which he speaks of the work of Christ. Thus, in contrast with Adam, He is the Head of a redeemed humanity, the 'Second Adam', who not only brings the resurrection (1 Corinthians xv. 21), but also, as by implication Romans v. 12 suggests, righteousness and through righteousness life.[3] As opposed to the hostile law in our members, Christ is the power of God whereby we are delivered 'out of the body of this death' (Romans vii. 24), the personal agent through whom God condemns sin in the flesh (Romans viii. 3). Ranged against the

---

[1] Cf. Moore, *op. cit.*, i, pp. 479 *ff.*; C. G. Montefiore, *Rabbinic Literature and Gospel Teachings*, pp. 164–6, 180–3.

[2] Cf. Sanday and Headlam, *I.C.C., Romans*, p. 132. For similar tendencies in Judaism, see Moore, *op. cit.*, i, pp. 492 *f.*

[3] Cf. Sanday and Headlam, *op. cit.*, p. 132.

F

hostile spirits who seek man's enslavement, He is the victorious Lord who despoils his foes and leads them broken and defeated in triumph (Colossians ii. 15). It will be seen, however, that while St. Paul's conceptions of sin determine the forms in which he presents the work of Christ, they do not disclose its inner character as he sees it. To determine this, it is necessary to consider, not only what he actually says about the Cross, but his teaching concerning forgiveness, justification, and reconciliation.

(4) *Forgiveness, Justification, and Reconciliation.* There can be no better way of approaching St. Paul's distinctive teaching concerning the death of Christ than to consider in detail all that he says about these great themes. This fact was perceived by Ritschl in his great work, *Justification and Reconciliation,*[1] and all subsequent work on Pauline theology has made it more evident still. St. Paul's teaching, however, on these subjects, especially the second and third, is so detailed, and is so closely allied to his presentation of other themes, including sonship, sanctification, and fellowship with Christ, that it would throw our present investigation entirely out of focus to attempt such an approach here;[2] and all that can be done at this point is to bring out the main points which illuminate his treatment of the work of Christ.

Concerning forgiveness he has very little to say, and he never represents it as the object for which Christ died. Apart from the passages in which χαρίζομαι is used (2 Corinthians ii. 7, 10, xii. 13, Ephesians iv. 32, Colossians ii. 13, iii. 13), he uses the noun 'forgiveness' (ἄφεσις) twice only (Ephesians i. 7, Colossians i. 14) and the verb 'to forgive' (ἀφίημι) once in a quotation (Romans iv. 7). The explanation is that he regards forgiveness as the remission of sins, a gift of the grace of God especially associated with the salvation which Christ brings, but not the precise end for which He suffered. This purpose is much more intimately connected with justification and reconciliation.

Justification is sometimes described as if it were another name for forgiveness, but to do so is only to obscure the Biblical meaning of each. Justification is much more than the remission of sins; it is the sovereign and yet gracious act of God by which He accepts men as righteous, so that, without the sacrifice of ethical realities they can enter into fellowship with Himself. He does this, accord

---

[1] The English translation of Part III of his *Rechtfertigung und Versöhnung.*
[2] I have treated these themes in *Forgiveness and Reconciliation* (1941).

ing to St. Paul, not because of meritorious works, but because of faith in Himself active to redeem in Christ. This righteousness is not merely imputed, or credited to our account, though some of St. Paul's Old Testament illustrations have given rise to this disastrous interpretation. On the contrary it is true righteousness, not that of perfected achievement, but a righteousness of mind, thought, and will, like that of the prodigal who comes to himself, casts himself upon his father's grace, and says: 'I have sinned against heaven, and in thy sight.'

Reconciliation is the act of God in receiving men into fellowship with Himself. It is not, in Pauline thought, a process, although in actual fact it issues in a life of growing fellowship without which its meaning is lost. It is something done, once and for all, even if we cannot time it by the dial of a clock or date it by the page of a calendar. 'We were reconciled to God', 'We have now received the reconciliation' (Romans v. 10 f.)—these are the statements of the Pauline point of view.

St. Paul grounds both justification and reconciliation in the atoning work of God in Christ. We are justified freely by His grace 'through the redemption that is in Christ Jesus' (Romans iii. 24). God set Him forth 'as a means of atonement, through faith, by his blood' (Romans iii. 25). Christ was delivered up for our trespasses, and raised 'for our justification' (Romans iv. 25). We are 'justified by his blood' (Romans v. 9). Similar statements are made in connexion with reconciliation. In Christ, God was reconciling the world to Himself (2 Corinthians v. 19). We were reconciled to God 'through the death of his Son' (Romans v. 10). The divine purpose was to reconcile Jew and Gentile in one body 'through the cross' (Ephesians ii. 16), to make peace 'through the blood of his cross' (Colossians i. 20). How St. Paul understands this work of God in Christ, and with what success he unfolds its meaning, we have still to consider. Meantime, there can be no doubt that the substance of his doctrine is determined by his conceptions of the righteousness of God, of justification, and of reconciliation. These are the ideas which lead him to ascribe a mediatorial character to the death of Christ: through it the grace of God reaches men, and in dependence upon it men are received into fellowship with Him. Further, the dying is conceived as representative in a sense which has yet to be defined. The presence of these ideas in the Pauline theology is not accidental; they appear because St. Paul sees the need of an ethical and religious basis for the act of God in justifying and reconciling men to Himself. The controlling thought is that God must act, not in conformity to a standard external to Himself, but in harmony with His own nature as the God of righteousness, truth, and love. The need also is felt of a living way whereby man may approach God and find his blessedness in fellowship with Him. This need, we shall find, is met in St. Paul's teaching by the idea of faith-union with Christ; but the possibility of faith-union, as well as its meaning and depth, depends upon the nature of the work which Christ accomplishes for men. These ideas must now be examined more closely, and first of all, because it is fundamental and determinative, the character of the work of God in Christ.

(5) *The Work of God in Christ.* From beginning to end, according to St. Paul, the work of God in Christ is a work of grace. 'God commendeth his own love toward us, in that, while we were yet sinners, Christ died for us' (Romans v. 8). The fact of this love is the constant assumption of his doctrine, but it is not the revelation of the love in itself which occupies his mind, but rather the manner in which it is expressed in relation to sinners whom God desires to accept as righteous and bring into fellowship with Himself. It is this compelling ethical and religious interest, we have argued, which leads him to stress the representative character of Christ's death. The passages in his Epistles in which this thought is implied have already been mentioned in treating the relation of his teaching to the primitive preaching, but it is necessary to consider them again in order to see its true character. These passages are as follows:

Romans iii. 25: 'Whom God set forth to be a means of atonement.'
Romans v. 18: 'So then as through one trespass the judgement came unto all men to condemnation; even so through one act of righteousness the free gift came unto all men to justification of life.'
Romans v. 19: 'For as through the one man's disobedience the many were made sinners, even so through the obedience of the one shall the many be made righteous.'
Romans vi. 10 *f.*: 'For the death that he died, he died unto sin once: but the life that he liveth, he liveth unto God. Even so reckon ye also yourselves to be dead unto sin, but alive unto God in Christ Jesus.'
2 Corinthians v. 14: 'For the love of Christ constraineth us; because we thus judge, that one died for all, therefore all died.'
2 Corinthians v. 21: 'Him who knew no sin he made to be sin on our behalf ; that we might become the righteousness of God in him.'
Galatians iii. 13: 'Christ redeemed us from the curse of the law, having become a curse for us: for it is written, Cursed is every one that hangeth on a tree.'

St. Paul does not use the term 'mediator' with reference to Christ,[1] but his doctrine is essentially mediatorial since it is through Christ and His work for them that men enter into fellowship with God. The free gift came to all 'through one act of righteousness'; the many were constituted righteous 'through the obedience of the one'. The One through whom such blessings come to men is undoubtedly a Mediator whether the term is used or not, although the absence of the terminology may be significant.

Is St. Paul's doctrine also substitutionary? Here again the distinctive vocabulary is wanting or almost wanting. The preposition ἀντί is not used, the nouns λύτρον, ἀντίλυτρον, λύτρωσις, λυτρωτής are not employed, and the verb λυτροῦσθαι ('to ransom' or 'redeem') nowhere appears. The noun ἀπολύτρωσις ('redemption'), where it is not employed in an eschatological sense, emphasizes the idea of deliverance from sin[2] rather than substitution (cf. Ephesians i. 7; Colossians i. 14), although in Romans iii. 24, 'through *the* redemption that is in Christ Jesus', the reference appears to be to the costly act more than to the freedom which it secures.[3] Instead of words which suggests the thought of a 'ransom', St. Paul prefers words which imply the idea of 'purchase',[4] and the one instance in which he uses a word apparently open to the suggestion of substitutionary action is ἱλαστήριον in Romans iii. 25, about the true meaning of which commentators are so sharply divided.[5] His linguistic usage, therefore, strongly suggests that his doctrine is not substitutionary in character.

This conclusion is sustained by his teaching which only has the appearance of substitution, but actually is best explained otherwise. He claims that, in view of the death which Christ died, and the life which He lives, we are to account ourselves dead unto sin, but alive unto God in Christ Jesus (Romans vi. 10 *f.*) The activity here described is vicarious, and probably representative, but it is far from being that of a substitute. So also when he says

[1] Μεσίτης is used of Moses in Galatians iii. 19, and generally in Galatians iii. 20. In the latter passage St. Paul seems unwilling to use it of God since He is One.

[2] See earlier, p. 61.

[3] Cf. Sanday and Headlam, p. 86; H. A. W. Meyer, i, p. 169; Boylan, p. 57.

[4] In 1 Corinthians vi. 20 and vii. 23 ἀγοράζω is used, and ἐξαγοράζω in Galatians iii. 13 and iv. 5.

[5] Sanday and Headlam, pp. 87 *f.*, support 'means of propitiation' (cf. Moffatt); Dodd, *The Bible and the Greeks*, p. 94, thinks that the meaning is that of expiation, not propitiation; Büchsel, *Theol. Wort.*, iii, p. 321, favours the rendering 'mercy-seat'. Probably 'means of expiation' or 'atonement' represents St. Paul's thought.

that 'one died for all', and 'therefore all died' (2 Corinthians v. 14); for in these terse sentences the word 'died' is probably used in different senses, the meaning being that Christ died a death on behalf of all, and therefore all *died to sin* in the power of His death.[1] The more difficult passages which assert that He was 'made to be sin on our behalf' (2 Corinthians v. 21), and became 'a curse for us' (Galatians iii. 13), will be considered later.[2] Words could hardly express more forcibly the thought of a service we are unable to render for ourselves, and which He, in the wonder of His grace, accomplishes for us, but there is no suggestion of penal suffering transferred from our shoulders to Him.

St. Paul's teaching and linguistic usage suggest that he shares the reluctance of the modern man to think of a redemption which is wrought entirely outside of, and apart from, ourselves so that we have nothing to do but to accept its benefits. A doctrine of this kind would have provided no adequate basis for his teaching concerning justification and reconciliation, since in these divine activities man is accepted as righteous, and received into fellowship with God, through the avenue of an active faith-relationship to the Crucified. If man cannot achieve his own salvation, neither can he obtain it as a purely external blessing; it is wrought in him as well as for him. St. Paul is in the dilemma, forced upon him by the greatness of his theme, of being compelled to describe the work of Christ as one which man cannot do for himself, but not as the work of a substitute in the exclusive sense of the term. It is for this reason that he avoids the vocabulary of substitution and does not even use the word 'mediator'.

Three considerations support this view. First, St. Paul does not present a theory of vicarious punishment, not even when he says that Christ was made sin on our behalf. Again, he refrains from developing the idea of Christ as the Second Adam in ways which would have suggested that in Him, as the federal Head of a redeemed Humanity, man's salvation is already complete. Further, as we have seen, he develops with the greatest freedom and variety the thought of the faith-union of the believer with Christ. In this way he suggests that man has a vital part,[3] although one that is the very opposite of a relationship of merit, in the divine plan of salvation.

---

[1] Cf. Plummer, *I.C.C., 2 Corinthians*, p. 174.   [2] See pp. 87 *f*.

[3] It is true that faith is represented as 'the gift of God' (Ephesians ii. 8), but by reason of its nature it is active, not passive.

In all circumstances it is best to avoid the word substitutionary and to describe the work of Christ as representative in character. It is true that this term also is not Pauline, probably because St. Paul has not made a marked use of the sacrificial principle is describing Christ's suffering. The term has the advantage of suggesting a close relationship between Christ and those whom He serves. Its weakness is that it does not so readily indicate a work of God in Christ for men, but rather a work of man in Christ directed Godwards. The same disability attaches itself to the word mediatorial. It is apparent, therefore, that if we give preference to the word 'representative', we must use it to describe the work of God in Christ for man, which man cannot render for himself, but in which in a true sense he can participate through the power of faith.

Discussions about terminology are apt to become tedious, but they are necessary in order to clear the issue by excluding alien suggestions. What, then, we may ask, is the central conception in St. Paul's account of the work of Christ, and in particular what does he mean when he says that He was 'made to be sin on our behalf' and became 'a curse for us'?

We have already said that St. Paul does not hold a theory of vicarious punishment. Such a theory is excluded, not only by his silence, but also by his emphasis upon the atonement as the work of God in Christ, not to speak of its fundamentally unethical character. Only the guilty can be punished.

The two passages in question use the language of paradox, perhaps the only kind of language suitable to such a theme. What St. Paul means when he says of God that He made Christ to be 'sin on our behalf' is that Christ voluntarily came under the blight of sin, entered into its deepest gloom, and shared with men its awful weight and penalty. The same idea is doubtless implicit in the statement of Galatians iii. 13, that He became 'a curse for us', although here the idea is expressed, not only in paradox, but also in the course of a polemical argument. Asserting on the ground of Deuteronomy xxvii. 26 that men who base their standing upon works of the law are 'under a curse', he claims that Christ has delivered us from this curse, 'having become a curse for us', since it is written: 'Cursed is every one that hangeth on a tree' (Deuteronomy xxi. 23). At first sight the argument seems trivial. Playing upon words, however, is a feature of St. Paul's style, and there is usually a deeper idea beneath the word-play.

It is so here.[1] In view of the quotation which follows, the words: 'having become a curse for us', might seem to mean no more than 'having been crucified for us'. When, however, we remember that elsewhere he speaks so strongly of the judgment of God resting upon sin,[2] and that already in this context he has spoken of a 'curse' resting upon those under the Law, we see that much more is in question than the tragedy of crucifixion. A spiritual experience of reprobation is meant, and since this cannot be personal, it must be participation in the reprobation which rests upon sin.[3] The thought is not clearly expressed because the Apostle is engaged in a cut and thrust rabbinical argument with those who exalt the claims of the Law; but in 2 Corinthians v. 21, in the words, 'made to be sin on our behalf', it is more evident, though still veiled in the language of paradox and epigram.

These words of St. Paul mark the nearest point to which he comes in his Epistles to the idea of sin-bearing. He never actually uses this particular image. A sentence like 1 Peter ii. 24, 'Who his own self bare our sins in his body up to the tree', is, in form at least, un-Pauline. The same also is true of John i. 29: 'Behold, the Lamb of God, which taketh away the sin of the world!' That, however, which is fundamental to these passages, the thought of submission to the dire consequences of sin, including spiritual suffering and death, is found also in St. Paul's thought in a form peculiar to himself. His conviction must be that the righteousness of God, and His purpose to justify men and reconcile them to Himself, required that Christ should suffer the condemnation of sin and come under its curse. This, in effect, is what he is saying, in a context, be it noted, in which reconciliation is the main theme, when he declares: 'Him who knew no sin he made to be sin on our behalf; that we might become the righteousness of God in him.'

Insistent questions crowd upon the mind as one considers this Pauline conception. The only passage in which St. Paul has treated it further, and here without direct reference to sin, is Romans iii. 25 f., a passage full of exegetical problems to which we must return in due course. Even in passing it may be useful to remember that not a few of the difficulties of the doctrine of

[1] See the careful discussion of E. de Witt Burton, *I.C.C.*, *Galatians*, pp. 163–77, and for an account of St. Paul's style, J. Weiss, *The History of Primitive Christianity*, pp. 399–421.

[2] Cf. Romans i. 18–32 and the references to the Wrath mentioned on p. 62.

[3] Cf. Burton, *op. cit.*, p. 172.

the Atonement are really problems of the Incarnation; and, further, that they are the more evident in the Pauline theology because, with all his insistence upon the Atonement as the work of God in Christ, there is an intractable element of subordination in the functions which he assigns to the Son (cf. 1 Corinthians xv. 27 f.). It would have been in harmony with one element in his thought, and that the deepest, to say that in Christ God Himself submits to the consequences of human sin; but St. Paul does not say this, and we must not represent it as his teaching. What he affirms is that Christ was made to be sin on our behalf.

The question arises whether, in Pauline thought, the sufferings to which Christ submitted are penal. This question is not fore-closed by the recognition that His experience was not one of punishment; unless, contrary to the facts of life, we regard pun-ishment and penal suffering as co-extensive. Without being punished, an innocent and sinless person can be involved in the penal sufferings of others either by the accidents of circumstance or because through love he makes himself one with sinners. Ritschl's submission, that the suffering of the innocent is affliction, not penalty,[1] fails because it does not take account of this possi-bility. Such suffering is certainly not penalty, and it may be affliction; but to the extent that the innocent person loves the wrongdoer, he shares in his penal sufferings.

In earlier discussions I have argued that much depends on whether it is right to describe the consequences of sin as penal.[2] These consequences are disciplinary only in so far as they are deserved, and if they are deserved they are retributive and there-fore penal. Every one desires a better word than penal,[3] but until we find it we ought not to abandon it because it has been used in ways which revolt the conscience or under the delusion that we can account better for the consequences of sin by invoking the operation of an inevitable law of cause and effect in the moral universe rather than the activity of God.

Much more than the meaning of words, however, is at stake in this question. All the difference in the world is made to our sense of abiding gratitude to Christ if we think that His experience was, not penal suffering freely accepted through love for men, but rather affliction. The deep sense of debt to Him, everywhere

---

[1] *Justification and Reconciliation* (Eng. Tr.), p. 479.
[2] *Jesus and His Sacrifice*, pp. 286 ff.; *The London Quarterly and Holborn Review*, January, 1939, pp. 49 f.
[3] But no one supplies it.

perceptible in St. Paul's Epistles, has its roots in the belief that
He embodied the love of God by enduring suffering for men at
supreme cost to Himself. We cannot tell, of course, if St. Paul
would have described these sufferings as penal, since he does not
employ the term; but we are entitled to say that the kind
of suffering implied when he speaks of Christ being 'made
sin on our behalf' and having become 'a curse for us', while
not punishment, is penal suffering in the sense defined above.
In perfect filial accord with the Father's will, and moved
by the greatness of His love for sinners, Christ came under the
curse of sin and shared its penalty. There is no question of the
transference of punishment from their shoulders to His own, still
less any thought of a measured equivalent of suffering: what is
meant is that in the work of redemption Christ submitted to the
judgment of God upon sin.

The end fulfilled by this suffering is not formally discussed by
St. Paul, and in a very important sense it does not need to be discussed since the suffering is the inevitable expression of the love of
Christ for men. It has other aspects, however, in relation to the
righteousness of God and His redemptive work for men; and on
these points the outlines of St. Paul's thought are discernible in
Romans iii. 25 *f.*, to which reference has already been made:

'Whom God set forth to be a means of atonement, through faith, by his
blood, to shew his righteousness, because of the passing over of the sins done
aforetime, in the forbearance of God; for the shewing, I say, of his righteousness at this present season: that he might himself be just, and the justifier of
him that hath faith in Jesus.'

Every important word in this passage is a battle-ground, and
many interpretations have been offered which have the general
effect of representing St. Paul's words as nothing other than a
declaration of the gracious purpose of God towards men, comparable to 2 Corinthians v. 19. This exegetical legerdemain is
accomplished by assigning to most of the important Greek words
and to some of the constructions meanings which in some cases are
highly doubtful, and in others are barely possible, with the result
that St. Paul is made to say almost the opposite of what a judicial
exegesis must take to be the meaning of his words.

I have discussed this passage in considerable detail in a recent
article in the *Expository Times*,[1] and as it is not possible to repeat
the investigation here, I must content myself with the claim there

[1] Vol. l, pp. 295–300. Cf. also H. G. Meecham, *Expository Times*, l, p. 564.

made, that the probabilities are strongly in favour of the 'traditional interpretation' of the passage based on the Revised Version and Moffatt's translation. The one important point of difference is that St. Paul does not speak of the death of Christ as 'a propitiation' or 'the means of propitiation',[1] but as 'a means of expiation', in the sense of the covering of sins, or more generally as 'a means of atonement'. In substance, his argument is that 'God had shown Himself to be righteous in the fact that in Christ He had met the moral situation created by sin. He had confronted men with a means of expiation or atonement, operative in Christ and His sacrificial death, and effective in men in virtue of the faith-relationship between them and Him'.[2]

St. Paul's purpose is to show that God is both 'righteous' and 'the justifier' of men. In his view, He is righteous because He has not treated sin as of small account, but has accepted His own judgment upon it by setting forth Christ as 'a means of atonement'. No explanation of this activity is given in the passage beyond the use of the sacrificial phrase 'by his blood', but it is highly probable that St. Paul is thinking of that submission to the consequences of sin which he has in mind when he says that Christ was made sin on our behalf. If this view is warranted, we are justified in rendering ἱλαστήριον 'means of expiation', since by the obedience of Christ sin is thought of as covered. An ethical means of atonement is provided, and in consequence God is righteous. The righteousness of God, it should be noted, is conceived both as a quality of God and as His redeeming activity. The claim is that He is the Holy One and the Saviour because He deals adequately with the fact of sin.

Equally, St. Paul believes, God is shown to be 'the justifier' of men. There is nothing fictitious in His action in accepting men as righteous because by faith they enter into faith-union with One who was made sin on their behalf. The statement that He is 'the justifier of him that hath faith in Jesus' depends for its consistency upon that which God has done for men in Christ and upon their relation thereto. Not only because they believe in Christ, but also because they identify themselves with all that He has done on their behalf, are they 'righteous' in the sight of God. Such appears to be St. Paul's thought in this most important passage.

[1] Cf. C. H. Dodd, *The Bible and the Greeks*, pp. 82–95.

[2] *Expository Times*, l, p. 300.

In conclusion, reference must be made to a question of considerable difficulty in Romans iii. 25 *f.* which cannot be completely solved. In this passage St. Paul seems to suggest that before the Cross God's action was of one kind but afterwards of another kind; that then He was indulgent, but now He is righteous. God, so to speak, has redeemed His name. It is surely highly improbable that he means to suggest this, and it is important to ask rather why his words are open to such an interpretation. The answer cannot be in doubt. St. Paul is speaking, as he must speak, of the Cross as an event in time, and so long as it is apprehended as such the suggestion of a change of method is inescapable. It is only an accommodation of language to say that God's action before the Cross was prospective, contingent upon a work of atonement still to be consummated. The better view is that to the mind of God the meaning of the Cross is eternal, and that what happened on Calvary was the emergence upon the plane of history of His timeless activity. The peril, however, of such speculation is the danger of losing Christian truth in abstractions, and it is better to confess that the resolution of the antinomy is beyond human power because, as creatures of time, we cannot see things *sub specie aeternitatis.* Whether St. Paul perceived the problem we cannot say. It may be significant that in describing God's action in Christ he speaks of Him 'setting forth', rather than of 'sending forth', Christ as he does in Galatians iv. 4. Be this as it may, his main purpose in the passage is to describe the work of God *as men see it*, and to claim that it was in perfect conformity with the divine holiness. We must esteem his words in the light of what he seeks to do, and not refuse what is clear because further vistas are opened out where man must walk by faith or not at all.

(6) *Man's Appropriation of the Work of God in Christ.* The separation of St. Paul's account of the work of God in Christ from his treatment of the way in which it is appropriated by man, is necessary for clearness of thought, but in reality the two are intimately connected by him, so much so that the one cannot be appreciated fully without the other. Even in the passage we have just been considering, where the righteousness of God is the principal theme, along with His work as the justifier of men, he speaks of the man who has 'faith in Jesus', and this association of ideas is not accidental but necessary. For St. Paul the Atonement is not only a work of God accomplished *for man*, but also and at the same time a work of God wrought *in him*, and it is only when

both aspects are combined that the Pauline doctrine is complete.

This claim needs to be emphasized in view of the tendency inherited, in the opinion of Denney,[1] from Pfleiderer, to distinguish between the 'juridical' and the 'ethico-mystical' aspects of St. Paul's thought, as if these elements stood apart in his teaching separate and unrelated. Against this delusion the arguments of Denney's devastating pages hardly need to be repeated. Not only is it incredible that a virile thinker like St. Paul would have allowed his thoughts on these themes to remain in watertight compartments, but justice cannot be done to either apart from the other. St. Paul's teaching is 'juridical' only because he is intensely interested in righteousness and uses forensic terms in order to describe the work of God for man; and it is 'ethico-mystical' only because it has to do with the spiritual appropriation of this work, which certainly lies outside man's experience but is meant to be related thereto. In both realms God is active; both in his objective work for man and in the subjective conditions in which it is appropriated. In the latter, however, man himself has a part to play, in a response of his spirit which concerns every part of his being, his thoughts, feelings, and will; and this response is actually part of the atonement, if by this term we mean the restoration of sinners to fellowship with God.

The wealth of St. Paul's teaching on the appropriation of the blessings of Christ's work for men has already been indicated in discussing his use of the primitive Christian tradition. It includes all that he has to say about faith in Christ, fellowship with Him, and sacramental communion. His teaching about sharing in the fellowship of Christ's sufferings may also be included, since this experience brings with it a deeper understanding of His redemptive service and therefore a firmer hold upon its blessings. It would be wrong, however, to suggest that a mature enjoyment of these spiritual blessings is necessary before man is brought into fellowship with God. Faith-union with Christ, living, dying, and rising with Him, sacramental communion, and sharing in His sufferings belong to the entire course of the life of the believer; and the same may be said of the richer aspects of the life of sonship and of sanctification. The primary and fundamental relationship, by which the Christian experience is begun and continued, is that of faith, living trust in God and in His will and power to do all that is necessary for salvation. As presented to us

[1] *The Death of Christ*, pp. 179–86.

in Pauline teaching this faith is primarily faith in Christ as the One in whom and through whom God works for us; it is surrender to Him, reliance upon Him, cleaving to Him in deep love and devotion of spirit. While this faith arises within man and is the expression of his will, it is not surprising that St. Paul should also describe it as 'the gift of God', for when a man looks back upon it in the light of his Christian experience as a whole, he sees that what appears to be his own effort is at the same time the working of God. St. Paul is conscious of this when he says: 'Work out your own salvation with fear and trembling; for it is God which worketh in you both to will and to work, for his good pleasure' (Philippians ii. 12 f.); and no more than he can we isolate the constituent elements of faith and say where the work of God ends and the effort of man begins. In describing the character of faith perhaps his most illuminating word is that it is faith working through love' (Galatians v. 6),[1] for herein is seen its true nature, as not only confidence and trust, but as the complete abandonment of spirit in loving devotion to One upon whom the soul of man rests for time and eternity.

In the Pauline sense, however, faith in Christ must be interpreted in the light of all that St. Paul says of Christ and His work. It is easy for the modern man, who often thinks of Christ mainly as the supreme teacher and the Revealer of God, to think of faith in Him as the loyalty of a disciple and a recipient of truth. This it is, but in Pauline teaching how much more! As we have seen, St. Paul thinks of Christ as One who died for men, who suffered for them, and stands in a representative relation to God on their behalf. He bore upon His pure spirit the sorrows and the sufferings of human sin, and in His submission to all that is inherent in the work of salvation rendered unto the Father an act of complete obedience for the salvation of men (Romans v. 19). This teaching is the undertone in all that St. Paul says concerning faith in Christ. Sometimes, indeed, its notes are sounded, as when he declares that God set forth Christ by his blood as a means of atonement 'through faith' (Romans iii. 25) and speaks of Him as 'the justifier of him who founds on faith in Jesus' (Romans iii. 26), when especially he associates faith expressly with justification (Romans iii. 28, 30, v. 1; Galatians ii. 16, iii. 8, 24, etc.) and

---

[1] Cf. Burton: 'For the disclosure of the Apostle's fundamental idea of the nature of religion, there is no more important sentence in the whole epistle, if, indeed, in any of Paul's epistles' (I.C.C., Galatians, p. 279).

with access to God (Ephesians iii. 12: 'In whom we have boldness and access in confidence through our faith in him'). We may be sure, however, that in Pauline teaching even where faith is not characterized in this way, it is none the less devotion to Christ as the One through whom God has manifested and wrought His redemptive activity. Faith is the acceptance of that activity, reliance upon it, and participation in it, in the sense that where it exists the work of God in bringing men into fellowship with Himself is crowned and consummated. It is not too much to say that in the Pauline scheme without faith there is no atonement.

It is upon this fundamental basis of faith in Christ that the richer teaching of St. Paul concerning faith-union, fellowship with Christ, dying and living with Him, sacramental communion, and daily suffering with Christ, is to be understood. Both justification and reconciliation, as he presents these ideas in his Epistles, are acts of God accomplished in the spiritual moment, not necessarily a moment in time, when the strivings of the soul cease and it rests in faith in Christ. At once the believer has his standing with God and his entrance upon the blessedness of fellowship with Him. As the recognition by God of this standing justification by its nature has this note of immediacy, and the same also is true of reconciliation as St. Paul describes it (cf. Romans v. 10 f.). Reconciliation is the gift of His fellowship, entrance upon His peace, adoption into His family, a sovereign act of God and not a process of attainment. Just because it has this character, however, it is inseparably linked to a subsequent process, and loses its meaning without it. As a state of fellowship, it is meant to issue in a life of fellowship; blessedness must become beatitude; nothing less than sanctification is its ideal goal. Hence follows the abundance and the variety of the Pauline teaching concerning the ethical and spiritual ends to which the atonement in Christ is directed. It is to the maintenance and increase of this life, and not only to its beginnings, that much of St. Paul's teaching about fellowship with Christ is related. We cannot, of course, draw a sharp line of demarcation between faith and faith-union and say that the former is concerned with justification and reconciliation and the latter with more mature expressions of the ethical and spiritual life. Perhaps only when faith is a matter of simple belief is it, in St. Paul's usage, other than a form of faith-union, and always it implies some kind of fellowship. None the less, the distinction we are making is useful, if only to emphasize the maturity of some of the experiences in question and, what is more important, to guard against the mistake of supposing that a highly developed, if not mystical, type of faith is needed for the appropriation of the gifts offered to men in the work of God in Christ.

Like the faith by which a man is justified, faith-union with Christ, often expressed in the phrase 'in Christ', is union with the Crucified, and not only with Christ as the Revealer of God. This fact is especially clear in the fellowship with Him described by the expressions, peculiar to St. Paul, 'being crucified with Christ' (Romans vi. 6; Galatians ii. 20), 'dying' and 'suffering' with Him (Romans vi. 8, viii. 17; cf. 2 Timothy ii. 11), 'being buried' and 'rising' with Him (Romans vi. 4; Colossians ii. 12, iii. 1; Ephesians ii. 6); and the same fundamental relationship is implicit in passages which speak of 'being quickened together with Christ' (Ephesians ii. 5; Colossians ii. 13) and 'being glorified' with Him (Romans viii. 17). In these experiences the believer's fellowship with Christ is so close that he shares mystically in the experiences of His Passion and Exaltation. Out of the same relationship emerge also those experiences connected with missionary toil and responsibility in which St. Paul speaks of 'bearing about in the body the dying of Jesus' (2 Corinthians iv. 10) and of filling up on his part 'the residue of the afflictions of Christ for his body's sake, which is the church' (Colossians i. 24). When he refers to 'the care of all the churches', and cries: 'Who is weak, and I am not weak? who is made to stumble, and I burn not?' (2 Corinthians xi. 29), he is voicing feelings which he has come to understand more readily, and to experience more deeply, because through fellowship with Christ he has come to know that 'fellowship of his sufferings' which is the subject of his prayers (cf. Philippians iii. 10). In all these ways a vital experience of union with Christ is the medium through which he receives the blessings of His sacrifice, moral and spiritual power for the daily duties of life, and strength to live no longer unto himself, but unto Him who for our sakes 'died and rose again' (2 Corinthians v. 15). Through faith the work of God in Christ is crowned.

We are not moving to a lower level, or even turning to something essentially different, when to what is said above we add St. Paul's teaching about sacramental communion. The opportunity the Eucharist affords is highly esteemed by St. Paul. For him it is a means of communion with the body and blood of Christ that is, of participating in the dedicated and offered life of the Lord (cf. 1 Corinthians x. 16). This fact is all the more significant because for rites as such he does not appear to have had a high regard. He thanks God that he baptized no one at Corinth save Crispus and Gaius, and then remembers the household of Stephanus, and finally says: 'Besides, I know not whether I baptized any other' (1 Corinthians i. 14–17). Nevertheless, he speaks of baptism as baptism into the death of Christ; in the words of Denney:[1] 'Baptism and faith are but the outside and the inside of the same thing.' Clearly, it is the spiritual aspect of the rite which is his main concern. Exactly the same is true of his estimation of the Eucharist. Any thought of a mechanical means of grace is entirely foreign to his mind; but he does believe that, just as by eating the sacrifices Israel has communion with the altar, that is, with God (cf. 1 Corinthians x. 18), and just as things sacrificed to idols expose the Corinthians to the perils of communion with evil powers (1 Corinthians x. 20), so the Bread and the Cup bring the believer into a vital relation with the Crucified Saviour (1 Corinthians x. 16, 21). Communion of this kind is not an alternative to faith-union with Christ, still less a lower and secondary means of approach; it is, like faith itself, an appropriating of all He has done for men by the aid of the symbols of His appointing. Through the Eucharist we receive the blessings of the work of God in Christ.

Such, then, is St. Paul's teaching as to the way in which the Atonement becomes a reality in the Christian experience. In variety and in extent it surpasses his explanation of the character of the work of God in Christ which, as we have seen, is conveyed by allusions and epigrams rather than by a detailed exposition. In this fact is seen the distinctive bent of his mind which is practical rather than speculative, religious more than theological. It is legitimate to infer that his teaching on faith-union in itself, alike by reason of its depth and range, implies a work of God in Christ which is not only a revelation of His love, but also and at the same time the provision of a living way whereby man may know the wonder of abiding fellowship with Himself.

(c) Summary

The investigation, it may be claimed, has shown that St. Paul's debt to the primitive Christian tradition is much greater than has often been supposed, and that his distinctive teaching concerns

[1] *The Death of Christ*, p. 185.

special points arising out of that tradition, notably on the side of the Christian experience. Justification, reconciliation, union with Christ, and life in the Spirit are all experiences in which God is active in the life of man with a view to fellowship with Himself. It is with the question, how man in spite of his sin can know this fellowship, that St. Paul above all else is concerned, and his conviction is that at every point its realization is bound up with the work of Christ. This practical interest gives a greater unity to his teaching than is commonly recognized. In works of Biblical theology it is usual to distinguish a number of separate ideas as illustrative of St. Paul's soteriology. Thus, his statements are gathered under such headings as (1) Salvation from sin, (2) Redemption, (3) Reconciliation; while Justification is treated separately.[1] This practice has the great advantage of simplicity, but it tends to suggest that his thought is lacking in unity. Paulinism, of course, is not a closely wrought system, but neither is it a collation of unrelated ideas.

The vital link which binds together the main elements in St. Paul's teaching is his emphasis upon the idea of the redemptive work of God in Christ for men, a work which reveals and expresses His righteousness and manifests the wonder of His love for sinners. This work of God presupposes the truth of the Incarnation; it is accomplished in the person of His Son, who in obedience to the Father's will identifies Himself with sinners and burdens Himself with their sorrows and sufferings in the greatness of His love. As the Christ who died for sins, He is 'a means of atonement', the medium of reconciliation between men and God; and this work He accomplishes in virtue of a faith-relationship between men and Himself. It is on the ground of this faith that God can accept men as righteous, and so bring them into fellowship with Himself; and an ever-deepening union between believers and Christ, always resting upon the reality of His work for men, is the source of a continuous ethical and spiritual growth which has nothing less than sanctification, or the life of perfect love, for its goal. Such, in brief, appears to be the idea of atonement implied in St. Paul's Epistles.

On reflection several points connected with this summary are seen to call for further notice. (1) First, summaries of this kind

---

[1] Cf. G. B. Stevens, *The Theology of the New Testament*, pp. 407–9, 417–30; H. A. A. Kennedy, *The Theology of the Epistles*, pp. 131, 135–8; H. J. Holtzmann, *Lehrbuch der neutestamentlichen Theologie*, ii, pp. 97–121, 124–43.

must always contain an interpretative element due to the point of view of the investigator. This should be frankly admitted. In such circumstances the only thing to do is to seek to exclude bias by repeated study of St. Paul's words. (2) Again, the summary has a precision greater than anything we can find in St. Paul's Epistles. This also must necessarily be the case. The Apostle has nowhere presented his views in the form of a theory; and, in consequence, the only course open to us is to consider whether his utterances can justly be treated as the detached fragments of a larger whole. Although he is not a systematic theologian, it is highly probable that, consciously or unconsciously, what he says about the death of Christ will belong to relatively uniform conceptions or patterns of thought. (3) Further, other ideas are expressed in his Epistles which cannot easily be brought within a common outline. In particular, his representation of the work of Christ as His victory over sin and powers hostile to man, is part of a different theory. The same also must be said of the view that the salvation of man is implicit in the person of Christ, as the Representative of humanity, just as the sin of the race is implicit in Adam. Although this view, adumbrated in Romans v. 12, is not developed, and does not represent the main current of Pauline teaching, the signs of its presence strengthen the belief that St. Paul did assign a representative function to the ministry of Christ for men. (4) Lastly, there are points within the summary itself which, while required by St. Paul's statements, are not fully represented in them. What, for example, is the work of Christ for men ambiguously indicated in Romans iii. 25 in the word ἱλαστήριον? We have claimed, as we are entitled to do, that it entailed submission to the consequences of sin. And on the basis of Romans v. 19 we can say that it was an act of obedience. But must not its content be even richer? It is a false reverence which stays this question, since at this point we lay our finger on the element most wanting in the Pauline theology. A faith-relationship so profound as that which St. Paul describes must mean, in addition to devotion to Christ's person, the affirmation of all the values implicit in His representative ministry for men. For salvation happily it is not required that we should first be able to apprehend these values, but for the purposes of a complete theology the case is otherwise. The faith in Christ which is the basis on which sinners are accepted as righteous by God requires for its foundation a work of Christ which expresses all that penitent

men are unable to utter save in Him. Would St. Paul have
questioned this? One cannot feel that he would. And yet, in
harmony with his express statements we can describe these values
only as submission and obedience. Of man's sorrow, penitence,
and longing after God there is no echo in the voice of the Pauline
Christ. In other words, the representative aspect of the ministry
of Christ for men is only partially presented in St. Paul's teaching.
Explanations of this fact must always remain speculative. Is it
due in part to the limitations which some theologians have
detected in his doctrine of the Incarnation?[1] Is it occasioned by
his restricted use of the sacrificial principle, of the idea, that is,
of an offering with which the worshipper can identify himself in
his approach to God? Is it influenced by his virtual neglect of the
concept of the Suffering Servant of the Lord? It is in the two
points just mentioned that we are conscious most of the differences
between St. Paul and Jesus,[2] or, if we prefer to put it so, between
St. Paul and the beliefs of primitive Christianity. If these suggestions are in any way justified, the neglect was costly, and the
inference is prompted that the theology which will fail least
lamentably in presenting the doctrine of the Atonement is one
which makes full use of the idea of sacrifice.

The immediate influence of St. Paul's teaching was not great
if we measure its extent by its effect upon the later New Testament
writers, apart from the Fourth Evangelist. As we have seen, the
writers of the Acts, 1 Peter, the Apocalypse, and the Pastoral
Epistles are dependent upon the common faith of the primitive
Church more than upon St. Paul's teaching. Its subsequent
influence has been profound, and its character has been determined by the peculiar features brought out in the above summary.

The doctrine of the Second Adam occupies an important place
in the recapitulation theory of Irenæus,[3] and in modern times,
along with other ideas, it has received special emphasis in the
discussions of W. P. Du Bose[4] and R. C. Moberly.[5] The idea of a
victorious conflict over hostile powers, coupled with various forms
of the 'ransom' theory, dominated the theology of the ancient
Church for a thousand years until the time of Anselm (A.D.
1033–1109), and recently has found renewed expression in
writings of G. Aulén[6] and S. Cave.[7] Each of these theories

[1] Cf. J. Weiss, *The History of Primitive Christianity*, pp. 489 f.
[2] Cf. *Jesus and His Sacrifice*, pp. 294–8.   [3] *Adv. Hær.*, v, 16, 3.
[4] *The Gospel in the Gospels*, p. 157.   [5] *Atonement and Personality*, p. 86
[6] *Christus Victor*.   [7] *The Doctrine of the Work of Christ*.

represents only a part of St. Paul's teaching, and, as we have seen, one which is not integrated with his main contentions, with the result that their adoption, as the basis of a modern theory, entails the neglect of the greater and more important part of his theology. Even more true is this of the view that the Cross is the revelation of the love of God, emphasized by Abailard (A.D. 1079–1142) and his disciple Peter Lombard, and with various modifications by a host of modern writers, including H. Bushnell,[1] H. Rashdall,[2] and R. S. Franks.[3] This great and moving idea, we have seen, is the prolegomena of Pauline doctrine, its fundamental assumption, but when it is made the whole truth of the Atonement, most of that teaching becomes mainly of historical and academic interest. The future, as it seems to the present writer, lies with a theology which grapples with the same ultimate problems of God, man, and sin as those with which St. Paul wrestles, and in agreement with his fundamental conception of a representative ministry of God in Christ, as the basis of faith-union and of reconciliation with God, is ready to hazard failure in an attempt to give to it a modern setting.

2. THE TEACHING OF THE WRITER OF THE EPISTLE
TO THE HEBREWS

In studying the Epistle to the Hebrews, we ought constantly to keep in mind the fact that we are dealing with the teaching of a single Epistle as compared with the ten which form the Pauline collection. This fact is most important when we are thinking of elements of primitive belief which are wanting in its teaching. Their absence from the Epistle can be pressed only when it is highly significant in the light of what is actually taught and the writer's intellectual and religious presuppositions.

By wide consent the Epistle is to be dated *c.* A.D. 80.[4] All that we can say of the writer is that he was a teacher of the Pauline circle whose point of view is distinctively Alexandrian.[5] A con-

[1] *The Vicarious Sacrifice.* Bushnell also emphasizes the truth that the Cross is the moral power of God and uses to some extent the idea of sacrifice.

[2] *The Idea of Atonement in Christian Theology.* A naked presentation of the theory.

[3] *The Atonement.* Dr. Franks seeks to combine with the teaching of Abailard the method of Anselm, and advocates the term 'experiential theory'.

[4] Cf. Moffatt, *I.C.C., Hebrews,* p. xxii; McNeile, *Introduction,* p. 224; Peake, *Introduction,* pp. 82 *f.*; E. F. Scott, *Introduction,* p. 199. Westcott dates the Epistle A.D. 64–7, *The Epistle to the Hebrews,* p. xlii, and T. W. Manson, A.D. 58–70, 'perhaps 58–66', *A Companion to the Bible,* p. 114.

[5] 'The more he differs from Philo in his speculative interpretation of religion, the more I feel, after a prolonged study of Philo, that our author had probably read some of his works', Moffatt, *op. cit.,* p. lxi.

vinced Christian, well versed in the knowledge of the Septuagint, his aim is to present the new faith in terms which have been suggested by the Platonic philosophy. He may not have read the writings of Plato, but he is certainly influenced by the Platonic principle of the antithesis between the heavenly Idea, which is real, and the earthly Copy, which is transient and temporal. Thus it is that in ix. 23 we read of the cleansing of 'the copies of the things in the heavens', and in x. 1 of the Law as 'having a shadow of the good things to come, not the very image of the things'. More important is the distinction between the present age and 'the age to come' (vi. 5), which is thought of as already existing, though not realized in time. It is on this basis that the writer argues that Christianity is superior to Judaism. The Levitical priesthood and the Jewish sacrificial system belong to the present age and are only copies of eternal realities, whereas Christ and His sacrifice belong to the heavenly order. His sacrificial offering is that of a high priest, and because He has opened up a living way to God, Christians, while living upon earth, belong already to 'the age to come'. 'We which have believed', the author says, 'do enter into that rest' (iv. 3). 'We have not here an abiding city, but we seek after that which is to come' (xiii. 14). Meantime, we have hope 'as an anchor of the soul', 'a hope both sure and steadfast and entering into that which is within the veil; whither as a forerunner Jesus entered for us, having become a high priest for ever after the order of Melchizedek' (vi. 18–20). It is in such passages as these that we see best the author's characteristic ideas, and it is from this standpoint that he treats the meaning of the death of Christ.

(a) The Use made of Primitive Christian Tradition in the Epistle to the Hebrews

Perhaps the simplest way of studying the use which the author makes of primitive Christian ideas is to indicate the passages in the Epistle which correspond with the several ideas included in the list printed on pp. 50 f.

1. The idea of the divine purpose.	ii. 9, 10.
2. Messianic character.	(i. 1, v. 8, vii. 28) (n. 1).
3. Vicarious nature.	ii. 9, vi. 20, vii. 25, ix. 14, 24.
4. Representative aspect.	ii. 17, iii. 1, iv. 14–16, v. 5 f., 9 f., vi. 20, vii. 22, 26, viii. 1 f., 6, ix. 11, 15, 24–8, x. 21, xii. 24.
5. Relation to sin.	i. 3, ii. 17, vii. 27, ix. 11 f., 14, 26, 28, x. 12, xiii. 11 f.

6. Sacrificial significance.	i. 3, ii. 17, vii. 27, ix. 11 *f.*, 14 *f.*, 24–8, x. 10, 12, 14, 19–23, xii. 24, xiii. 11 *f.*, 20 *f.*
7. Servant-conception.	ix. 28 (*n.* 2).
8. The Resurrection.	xiii. 20 (*n.* 3).
9. Idea of a faith-relationship.	
10. Eucharistic teaching.	(*n.* 4).
11. Suffering with Christ.	
12. Relation to the love of God.	(ii. 9) (*n.* 5).
13. Ethical and spiritual ends.	ii. 15, ix. 14.
14. Universality.	ii. 9 (ii. 17, vii. 27, xiii. 12) (*n.* 6).

NOTES

1. Although the term 'Son' in the passages cited is Messianic in origin, the writer's Christology, and therefore his doctrine of Christ's mediatorial work, transcend Messianic categories.

2. While the language of ix. 28: 'So Christ also, having been once offered *to bear the sins of many*, shall appear a second time . . .', reflects the influence of Isaiah liii. 12, it cannot be said that the Servant-conception enters into the writer's account of the work of Christ.

3. The Resurrection is mentioned in xiii. 20: 'Now the God of peace, who brought again from the dead the great shepherd of the sheep with the blood of the eternal covenant, . . .', but otherwise it is not related by the writer to the death of Christ. His continued presence at 'the right hand' of God is frequently mentioned and is a fundamental element in His mediatorial ministry (cf. i. 3, viii. 1, x. 12, xii. 2).

4. The difficult passage, xiii. 10, 'We have an altar, whereof they have no right to eat which serve the tabernacle', is discussed later. See pp. 105–110.

5. The thought of the love of God is implied in ii. 9, 'that *by the grace of God* he should taste death for every man', but otherwise is not mentioned in the Epistle.

6. The universality of Christ's work is definitely expressed in ii. 9 (cited above) and the references to 'the people' in the passages mentioned are in no way intended to suggest a limited atonement.

Provided it is rightly interpreted, this list is most instructive. Some of its omissions are surprising and are a challenge to thought. On the other hand, the prominence given to the relation of the death of Christ to sin and to its vicarious, representative, and sacrificial aspects is only what we might expect in such an Epistle. The idea of atonement as the purpose of God has nothing like the emphasis it receives in the Pauline Epistles, but it is implied in the assertion that it was 'by the grace of God' that Christ tasted death for every man (ii. 9), and in the statement that it 'became' the One for whom and through whom are all things 'in bringing many sons unto glory, to make the author of their salvation perfect through sufferings' (ii. 10). The former passage, in its reference to God's 'grace', is also the only allusion to the love of God as the motive power of the work of Christ.[1] The resurrection is another idea which falls into the background

[1] The alternative reading: 'without God' (χωρὶς θεοῦ) read by M 424** sy^pe (three codices), and attested by Origen, Theodoret, Ambrose, Jerome, and Theodore of Mopsuestia, is probably a scribal corruption. The meaning of the phrase is variously explained as 'except God', 'forsaken by God', and 'apart from his divinity'. For critical discussions, see Moffatt, pp. 26 *f.*; Westcott, pp. 60–2; Peake, pp. 102 *f.*; Rendall, p. 19

(cf. xiii. 20), probably because the writer's attention is concentrated upon that which follows the resurrection, namely, the
exaltation and the session of Christ on high. Thus, it is emphasized that 'when he had made purification of sins', the Son 'sat
down on the right hand of the Majesty on high' (i. 3; cf. viii. 1,
x. 12, xii. 2), and that because 'he ever liveth to make intercession
for us', He is able to save to the uttermost those who enter into
communion with God through Him (vii. 25). This emphasis,
however, could hardly have led to a neglect of the resurrection
if, like St. Paul, the writer had thought of it as the victory of
Christ over sin and death, and, in consequence, as a vital part
of His redeeming work.

The very limited use which is made of the Servant-conception
(cf. ix. 28) seriously affects the writer's teaching, although he
expresses some of its essential ideas in other ways, by the use of
the term 'mediator' and the thought of a new covenant-relationship between God and men effected by Christ's sacrifice. The
same must also be said of his failure to use the idea of an intimate
faith-relationship with Christ, to develop eucharistic teaching,
and to speak of the experience of suffering with Christ. If any
one of these omissions stood alone, we might invoke the argument
already mentioned, that, since we possess only a single writing
from the author's pen, the silence may be accidental. But the
signs we have already noted of a close connexion between faith-
union and sacramental communion warn us against the adequacy
of this explanation, and suggest that the omissions may be due to
the peculiar character of the mediatorial ministry which is
assigned to Christ in the Epistle. The cause may be doctrinal.
This possibility cannot be considered further until the writer's
distinctive teaching has been examined. At the present stage we
must ask whether, in fact, teaching about faith-union and the
Eucharist is wanting.

As regards faith-union there can be no uncertainty. Faith, as
the writer of the Epistle to the Hebrews understands it, is not
trust in, and self-committal to, Christ in the Pauline sense; it is
rather confidence in the reality of the unseen, in the certainty of
God's promises, in the truth of Christ's redemptive work. In the
rendering of xi. 1 proposed by J. H. Moulton:[1] 'Faith is the *title-
deeds* of things hoped for.' Moffatt's translation of the verse is:
'Now faith means we are confident of what we hope for, convinced

---

[1] *The Vocabulary of the Greek Testament*, p. 660; *From Egyptian Rubbish-heaps*, pp. 27-9

of what we do not see.'[1] It is not that which gives substance to the unseen, but the habit of mind to which the unseen is the real, together with a strong and unyielding reliance upon its reality, as may clearly be seen in the roll of the heroes of faith unfolded in chapter xi. This is precisely the relationship in which the believer stands to the sacrifice of Christ described in the Epistle, as is indicated in the exhortation of x. 19 ff.: 'Having therefore, brethren, boldness to enter into the holy place by the blood of Jesus, by the way which he dedicated for us. . . let us draw near with a true heart *in fulness of faith* . . . let us hold fast the confession of our hope that it waver not. . . .' Faith is not, as in St. Paul's Epistles, a spiritual appropriation of Christ's redemptive service, a fellowship with Himself in the mystery of His sufferings, but rather a confident belief that in the unseen world He intercedes with the Father on the basis of all that He has accomplished for men. It would be folly to set these two conceptions in opposition, since both are needed, along with that practical presentation of faith in the Epistle of James, to set forth in its fulness the wealth of New Testament teaching; but the recognition of the absence of the Pauline idea in the Epistle to the Hebrews is essential to an intelligent appreciation of its teaching concerning the sacrifice of Christ.

Whether the Epistle refers to the Eucharist depends on the interpretation of a single text, xiii. 10: '*We have an altar, whereof they have no right to eat which serve the tabernacle.*' From Chrysostom[2] to Bishop Westcott,[3] this passage has been often interpreted as a reference to the Christian Eucharist in contrast with the sacrificial feasts of Judaism. On this interpretation the 'tabernacle' is that described in the Pentateuch,[4] those who 'serve' it are the sacrificing priests of Judaism,[5] and the 'altar' is the sacrifice of Christ upon the Cross[6] which is pledged to the believer in the

[1] Moffatt, p. 159, quotes Tyndale's translation: 'Faith is a sure confidence of thynges which are hoped for, and a certaynetie of thynges which are not seyne.'

[2] *In Epist. ad Hebr.*, hom. xxxiii, 304A.

[3] *The Epistle to the Hebrews*, pp. 437–9, 453–62.

[4] So Lünemann, p. 482; Alford, iv, p. 267.

[5] So Alford, iv, p. 266; Vaughan, p. 298; Westcott, p. 439. Dods, *Expositor's Greek Testament*, iv, p. 377, on the contrary, holds that to refer the words to the O.T. priests 'is to shatter the argument'.

[6] The view that the 'altar' is the Cross is supported by Bengel, F. Bleek, Alford, iv, p. 266; Lünemann, pp. 482 f.; and others. Thomas Aquinas held that it is either the Cross or Christ Himself. Many commentators have preferred to see in it a reference to the atoning sacrifice of Christ, e.g. T. C. Edwards, p. 321; A. B. Bruce, p. 426.

Christian Eucharist.[1] In support of this view, Westcott para-phrases the passage as follows: 'We Christians *have* an altar, from which we draw the material for our feast. In respect of this, our privilege is greater than that of priest or high-priest under the Levitical system. Our great sin-offering, consumed in one sense outside the gate, is given to us as our food. The Christian there-fore who can partake of Christ, offered for his sins, is admitted to a privilege unknown under the old Covenant.'[2] This exegesis, I think, is not only true in substance, but also adequately explains the passage, so long as it is taken by itself; it is more difficult, however, and indeed impossible to accept it as representing the writer's thought. Amid much that is obscure the context seems clearly to indicate that, in the writer's view, Christians as such have no sacrificial meal in the material sense of the term. The passage is immediately preceded by the injunction: 'Be not carried away by divers and strange teachings: for it is good that the heart be established by grace; *not meats*' (βρώμασιν). We cannot be certain whether the reference here is to Jewish ascetic regulations about food (cf. Colossians ii. 20–3) or to pagan cult-feasts (cf. 1 Corinthians x. 20–2); but in either case it is against the observance of religious practices connected with food that the writer is contending,[3] and this consideration must determine our interpretation of xiii. 10. The same conclusion is suggested by the words which immediately follow. In xiii. 11 *f.* the writer refers to the sin-offering, pointedly explaining that the bodies of the victims were burned without the camp of Israel, and identi-fying the sacrifice of Jesus, who 'suffered without the gate', with this type of offering. The readers are urged to go forth unto Him 'without the camp, bearing his reproach' (xiii. 13), and they are exhorted to offer up a sacrifice which, so far from being a feast, is described as 'a sacrifice of praise to God continually', and is interpreted by the writer himself in the words: 'that is, the fruit of lips which make confession to his name' (xiii. 15). As if to indicate the kind of spiritual sacrifice he has in mind, the writer adds: 'But to do good and to communicate forget not: for *with*

---

[1] For the view that the 'altar' is the Eucharist, see the references given by J. Behm, *Theol. Wort.*, iii, pp. 182 *f.* Westcott appears to combine this view with those noted in the preceding footnote. Nairne, p. 130, speaks of the imagery as 'thoroughly sacramental'.

[2] *The Epistle to the Hebrews*, p. 439. See also F. C. N. Hicks, *The Fullness of Sacrifice*, pp. 235–7.

[3] The probability that the reference is to the Lord's Supper interpreted in a realistic sense is considered later.

such sacrifices God is well pleased' (xiii. 16). Is it possible, we must ask, without some strong indication within the passage itself, to infer that in xiii. 10 his intention is to claim that in the Eucharist his readers actually possess a sacrificial meal which Jewish priests have no right to eat? The presumption must surely be that his aim is to say something quite different.

Bishop Westcott argues that the point of the passage is that the Gospel as compared with the Law offers more to the believers in respect of social worship. 'The Christian enjoys in substance that which the Jew did not enjoy even in shadow.'[1] In the words already quoted: 'Our great sin-offering, consumed in one sense outside the gate, is given to us as our food. The Christian therefore who can partake of Christ, offered for his sins, is admitted to a privilege unknown under the old Covenant.' The Bishop of Lincoln argues to the same effect when he writes: 'What he seems to say, therefore, is that it is just at the point of communion that the sin-offering breaks down. Those for whom it was offered might not eat of the sacrifice; and when the priest offered it for himself, or for the people including himself, even he might not eat of it.'[2] 'Christ is no mere sin-offering. He fulfils the idea of sacrifice in all its forms. He gives Himself as our food: His flesh, no longer too holy for the forgiven sinner to receive, becomes part of ours; and, as might have been added, even His blood itself, the very Life of the sacrifice, too holy in the old days ever to be received, and never imparted to any offerer, priest, or layman, more closely than by an external sprinkling, is given to every Christian worshipper to drink'.[3]

This attractive argument, and especially the claim that Christ is no mere sin-offering, but 'fulfils the idea of sacrifice in all its forms', for all its truth is, I think, a doctrinal invasion upon the rights of sober exegesis. Throughout the whole of the passage, xiii. 9–16, the writer's contention is that Christ's sacrifice *is* the perfect sin-offering, and while, of course, it is much more than this, he has given us no indication of his intention in this context to make the wider claim. In order to find a reference to the Eucharist in xiii. 10, we are compelled, in fact, to invert his argument, and to do it without his consent. In this matter we must agree, I think, with the opinion of the late Canon J. M. Creed: 'But it must be admitted that the author gives no direct indication that he intends to qualify what he has already asserted;

[1] *Op. cit.*, p. 439.   [2] *The Fullness of Sacrifice*, p. 236.   [3] *Op. cit.*, p. 237.

on the contrary the connexion of the sentences suggests rather that he is developing a single line of thought in an even style.'[1] As a matter of exegesis, we must conclude that in xiii. 10 the author is not claiming that Christians possess a sacrificial meal. This view is confirmed by the fact that nowhere else in the Epistle does he refer to the Eucharist, not even when he speaks of the death of Christ under the analogy of covenant-sacrifice (cf. vii. 22, viii. 6, ix. 15).

The question indeed arises whether there is not in the passage a polemic against a materialistic interpretation of the Eucharist as an actual 'eating' of the Lord's body. Among English commentators this view is taken by A. S. Peake, J. Moffatt, and T. H. Robinson.[2] Peake writes: 'And thus the author would say, Because Jesus is the supreme sin-offering, it is impossible that his body should be eaten in a sacrificial meal', and he paraphrases the passage: 'We have an altar, but it is one with which no meal can be associated, for its sacrifice belongs to that class of most sacred sin-offerings, whose blood was brought into the Holy Place, and the bodies of which could not be eaten even by the priests, but had to be burnt outside the camp.'[3] Moffatt argues that the trend of xiii. 10 f. is that 'in real Christian worship there is no sacrificial meal; the Christian sacrifice is not one of which the worshippers partake by eating'.[4] Robinson goes so far as to say that the most natural interpretation, on the surface, is that the writer disapproved altogether of the celebration of the Supper as a special ritual, but that it is also possible that he found what he considered to be superstitious ideas gathering round it. 'He may have been faced with people who believed that the very body and blood of Christ, present in the consecrated elements, gave a profoundly real vitality to the heart.'[5]

Canon Creed thinks that such a polemic as that described is unlikely on the twofold ground that, if the writer had had this definite aim he would not have expressed himself so allusively and obscurely, and that there is very little reason to suppose that beliefs with regard to the Eucharist were of controversial interest in the first century.[6] As regards the second point, one must recognize that the Fourth Evangelist, himself a sacramental

---

[1] *The Expository Times*, l, p. 14.
[2] Among Continental scholars who hold the same opinion are F. Spitta, O. Holtzmann, H. Windisch. Cf. Moffatt, pp. 233 f.
[3] *The Century Bible*, *Hebrews*, pp. 240 f.   [4] *Op. cit.*, p. 234.
[5] *The Moffatt New Testament Commentary*, *Hebrews*, p. 201.   [6] *Op. cit.*, p. 15.

mystic, appears to presuppose such a polemic[1] twenty years later, and there is nothing to exclude the possibility that it is implied by the reference to 'divers and strange teachings' in xiii. 9. Moreover, the allusive and obscure language of xiii. 10 may be held to support rather than weaken this inference. Had the writer meant what Westcott understands him to mean, or had he altogether repudiated the Eucharist as a rite, we might reasonably look for much clearer language in the passage; but if, while recognizing the place of the Eucharist in the corporate worship of the Church, but not as a partisan and certainly not as a 'sacramental mystic', he was opposing what he believed to be crude teaching, the language which he uses is precisely that which we might expect him to employ. His readers would understand exactly what he meant, that he was not attacking a rite justly prized within the Church, but an interpretation which he believed to be mischievous.

If the position I have outlined is sound, we obtain a clear and consistent interpretation of xiii. 7–17. The writer sees his readers exposed to teaching which he believes to be materialistic relating to the Eucharist; they are being invited to think that in the Supper they are eating the body of Christ in a carnal sense. It is for this reason that he reminds them of the teaching of their departed leaders, and asserts that Jesus Christ is 'the same yesterday and to-day, yea and for ever' (xiii. 7 f.). Warning them against 'divers and strange teachings', he says pointedly: 'It is good that the heart be established by grace; not by meats', and declares that those who walk in this way were not profited (xiii. 9). The word 'meats' is his word, a sharp polemical word, and it may be that the word 'altar', which he had already used in vii. 13 of the Old Testament altar, is wrested from their vocabulary. 'Yes', he says in effect, 'we have an "altar"'; but it is not one with which sacrificial meals are to be associated, since our Sacrifice is a sin-offering' (xiii. 10–2). By the word 'altar' he is not thinking of any object either on earth or in heaven, but of the sacrificial death of Christ upon the Cross, and by 'those who serve the tabernacle' he may mean either Jewish priests[2] or Christians or the false teachers who used this language of themselves. In any case, his

---

[1] Cf. W. F. Howard, *The Fourth Gospel in Recent Criticism and Interpretation*, pp. 146, 213 f.

[2] A reference to contemporary Jewish priests is improbable since the 'tabernacle' is mentioned. A reference to Christians, however, is not easy, and, on the whole I am inclined to think that the phrase is polemical.

plea is for loyalty to Jesus who 'suffered without the gate' (xiii. 12.) They are to 'go forth unto him without the camp, bearing his reproach', since they are the citizens of the city which is to come (xiii. 13 f.). The 'reproach' is any depreciation to which they might be exposed because of their refusal to accept novel doctrines. Meantime, as we have pointed out, he claims that they do possess true sacrifices, the ancient peace-offering in the form of continual praise to God and the opportunity to do good and to relieve the needs of their fellows (xiii. 15 f.). In harmony with this interpretation is the final exhortation to obey those who have the rule over them, since they watch over their souls as 'they that shall give account'. The idea of what is profitable for them persists to the end of the section. They are to obey their rulers that these may watch over them 'with joy, and not with grief', for 'this', says the author, himself a shepherd of souls, 'were unprofitable for you' (xiii. 17).

I have given considerable attention to xiii. 10, not only because it is a *crux interpretum* which if it is treated at all, must be treated fully,[1] but also because it is vital to a full understanding of the teaching of the Epistle in relation to the Atonement. To a degree unparalleled elsewhere in the New Testament the writer has drawn upon the traditional teaching of the Church in respect of the vicarious, representative, and sacrificial aspects of the work of Christ without developing to the slightest extent, or even introducing, any doctrine of faith-union or sacramental communion as the means whereby the blessings of Christ's work may be appropriated by the believer. The same also is true of the idea of suffering with Christ. The one passage in which he speaks of Christians as 'partakers (μέτοχοι) of Christ' (iii. 14), like the similar phrases 'partakers of a heavenly calling' (iii. 1) and 'partakers of the Holy Spirit' (vi. 4), indicates association with Christ rather than union with Him in respect of His suffering life and death. Moffatt is entirely right in saying that 'he is devoid of the faith-mysticism which characterizes Paul',[2] and at the same time in claiming that he has 'a mystical or idealistic bent, to which the sacramental idea is foreign'.[3] A refusal to recognize this fact, in the supposed interests of eucharistic doctrine, seems to me to be mistaken because it thereby conceals from us the peculiar

---

[1] I have used the first person freely in discussing this passage in order to indicate that the views expressed are *personal* opinions with no more weight than their truth.
[2] *Op. cit.*, p. liv.
[3] *Op. cit.*, p. 234. Cf. Creed, *op. cit.*, p. 14.

character of the sacrificial teaching of the Epistle, a teaching which stakes everything upon the fact of Christ's sacrificial offering of Himself for men without raising the question how that self-offering becomes a vital reality in the experience of believers.

Already it has become evident that the teaching of the Epistle is based on a conscious selection of important elements in the primitive Christian belief. No attempt is made in it to deal fully with all that was believed and taught in the Churches of the ninth decade of Christianity. If any further proof of this claim is needed it is afforded by the attitude of the writer to two other convictions of the Churches of his time. Only once, but with definiteness, does he refer to the universality of Christ's redeeming work, in the statement that, by the suffering of death, He was 'crowned with glory and honour, that by the grace of God he should taste death *for every man*' (ii. 9). The controversy about the Law in relation to Jew and Gentile lies in the past, and the victory of Pauline teaching is tacitly assumed. More remarkable is the slight extent to which the writer has referred to the ethical and spiritual ends of the atoning ministry of Christ. Almost in passing he says that Christ partook of flesh and blood 'that through death he might bring to nought him that has the power of death, that is, the devil; and might deliver all them who through fear of death were all their lifetime subject to bondage' (ii. 14 *f.*). He also speaks of the blood of Christ cleansing the conscience in the words: 'How much more shall the blood of Christ . . . cleanse your conscience from dead works to serve the living God?' (ix. 14). Otherwise, all his interest is concentrated upon the purification and cleansing from sin to which the sacrifice of Christ is directed. No references to peace with God, justification, reconciliation, eternal life, or living unto righteousness are to be found in the Epistle. The writer devotes all his attention to one cycle of ideas, the vicarious, representative, and sacrificial offering of Christ, and in comparison with this all else falls into the background. Instead of making this a ground for complaint we ought rather to welcome a positive and highly individual attempt to deal with a central aspect of the work of Christ and to base our appreciation of the teaching of the Epistle upon what it actually contains and upon what the writer seeks to do.

(b) *The Distinctive Teaching of the Epistle to the Hebrews*

It will be of advantage to preface the discussion of the distinctive teaching of the Epistle by considering the writer's doctrine of God, of Christ, and of sin. Only so can we justly appraise his teaching on the work of Christ as vicarious, as representative, and as sacrificial.

(1) *God.* As described by the writer, God is essentially the revealing God who spoke to the fathers in the prophets 'by divers portions and in divers manners' and now in the New Age to which Christianity belongs has spoken to us 'in a Son' (i. 1 *f.*). It is characteristic that His glory and majesty are mentioned at the beginning of the Epistle (i. 3; cf. viii. 1), for it is His transcendent greatness which most of all has impressed the writer. He is the builder of all things (iii. 4; cf. xi. 10, 16), and by His word the world has been framed (xi. 3). Especially is He 'the living God' (iii. 12, ix. 14, x. 31). His word is 'living and active', sharper than any two-edged sword, and piercing 'even to the dividing of soul and spirit' (iv. 12). There is no creature that is not manifest in His sight, and all things are 'naked and laid open before the eyes of him with whom we have to do' (iv. 13). His counsels are immutable (vi. 17). He is the Judge of all (xii. 23; cf. xiii. 4) and apostates are faced with 'a certain fearful expectation of judgment' (x. 27, cf. ii. 1–3). 'It is a fearful thing', he says, 'to fall into the hands of the living God' (x. 31). God is about to make to tremble both the earth and the heaven, and the readers must have grace to offer service well-pleasing to Him 'with reverence and awe', for He is 'a consuming fire' (xii. 26–9). The writer speaks of Him as 'the Father of spirits' who treats us 'as sons'; but it is the disciplinary aspect of His dealings which he emphasizes. He chastens us 'for our profit, that we may be partakers of his holiness' (xii. 9 *f.*). Without 'sanctification' no man shall see Him, and it is necessary to look carefully lest there be any man that falleth short of His grace (xii. 14 *f.*).

All that has been mentioned thus far represents only part of the writer's teaching, but none the less it is opportune to point out the strength and sublimity of his conception. The God he describes is a Being of supreme power and dignity, to be reckoned with by men and to be approached with feelings of reverential awe. It cannot be denied that the picture is austere; but, on the other hand, there is no suggestion of an offended Deity who needs to be appeased before men can approach Him in penitence and hope. His wrath, as Moffatt has said, 'is reserved for the apostates; it does not brood over unregenerate men, to be removed by

Christ'.[1] There is nothing in the representation that is unworthy and much that is essential to any true doctrine of God.

Moreover, there are other elements in the writer's teaching which soften the outlines of the portraiture. It is assumed that God is One to whom men 'draw nigh' (vii. 19, xi. 6), and His purpose, as Jeremiah foretold, is to establish a 'new covenant' with them (viii. 8–13). Faith is well-pleasing to Him, and He is 'a rewarder of them that seek after him' (xi. 6). By His 'grace, Christ tasted death for every man' (ii. 9). God is 'the God of peace, who brought again from the dead the great shepherd of the sheep with the blood of the eternal covenant, even our Lord Jesus Christ', and who is ready to make men perfect in every good thing to do His will, working in them that which is well-pleasing in His sight (xiii. 20 f.).

One cannot fail to recognize the nobility of this conception of God. At the same time, however, it undeniably lacks those warmer notes which belong to the teaching of Jesus and of St. Paul. There is nothing in the Epistle comparable to the picture of the Father in heaven who 'maketh his sun to rise on the evil and the good, and sendeth rain on the just and on the unjust' (Matthew v. 45), and this is the more significant because there are also stern elements in the teaching of Jesus concerning God, as, for example, when He says: 'Fear him, which after he hath killed hath power to cast you into hell' (Luke xii. 5). The teaching of the writer differs also from that of St. Paul. It would hardly have occurred to the former to write such a sentence as: 'God commendeth his own love toward us, in that, while we were yet sinners, Christ died for us' (Romans v. 8), although he would not have questioned its truth. It is not accidental that he uses ἀγαπᾶν ('to love') twice only, and in both cases in Old Testament quotations (i. 9, xii. 6), and that similarly the noun ἀγάπη is used but twice (vi. 10, x. 24), and in neither case of man's attitude to God.[2] The name 'Father' is found only in the phrase 'the Father of spirits' (xii. 9) and by implication in xii. 7 and 9. No doubt the Fatherliness of God is made to shine 'through the awfulness of His spiritual and moral perfection',[3] but the doctrine is not characteristic of the Epistle except so far as it is presupposed in the relationships of the Father and the Son. A. B. Bruce,[4] who held that the author

[1] *Op. cit.*, p. xxxv.
[2] Cf. Moffatt, *op. cit.*, p. xxxvi.
[3] Cf. J. Scott Lidgett, *Sonship and Salvation*, p. 245.
[4] *The Epistle to the Hebrews*, pp. 445 f.

H

believed with all his heart in 'the Father-God of Jesus', none the less recognized that this conception lies in the background, and he ascribed the fact to 'the exigencies of the apologetic argument' in the Epistle, 'the first apology of Christianity'. It would perhaps be truer to reverse the relationship and say that the argument takes the form it does because of the predominantly transcendental character of the author's idea of God. The consequences are seen in the limitations of his argument. None the less, he has richly served the cause of Christian truth by emphasizing noble aspects of God's Being, and therefore of redemption, which are easily lost sight of by the sentimentalism which accepts His Fatherhood without adequately recognizing its strength as well as its graciousness.

(2) *Christ.* The writer's doctrine of Christ is part of his doctrine of God, and the one cannot be understood apart from the other. In the majestic prologue there is complete unity of operation between God and His Son. God has spoken to us in a Son whom He appointed 'heir of all things' and who was His agent in creation. He is the radiance of His glory, the impress of His Being, upholding all things by the word of His power, and when He had accomplished purification of sins, He 'sat down on the right hand of the Majesty on high' (i. 1–3). This language is undoubtedly suggested by Wisdom vii. 25 f., where Wisdom is described as 'a clear effluence of the glory of the Almighty', 'an effulgence from everlasting light', 'an unspotted mirror of the working of God', and 'an image of his goodness'. There is thus every reason to say that the Epistle contains a Wisdom-Christology which strongly emphasizes the divinity of Christ.[1] An equally marked feature of the Epistle is its insistence upon the reality of His humanity. He sprang from the tribe of Judah (vii. 14). He was touched with the feeling of our infirmities, and was tempted in all points like as we are, yet without sin (iv. 15). In the days of His flesh He offered up prayers and supplications with strong crying and tears unto Him that was able to save Him from death; and having been heard for His godly fear, though He was a Son, yet learned obedience by the things which He suffered (v. 7 f.). He endured the gainsaying of sinners (xii. 3), and suffered outside Jerusalem (xiii. 12). In these statements a knowledge and an appreciation of the details of the Gospel Story are clearly implied.

It will be seen how fully this Christology is attuned to the idea of

[1] Cf. A. E. J. Rawlinson, *The New Testament Doctrine of the Christ*, pp. 186–9.

sacrificial redemption which it is the writer's purpose to describe. On the one hand, the offering, whatever its nature, is made not by man, but by God in the person of His Son; on the other hand, it is made by One who by the reality of His humanity is in perfect sympathy with sinful men and can offer Himself on their behalf. The terms by which Jesus is described are in perfect harmony with this Christology. On the divine side He is the 'radiance' or 'effulgence' of God's glory (i. 3), the 'impress' of His essence (i. 3), the 'Son',[1] and 'the Son of God'.[2] On the human side He is the 'author' or 'pioneer'[3] (ii. 10, xii. 2), the 'forerunner' (vi. 20), the 'mediator' of a new or better covenant (viii. 6, ix. 15, xii. 24), and, above all, a 'high priest'[4] after the order of Melchizedek. The author's usage thus brings into prominence the thought of One who comes to us out of the depths of God's Being, and yet is able in virtue of His humanity, to represent man before Him. It is therefore with much justice that A. E. J. Rawlinson writes: 'In combining a "Wisdom" Christology with so strong an insistence upon the importance of the human story of our Lord's life the writer of Hebrews may be regarded as having anticipated, and perhaps actually influenced, the theology of the Fourth Gospel'.[5]

One important difference, however, between the writer and St. John and St. Paul must be noticed. As in his doctrine of God, so also in his teaching concerning Christ, he does not mention love. There is nothing in the Epistle corresponding to the statement of the Fourth Evangelist that Jesus, knowing that His hour was come, 'having loved his own which were in the world, loved them to the uttermost' (xiii. 1); and, while like St. Paul he teaches that 'one died for all', he does not say: 'The love of Christ constraineth us' (2 Corinthians v. 14). He is not filled with awe at 'the love of Christ which passeth knowledge' (Ephesians iii. 19), and, while he speaks of cleansing from sin, he has no song like that in the Apocalypse: 'Unto him that loveth us and loosed us from our sins by his blood' (i. 5). The point is not that he doubted this love, or would not have mentioned it in

---

[1] i. 2, 5, iii. 6, v. 8, vii. 28.

[2] iv. 14, vi. 6, vii. 3, x. 29.

[3] Peake, pp. 105 f., 226, renders ἀρχηγός 'captain' or 'leader'; Moffatt, pp. 31, 196, 'pioneer'; Westcott, p. 49, 'author' or 'captain', p. 395, 'leader'; see Moulton's discussion, Gr., ii, 277 f., and Vocab., s.v.

[4] A list of passages is given on pp. 119 f. The name 'Jesus' is used ten times, the name 'Christ' nine times, 'Jesus Christ' three times, 'Our Lord Jesus', 'Our Lord', and 'the Lord' once each.

[5] The New Testament Doctrine of the Christ, p. 189.

another Epistle, but that the thought of it does not control his soteriology. It is true that the new Covenant of which Christ is the mediator is a covenant of grace, but it cannot be said that the writer emphasizes this aspect of it. Dr. Moffatt[1] maintains that the author of Hebrews 'shows more originality in treating grace than any other writer of the New Testament after Paul'; but the originality does not extend to the thought of grace in the atoning work of Christ, apart from the reference to the 'grace of God' in ii. 9. Of the eight passages where χάρις is mentioned,[2] none speaks of 'the grace of Christ' as revealed in His sacrifice. The nearest approaches to a recognition of His love are in ii. 17, where it is said that 'it behoved him' in all things to be made like unto his brethren, 'that he might be a merciful and faithful high priest in things pertaining to God', and the denial in iv. 15 that we have a high priest 'that cannot be touched with the feeling of our infirmities'.

All this is not said in any disparagement of the writer's positive achievement, which we have yet to examine, and which indeed is of essential importance to a true understanding of Christ's atoning work. Since, however, it is his clear intention to describe the work of Christ as the priestly mediator, it is necessary to examine his Christology; and it is impossible not to observe that he is so intent upon his main objective that he loses sight of an element which is vital to it. Preoccupied with the work of theological construction, the brilliant Alexandrian teacher finds little room for his beliefs about the love of Christ. The effects of this omission upon his positive teaching have yet to be observed.

(3) *Sin.* In the author's view it is sin above all else which stands in the way of that relationship of man with God which it is the work of Christ to restore. It is necessary, therefore, to consider how he thinks of sin and its removal.

Of the seriousness with which he views sin there can be no doubt. Indeed, in this matter the only question which arises is whether he thinks of it with too great a severity, since in apostasy he sees a sin for which there is no forgiveness. 'If we sin wilfully', he says, 'after we have received the knowledge of the truth, there remaineth no more a sacrifice for sins, but a certain fearful expectation of judgment, and a fierceness of fire which shall devour the adversaries' (x. 26 f.). The existence of an unpardonable

[1] *Grace in the New Testament*, p. 345.

[2] ii. 9, iv. 16 (*bis*), x. 29, xii. 15, 28, xiii. 9, 25.

sin is taught by Jesus Himself (Mark iii. 29), but whether He would have included apostasy under this category is open to question, unless, in some particular case, it merits the writer's description of treading underfoot the Son of God, counting the blood of the covenant a common thing, and doing despite unto the Spirit of grace (cf. x. 29). This is how the writer understands apostasy, and it should be remembered that he is speaking of an attitude that is wanton and deliberate.[1]

Sin is nowhere defined in the Epistle either in relation to law or to God, but it is everywhere assumed that it constitutes a barrier to fellowship with God. It is something which 'besets' or 'clings closely'[1] to man as he seeks to run his appointed course (cf. xii. 1). The writer is fully convinced of its deceitfulness (iii. 13), the temporary character of its enjoyment (xi. 25), and the necessity of striving against it in deadly earnest (xii. 4). His frequent allusions to cleansing show that he thinks of it as leaving a stain upon human nature and especially upon the conscience of man (ix. 14, x. 22). His main interest, however, is in its removal. For this idea he uses a variety of expressions. Thus, he speaks of 'purification' or 'cleansing 'of sins (i. 3); of 'putting away (εἰς ἀθέτησιν) sins' (ix. 26); of 'bearing sins' (ix. 28, ἀναφέρειν); of 'taking away sins' (x. 4, ἀφαιρεῖν; 11, περιαιρεῖν); of sacrifices for sin (x. 6, 8, 18) or sins (x. 12, 26); and of 'making atonement' or 'expiation' for the sins of the people (ii. 17, εἰς τὸ ἱλάσκεσθαι τὰς ἁμαρτίας τοῦ λαοῦ). Everywhere he is thinking of an act of redemption which is wrought by Christ alone, for to him it is axiomatic that man is incapable of effecting the removal of sin. A simple doctrine of repentance followed by forgiveness is no part of his theology. He mentions forgiveness twice only (ix. 22, x. 18) in the sense of 'remission', and does not use the verb 'to forgive', although he twice quotes Jeremiah xxxi. 34: 'And their sin will I remember no more' (viii. 12, x. 17).[3] Moreover, of his three references to repentance two are negative and the third is almost disparaging. The first two are the statement that it is impossible to renew again apostates to repentance (vi. 6) and the reference to Esau who 'found no place of repentance' (xii. 17).

---

[1] Cf. ἑκουσίως which stands first in x. 26 for the sake of emphasis.

[2] For the meaning of εὐπερίστατος see Moulton, *Grammar*, ii, p. 282; Moffatt, pp. 194 f.; Westcott, pp. 393 f.; Peake, pp. 225 f.; Moulton and Milligan, *The Vocabulary of the Greek Testament*, p. 264.

[3] In viii. 12 the writer follows the Septuagint text of Jeremiah xxxi. 34: 'For I will *be merciful* to their iniquities' (Hebrew text: 'For I will *forgive* their iniquity').

The third appears in the exhortation to cease to speak of 'elementary Christian doctrine'[1] and to pass on to what is mature, 'instead of laying the foundation over again with repentance from dead works . . .' (vi. 1). The inference is inescapable that, to the writer's mind, much more than man's repentance is necessary if the barrier of sin between him and God is to be removed. Everything depends upon a decisive deed of Christ, the mediator of a new covenant and high priest of our salvation. Christ is the 'pioneer' (ii. 10) and the 'cause' or 'source' of eternal salvation unto all them that obey Him (v. 9). 'How shall we escape', asks the writer, 'if we neglect so great salvation?' (ii. 3).

(4) *The Vicarious Act of Christ.* While the vicarious aspect of Christ's death is part of the common faith of the primitive Church, the writer's use of this idea is so emphatic that it is necessary to include it in any detailed account of his distinctive teaching. Everywhere it is the presupposition of his argument, but in the following passages it is clearly expressed:

ii. 9: 'But we behold . . . Jesus, because of the suffering of death crowned with glory and honour, that by the grace of God he should taste death *for every man.*'

vi. 20: 'Whither as a forerunner Jesus entered *for us*, having become a high priest for ever after the order of Melchizedek.'

vii. 25: 'Wherefore also he is able to save to the uttermost them that draw near unto God through him, seeing he ever liveth to make intercession *for them.*'

ix. 14: 'How much more shall the blood of Christ, who through the eternal Spirit offered *himself* without blemish unto God, cleanse *your* consciences from dead works to serve the living God?'

ix. 24: 'For Christ entered not into a holy place made with hands, like in pattern to the true; but into heaven itself, now to appear before the face of God *for us.*'

In all these passages the preposition 'for' is the Greek ὑπέρ, 'on behalf of', but, apart altogether from the linguistic usage, there is a strong emphasis upon the thought of a saving deed, which men are not able to accomplish for themselves, and which Christ does on their behalf. This impression is deepened by the clear signs that His ministry is representative, and also by the stress laid by the writer upon the *finality* of Christ's redemptive act. 'This he did *once for all*', he says, 'when he offered up himself' (vii. 27). Through His own blood, He 'entered in *once for all* into the holy place' (ix. 12). By His acceptance of the will of God 'we have been sanctified through the offering of the body of Jesus

[1] Moffatt.

Christ *once for all*' (x. 10). The same truth is powerfully expressed by St. Paul when he writes: 'For the death that he died, he died unto sin once for all' (Romans vi. 10). A redemptive act so decisive that it cannot be repeated is by its nature a deed done for us. In it we rest and upon it we rely. Its meaning and its blessings are offered to us for our acceptance, in the spirit of childlike trust. Doubtless, there is much more to be said than this, and there is further teaching in the Epistle. Meantime, it is true to say that the heart of its message, and the Gospel itself, is that a finished work, perfect in itself, and therefore incapable of supplement, has been wrought by Christ on our behalf. A Christianity without this conviction is crippled, since it is wounded at the heart; with this belief, it is strong, even when its pronouncements are crude; but when this truth is integrated with its revelation as a whole, it is strongest of all.

(5) *The Representative Ministry of Christ.* Already from the account of Christology of the Epistle it is apparent that Christ is thought of as the representative of man before God. It is necessary, however, to consider this aspect of His ministry in greater detail. The passages in which He is described as 'high priest' naturally claim attention first, for in them can be seen the kind of service which the writer has in mind.

ii. 17: '. . . that he might be a merciful and faithful *high priest* in things pertaining to God, to make expiation for the sins of the people.'

iii. 1 *f.*: 'Consider the Apostle and *High Priest* of our confession, Jesus; who was faithful to him that appointed him, as also was Moses in all his house.'

iv. 14–16: 'Having then a great *high priest*, who hath passed through the heavens, Jesus the Son of God, let us hold fast our confession. For we have not a high priest that cannot be touched with the feeling of our infirmities; but one that hath been in all points tempted like as we are, yet without sin. Let us therefore draw near with boldness unto the throne of grace. . . .'

v. 5 *f.*: 'So Christ also glorified not himself to be made a *high priest*, but he that spake unto him, Thou art my Son. . . .'

v. 9 *f.*: '. . . the author of eternal salvation; named of God a *high priest* after the order of Melchizedek' (cf. v. 6, vi. 20).

vi. 20: 'Whither (within the veil) as a forerunner Jesus entered for us, having become a *high priest* for ever after the order of Melchizedek.'

vii. 26: 'For such a *high priest* became us, holy, guileless, undefiled, separated from sinners, and made higher than the heavens.'

viii. 1 *f.*: 'We have such a *high priest*, who sat down on the right hand of the throne of the Majesty in the heavens, a minister of the sanctuary, and of the true tabernacle, which the Lord pitched, not man.'

ix. 11: 'But Christ having come a *high priest* of the good things to come, through the greater and more perfect tabernacle, not made with hands. . . .'

x. 21: 'And having a *great priest* over the house of God' (cf. v. 6).

From these passages it will be seen that, not only is Jesus given a name which itself implies a representative office, but He is also described in terms which show that He stands for men before God. He is appointed by God (iii. 2, v. 5*f.*); He 'makes expiation' (ii. 17); He lives in the real but unseen world (iv. 14, vi. 20); and because of Him men can 'draw near' to God (iv. 16). Separated from sinners, and made higher than the heavens, He sits on the right hand of the throne of God, a minister of the sanctuary and of the true tabernacle of God (viii. 1 *f.*, ix. 11).

Full and clear as these passages are, they are supported by others in which the term 'high priest' does not appear. Thus, Christ as the Son is said to be over the house of God, 'whose house', says the writer, 'are we' (iii. 6; cf. x. 21). The session of the Son on high is mentioned in i. 3, x. 12, xii. 2, and is implied in ix. 24; and in the latter passage it is said that Christ has entered into heaven itself 'now to appear before the face of God for us'. The references to Christ as the 'surety' or 'mediator' belong to a somewhat different order of thought. In this Epistle Christ is not spoken of, as He is in 1 Timothy ii. 5, as the 'mediator between God and men'. He is the surety or mediator of a 'new' or 'better covenant' (vii. 22, viii. 6, ix. 15, xii. 24), the one who guarantees it and through whom it is brought into being. The writer appears to avoid the direct phrase 'mediator between God and men', perhaps because the noun suggested to him the idea of settling differences between equals or the thought of an 'arbiter' as it does in the Papyri.[1] The representative ministry of Christ, as he sees it, provides a means of approach for sinful men to the God of infinite holiness and majesty. Moreover, while it rests upon an act done 'once for all', it is also continuous, since, as the writer says, He 'ever liveth to make intercession' for 'them that draw near unto God through him' (vii. 25).

If we ask further regarding the character of this ministry, the answer, according to the teaching of the Epistle, is that it is of the nature of a sacrificial offering. To this teaching, therefore, we now turn.

(6) *The Sacrifice of Christ.* That the vicarious deed of Christ is an act of sacrifice for sinful men is the most fundamental note in the teaching of the Epistle. Quite apart from express statements which are capable of no other interpretation, this fact is made plain by the cumulative use of a number of terms and expressions

---

[1] *The Vocabulary of the Greek Testament*, p. 399.

each one of which is significant in itself: the use of the noun 'offering' (προσφορά)[1] and 'sacrifice' (θυσία),[2] and of the verbs 'to offer up' (ἀναφέρειν),[3] 'to offer' (προσφέρειν),[4] and 'to make expiation' (ἱλάσκεσθαι),[5] all with reference to the work of Christ; the allusions to the sin-offering[6] and the covenant-sacrifices;[7] and the use of the word 'blood'[8] in relation to Christ in a sense entirely transcending the suggestion of a violent death. The important passages include the following:

i. 3: 'When he had made *purification of sins*.'

ii. 17: 'Wherefore it behoved him in all things to be made like unto his brethren, that he might be a merciful and faithful high priest in things pertaining to God, *to make expiation for the sins of the people*.'

vii. 27: 'This he did once for all, *when he offered up himself*.'

ix. 11 f.: 'But Christ having come a high priest of the good things to come, through the greater and more perfect tabernacle . . . *through his own blood*, entered in once for all into the holy place, *having obtained eternal redemption*.'

ix. 14: 'How much more shall *the blood of Christ*, who through his eternal spirit *offered himself* without blemish *unto God, cleanse your conscience* from dead works to serve the living God.'

ix. 26: 'But now once at the end of the ages hath he been manifested *to put away sin by the sacrifice of himself*.'

ix. 28: 'So Christ also, *having been once offered to bear the sins of many*, shall appear a second time, apart from sin, to them that wait for him, *unto salvation*.'

x. 10: 'By which will we have been sanctified *through the offering of the body of Jesus Christ once for all*.'

x. 12: 'But he, *when he had offered one sacrifice for sins for ever*, sat down on the right hand of God.'

x. 14: 'For *by one offering* he hath perfected for ever them that are sanctified.'

x. 19-23: 'Having therefore, brethren, boldness to enter into the holy place *by the blood of Jesus*, by the way which he dedicated for us, a new and living way, through the veil, that is to say, his flesh; and having a great priest over the house of God; let us draw near with a true heart in fulness of faith, *having our hearts sprinkled from an evil conscience*, and our body washed with pure water: let us hold fast the confession of our faith that it waver not; for he is faithful that promised.'

xii. 24: 'And to Jesus the mediator of a new covenant, and to *the blood of sprinkling* that speaketh better than Abel.'

xiii. 11 f.: 'For the bodies of those beasts, whose blood is brought into the holy place by the high priest as an offering for sin, are burned without the camp. Wherefore Jesus also, that he might *sanctify* the people *through his own blood, suffered* without the gate.'

xiii. 20 f.: 'Now the God of peace, who brought again from the dead the great shepherd of the sheep *with the blood of the eternal covenant*, even our Lord Jesus, make you perfect in every good thing to do his will, working in us that which is well-pleasing in his sight, through Jesus Christ; to whom be the glory for ever and ever. Amen.'

---

[1] x. 10, 14.

[2] ix. 26, x. 12.

[3] vii. 27, and, in the sense of 'bearing' sins, in ix. 28.

[4] ix. 14, 28, x. 12.

[5] ii. 17.

[6] xiii. 10-12.

[7] ix. 11-28.

[8] ix. 12, 14, x. 19, xii. 24, xiii. 20.

This list, which cannot be studied too carefully, supplies conclusive evidence that, in the writer's belief, 'all hope for the Christian rests in what Jesus has done in the eternal order by his sacrifice'.[1] In no way is this conclusion shaken by his use in x. 5-7 of Psalm xl. 7-9, and especially the words: 'Sacrifice and offering thou wouldst not', and: 'In whole burnt offerings and sacrifices for sin thou hadst no pleasure', for the writer's purpose is not to assert that obedience is better than sacrifice, but to claim that, in that it fulfilled the will of God, Christ's sacrifice of Himself surpassed and superseded the Levitical sacrifices. The point in which he is mainly interested is not the Psalmist's suggestion that sacrifice is non-essential, but the words: 'Then said I, Lo, I am come . . . *to do thy will*, O God',[2] and the mistranslation of the Septuagint: 'But a *body* didst thou prepare for me',[3] which leads him to think of the coming of Christ in flesh to die for sinful men.[4] Nor must the words: 'It is impossible that the blood of bulls and goats should take away sins' (x. 4), be read as a repudiation of sacrifice, but in harmony with what the writer says elsewhere when he declares that 'gifts and sacrifices' 'cannot, as touching the conscience, make the worshipper perfect' (ix. 9; cf. x. 1).[5] His argument, '*How much more* shall the blood of Christ . . . cleanse your conscience' (ix. 13 *f.*), and his declaration that 'apart from shedding of blood there is no remission' (ix. 22), imply that he sees a relative efficacy[6] in the Old Testament sacrifices.

The references to 'blood' in the passages cited above are especially striking. Some scholars have held that, influenced by later rabbinical teaching,[7] the writer believed that since blood contains the vital principle, it is 'efficacious as an atonement',[8] and that he did not ask why sacrifice is essential, but was content with the fact that it is commanded in Scripture. In this matter speculation is hardly profitable, and we must be guided by what he actually says regarding (1) the sacrifice of Christ, and (2) the effects which it produces in men, and, in consequence, in their

---

[1] Moffatt, p. 89.

[2] Hebrew text: 'I delight to do thy will, O my God.'

[3] Hebrew text: 'Mine ears hast thou opened' (R.V.). R.V., marg., reads: 'Ears hast thou digged (or, pierced) for me.'

[4] Moffatt, pp. xli, 139; Peake, p. 197.

[5] In ix. 10, however, he speaks of gifts and sacrifices as 'only (with meats and drinks and divers washings) carnal ordinances, imposed until a time of reformation'.

[6] On this question there are signs of an unresolved tension in the writer's mind. Note especially the phrase quoted above, 'until a time of reformation'.

[7] *Yoma*, v. 1, cited by Moffatt, p. 131.

[8] Cf. Moffatt, p. 131. See Leviticus xvii. 11.

relationships with God. In the light of this teaching it will be found, I think, that when he uses the term 'blood' his main emphasis is upon the idea of life freely surrendered, applied, and dedicated to the recovery of men.

The writer's main contention is that Christ's sacrifice is the offering of Himself for men (ix. 14, 26, x. 10) in complete obedience to the will of God. 'By which will', he says, 'we have been sanctified through the offering of the body of Jesus Christ once for all' (x. 10). This teaching is often interpreted to mean that His sacrifice is the offering of His perfect obedience, but this statement is meaningless unless it is defined more closely, and misleading if it means no more than it says. It is not only in His obedience, as a moral quality, but in His perfect fulfilment of the redemptive will of God for men that His sacrifice consists. The writer shows us clearly that this will involved the self-offering of Jesus and that its nature was entirely spiritual, since it was made 'through his eternal spirit[1]' (ix. 14); but, unfortunately, he nowhere tells us how the offering fulfils the divine will, except in so far as he indicates its effects in determining human relationships with God.

These effects are described in several ways. Purification of sins is accomplished (i. 3), a phrase which may indicate either the cleansing of sins or deliverance from them.[2] Eternal redemption is obtained (ix. 12), a statement which is probably too general for us to be sure that the idea of the payment of a ransom is in mind.[3] The conscience is cleansed from 'dead works' so as to make possible the service of a living God.[4] By the sacrifice of Christ sin has been 'put away' (ix. 26), its consequences 'borne' (ix. 28),[5] and men have been 'sanctified' (x. 10) and 'perfected' (x. 14).[6] A more positive claim is that 'a new and living way' has been opened into the world of eternal realities by the blood of Jesus, in consequence of which men can draw near to God 'with a true heart

---

[1] The reference is to Christ's spirit, not to the Holy Spirit. Cf. Moffatt, p. 124; Westcott, pp. 259, 261; Peake, p. 185.

[2] Westcott, p. 15, prefers the former view; Moffatt, p. 8, and Peake, p. 77, leave both possibilities open.

[3] Cf. F. Büchsel, *Theol. Wort.*, iv, p. 354.

[4] Cf. T. H. Robinson, p. 127.

[5] 'At any rate his suffering of death was vicarious suffering; he took upon himself the consequences and responsibilities of our sins', Moffatt, p. 134.

[6] 'The people were sanctified, not when they were raised to moral perfection, but when their sin had been so neutralized or annulled that they had access to God' (Flew, *The Idea of Perfection*, p. 86).

in fulness of faith'; their hearts have been 'sprinkled from an evil conscience', and, in baptism, their bodies 'washed with pure water' (x. 19–23). Above all, the 'new covenant', long foreseen by Jeremiah, has been established, in virtue of which God's laws are put into their minds and written on their hearts, and His forgiveness and fellowship are assured. The writer attached the greatest importance to this claim, for he twice quotes the words of the prophet (viii. 8–12, x. 16 *f.*) and, as we have seen, four times speaks of Jesus as the 'surety' or 'mediator' of a new or better covenant (vii. 22, viii. 6, ix. 15, xii. 24). These statements which are all based upon facts of the Christian experience as the writer had seen them in his own life and the lives of the Christians of his day, are related in the Epistle to the offering and sacrifice of Christ. The sacrifice is that which achieves these results; it is their ground and cause, and is not adequately interpreted until it is explained as such. This conviction, we must infer, was the firm belief of the writer. From his description of its effects we must conclude that he thought of the sacrifice as a work of Christ which annuls sin, cleanses the heart, and opens the way to God.

The question how these blessed results are accomplished he does not answer. His nearest approach to an explanation is ii. 17: 'Wherefore it behoved him in all things to be made like unto his brethren, that he might be a merciful and faithful high priest in things pertaining to God, to make expiation for the sins of the people'. The researches of C. H. Dodd and others, to which reference has been already made, have made it certain that there is no suggestion in ἱλάσκεσθαι of propitiation, no thought of appeasing the wrath of an angry God; but they have made it equally plain that the writer is thinking of 'expiation', in the sense of the 'covering' of sins conveyed by the Hebrew verb *kipper*. Of course, if we are to press the derivation of the Latin word 'expiation' and take it as the equivalent of 'propitiation', this word also must disappear from modern theology. In this case, we are left with the somewhat ambiguous word 'atonement', and on the whole it is best to retain 'expiation' with the understanding that it is to be read in the Hebraic sense of the 'covering' of sins in such a way that they no longer stand as a barrier shutting out the sinner from fellowship with a gracious and loving God. Just as there is no thought of propitiation in the passage, so neither is there any suggestion of a 'compensation' made to God. Had this idea been the thought of the writer, it could not have been left to a word which, from his knowledge of Greek, the writer knew that he was using in the sense in which it is employed in the Greek Bible, in which the object of the verb is not God but sins. Would it have been possible, moreover, for him to have held the belief that compensation must be made to a righteous God for sins without expressing it elsewhere in the Epistle in clear and unmistakable terms? It is true that, apart from avoiding the use of a personal object to the verb, he had not shown how the death of Christ 'covers' sin. Nevertheless, his emphasis on the necessity that Jesus should be 'made like unto his brethren', and his use in ix. 28 of the idea of 'bearing sins', that is, of submitting to their consequences, not to speak of his dominant conception of the work of Christ as that of a representative high priest, unmistakably suggest a racial act in which sin is annulled, without implying the necessity either of submitting to punishment or of offering its equivalent in compensation to God.

But how does the writer think that the sacrifice of Christ annuls sin? This is a question which the modern man, as distinct from the ancient man who took the necessity of sacrifice for granted, must press, not merely for the satisfaction of his intellectual demands, but in order to meet his religious needs as a sinner seeking fellowship with God. And, apart from fruitful suggestions contained in the Epistle, the author does not answer the question. It is, I believe, of the utmost importance, not only to be vaguely conscious of this fact, but to recognize it fully, because the reasons for his silence are of supreme importance for the formation of a modern doctrine of the Atonement. Many readers of the Epistle fill out the gaps in the writer's treatment by the aid of ideas derived from other parts of the New Testament. This procedure is essential to the construction of a theology, but fatal to the understanding of the Epistle to the Hebrews; it also makes the work of the theologian much more difficult because he has not inquired why so great a writing, to which he constantly turns with a sense of exhilaration, leaves upon his mind a furtive sense of disappointment. For theological purposes the most important question in connexion with the Epistle is why it fails, and to this problem consideration will be given in the Summary which follows. The question cannot usefully be treated, however, until every scrap of positive teaching in the Epistle has been patiently gleaned, and for this reason such an investigation as that made in the preceding pages is an indispensable discipline.

One issue, however, of essential importance still needs to be raised. Does the writer think of the sacrifice of Christ as accomplished on earth, or after He has entered into the eternal tabernacle of the unseen world? If we have to choose between these alternatives, we must choose the former. It was after He had made 'purification of sins' that He sat down on the right hand of the Majesty on high (i. 3; cf. x. 12). He entered once for all into the holy place 'having obtained eternal redemption' (ix. 12). The meaning of these and other passages is beyond dispute. But is it necessary to choose between the alternatives mentioned? It is the writer's firm conviction that the work of Christ is rooted in history, but it is equally his belief that for Christianity the New Age has already dawned in Christ whose ministry belongs to the eternal order. Between these conceptions he moves easily without any sense of constraint; he can speak of a work done once for all and a ministry of intercession which belongs to the eternal Now. Perhaps his greatest utterance is ix. 24: 'Christ entered not into a holy place made with hands, like in pattern to the true; but into heaven itself, now to appear before the face of God for us.'

(c) Summary

As in the case of the Pauline Epistles, no attempt will be made to summarize further the details discussed in the preceding sections. The point for special consideration is the writer's central theme of the One Offering by which men are sanctified and perfected, and in virtue of which Christ appears before the face of God on their behalf. We have seen that, apart from stressing the necessity that Christ should come as Man, and affirming that His sacrifice cleanses the conscience and annuls sin, the writer does not tell us how His offering avails for sinners in their approach to God. It may be that he thought of the offering as so complete in itself, and so immediately efficacious, that no further explanation was necessary or even possible. In this case our question must be, not so much why he is silent on the point which most concerns the modern reader of the Epistle, but rather why it was possible for him not to feel the need for further explanation. In any case, the answer must be found in his silences and omissions in general, in the elements which are but faintly represented or are entirely wanting in his teaching.

In our investigation the strictest care has been taken not to misconstrue the writer's omissions. We have found, however, that rarely indeed can we have confidence in the explanation that we are dealing with a single Epistle, and that in other writings he might well have given greater prominence to the subjects in question. This explanation may be true, but it does not answer the objection that treatment is wanting where it is most needed, and further that silence upon one aspect is accompanied by a corresponding silence upon a related theme. The omissions, therefore, are highly significant. If the positive teaching of the Epistle is of supreme importance, its reserves are no less instructive for the theologian.

(1) First, the small extent to which the love of God is prominent in the teaching of the Epistle[1] accounts for the limited degree to which the ideal of fellowship, implicit in the covenant-relationship, is treated, and explains the absence of any reference to His passionate yearning to restore the breach created by sin. If the writer belongs to the Pauline circle, he never understood, and perhaps did not sympathize with, his master's teaching about the nature of justification by faith. His God is a Being to whom men must draw near with reverence and with awe, but hardly One of whom the prodigal is likely to say: 'I will arise and go to my Father.' The consequence is that he does not envisage the problem of reconciliation as a personal problem, except in so far as the idea of the covenant pre-supposes a personal relationship; he is concerned with sin rather than with sinners, with its annulling more than with their recovery. It is possible, therefore, that he may not have been conscious of the fact that he has not shown how the One Sacrifice avails for penitent and despairing souls.

(2) Again, his silence concerning the love of Christ explains the fact that he nowhere speaks of His self-identification with sinners and consequent experience of the judgment which falls upon their sin. The Christ of the Epistle is merciful, compassionate, and sympathetic, but He is not marked by the utter abandon of the love which shares in the consequences of sin. For this reason the writer's one allusion to the Suffering Servant in ix. 28 ('once offered to bear the sins of many') is literary rather than of fundamental importance for his theology. The cultus, of course, taught him nothing about sin-bearing, except in the case of the scapegoat

---

[1] 'The one conspicuous point of incompleteness in the atonement theory of Hebrews is its failure to make evident how the whole work of atonement is from beginning to end the act of God's love. We miss in Hebrews just that vital element which St. Paul and St. John so clearly supply' (O. C. Quick, *Doctrines of the Creed*, p. 235).

on the day of Atonement, for the lamb of the Old Testament sacrifices did not 'bear sins', nor were sins 'laid upon' him;[1] while the doctrine of the Servant, central for the thought of Jesus but fast fading in the popular Christianity of his day, has little meaning for him. To how small a degree the idea of vicarious suffering is alive in his religious thinking is apparent in his allusion to Gethsemane in v. 7 f., where Jesus offers up prayers and supplications with strong crying and tears 'unto him that was able to save him *from death*'. In this passage 'death' is certainly more than physical death; it is death which comes to Him in the fulfilment of His vocation; but it has no penal character. For the writer, the 'cup' of the Synoptic story is personal, not vicarious, suffering; and its consequence is not redemption, but the perfecting of His obedience, in virtue of which He becomes 'the source (αἴτιος) of eternal salvation for all who obey him' (v. 9). The thought of the passage is that of salvation through obedience to the Incarnate Lord rather than through union with the Suffering Redeemer. Both truths are necessary to a full Christian doctrine, but they are very different, and the absence of the latter idea is due to a deficiency of emphasis on the love of Christ for sinners. In this connexion his use of πάσχω ('to suffer') is perhaps significant. He uses the verb four times, of Christ's temptations (ii. 18), of His agony in the face of death (v. 8), in a hypothesis (ix. 26), and as a synonym for 'died' (xiii. 12); but never of suffering for sins. Also he does not speak of Christ as 'Saviour', and his use of 'salvation' is eschatological.[2] These features are not accidental; they are integral to the writer's Christology and therefore determinative for his soteriology. It is the glory of his Epistle that he presents Christ as the One Sacrifice. If we are not able to see in what way the Sacrifice annuls sin, one reason is that he has not dwelt more fully upon the sacrificial love of Him who was 'once offered to bear the sins of many' (ix. 28).[3]

(3) Lastly, the most costly omission is the absence of teaching regarding faith-union, sacramental communion, and mystical suffering with Christ. As we have seen, for the writer faith is confidence in the unseen and complete loyalty to Christ; not

---

[1] Cf. W. F. Lofthouse, *Altar, Cross, and Community*, pp. 113, 151, 173.

[2] Moffatt says 'invariably eschatological', *I.C.C., Hebrews*, p. 16. Cf. i. 14, ii. 3, 10, v. 9, vi. 9, ix. 28.

[3] Note the eschatological context: 'So Christ . . . shall appear a second time, apart from sin, to them that wait for him, unto salvation' (ix. 28).

personal union with Him.[1] Of sacramental communion he has nothing to say, and it may be that in this matter he paid the price of victory over errorists through failure to apprehend the reality they misrepresented. Believing, like his Lord, in 'the blood of the eternal covenant' (xiii. 20), he does not dwell on the opportunity presented by the Eucharist to participate in the very sacrifice which it is his deepest desire to commend. On this question speculations may be idle, but one can with difficulty resist the conclusion that his theology suffers from too great a dependence upon that singularly unpromising sacrificial type, the Old Testament sin-offering, which in the ancient cultus availed for sins of inadvertence and for acts of ritual defilement, by the offering of beasts whose blood indeed was brought into the holy place, but whose bodies were 'burned without the camp' (xiii. 11). Was the writer the victim of his exegetical logic? Not essentially different from these omissions in respect of faith-union and sacramental communion, is the fact that, while he puts a tremendous emphasis upon loyalty to Christ and leaves his readers in no doubt about the sufferings it may entail,[2] he has nothing to say about the mystical suffering of the believer with the Lord in the agony of His redemptive ministry. Was he of those to whom this aspect of Pauline teaching is an insoluble mystery?

Once more it must be urged that these silences are not accidental. One cannot account for the facts by saying that the writer does not happen to mention faith-union, sacramental communion, and suffering with Christ; that he might have spoken of these truths elsewhere in another writing; and that, in any case, others had given them adequate attention. The writer does not mention them because he has not felt their relevance to his dearest purpose. And the consequence of his silence is deeper silence. He cannot tell us how the One great Sacrifice avails for sinners, how they can appropriate its blessings, and make it a vital factor in their approach to the Holy and Living God. He can affirm the utter necessity of the Sacrifice, describe its cleansing and annulling power, and trace its efficacy beyond the gates of heaven, but he is unable to show how it is apprehended by the guilty, how they can lay hold of it and find it the way to the peace and worship of the heavenly tabernacle.

---

[1] At the same time faith is represented as involving a call to personal suffering which is associated with the triumphant suffering of Christ (cf. xii. 2).

[2] Cf. x. 32-9, xii. 3-13.

I

In making these points it is not our intention to underrate or depreciate the greatness of this sublime Epistle, which indeed shines in its own light and is in no need of praise or panegyric. It is a point cardinal to the appreciation of any writing that it stands in virtue of what it contains, by what it says or teaches. Such is the basic canon of all literary and artistic appreciation. Theology, however, has needs of its own, and it learns from a writer's silences as well as his inspired utterances. So far as the Epistle to the Hebrews is concerned, the theologian has not gained all that it can teach him until he asks why in the end it leaves him with the feeling of something vital which is wanting. If he can answer this question he is well on the way to a worthy doctrine of the Atonement. It is in the highest degree significant that the silences of this Epistle are the utterances of St. Paul, and equally that what we find wanting in St. Paul's theology is the central truth of the Epistle to the Hebrews. St. Paul supplies all that we need concerning the love of God, the love of Christ, faith-union, sacramental communion, and living and dying with Christ; the Epistle to the Hebrews teaches the truth of the One Sacrifice; and both writers rest, for all their distinctive teaching, in the common faith of the primitive Church, itself based upon the mind and teaching of Christ. The lesson for the theologian is plain. Any success he may hope to gain in presenting to his own age the truth of the doctrine of the Atonement depends upon his fidelity to the teaching of the New Testament as a whole, and not upon his selection of those parts of its witness which make the greatest appeal to his susceptibilities. The reason for this is that the New Testament is not a collection of isolated proof-texts, but an organic whole.

3. THE TEACHING OF ST. JOHN

Of the five Johannine Writings the Apocalypse, as the work of a writer other than the Evangelist and a witness to primitive Christian belief, has already been considered separately. Like 2 Thessalonians, Philemon, James, and Jude, 2 and 3 John are without importance for our inquiry since these brief letters contain no reference to the death of Christ. In estimating the teaching of St. John, we are left therefore with the Fourth Gospel and 1 John, the significance of which for the purposes of our investigation can hardly be exaggerated.

The traditional opinion, which claims these writings as the work of a single author, is accepted by most New Testament scholars, but it has been seriously challenged by many critics, including H. J. Holtzmann,[1] P. W. Schmiedel,[2] J. Moffatt,[3] E. F. Scott,[4] Lord Charnwood,[5] and most recently by C. H. Dodd;[6] and, since this question must necessarily affect our discussion, it must receive careful attention. If both writings are the work of the Evangelist the area for the inquiry is broadened; if 1 John is the work of a different writer, this Epistle must be regarded as a late witness to primitive Christian belief.

Other critical questions connected with the Johannine problem need not be discussed here.[7] The position that is accepted in the following pages is that the author of the Gospel interprets, in the sense of bringing out the inner meaning, the Synoptic teaching and the special tradition of the Apostle John. His fundamental affinities are Jewish-Christian, although at the same time he is keenly responsive to Hellenistic influences.[8] In view of his supreme interest in the Gospel as the communication of life, his sublimation of primitive Christian eschatology, his conception of Christianity as a conflict between the powers of light and of darkness and, above all, his teaching concerning the Logos, the denial of this outlook and interest seems perverse. The Evangelist lives in two worlds, the Judaic and the Greek, and his endeavour to relate the one to the other marks the greatness of his achievement. The fundamentally Christian character of his beliefs, however, is manifest in the Gospel, and still more in the homily traditionally known as 1 John.

(a) The Authorship of the Fourth Gospel and of the First Epistle of St. John

The objections to the identity of authorship have usually turned on two issues, the vocabulary and style of the two writings

---

[1] *Jahrbuch für protestantische Theologie*, 1881, pp. 690 f.; 1882, pp. 128 f., 316 f., 460 f.

[2] *The Johannine Writings*, pp. 208–11.

[3] *Introduction to the Literature of the New Testament*, pp. 589–93.

[4] *The Fourth Gospel: Its Purpose and Theology*, pp. 88 f., 94. Scott, however, now thinks the two writings are the work of the same author. Cf. *Literature of the New Testament* (1932), p. 261.

[5] *According to St. John*, p. 79.

[6] See his article, 'The First Epistle of John and the Fourth Gospel', *Bulletin of the John Rylands Library*, vol. 21, no. 1, April, 1937, pp. 129–56.

[7] I have treated these questions in *The Gospels*, pp. 95–122, *The Formation of the Gospel Tradition*, pp. 113–18, 163–6, *Jesus and His Sacrifice*, pp. 218–49.

[8] For an attempt to explain the doctrine of the Word of God on a purely Old Testament basis, see Hoskyns and Davey, *The Fourth Gospel* (1940), pp. 152–64. See also F. C. Burkitt, *Church and Gnosis* (1932), pp. 92–9.

and a difference of theological standpoint, especially in relation to eschatology, the Atonement, the doctrine of the Spirit, and the attitude to Gnosticism.[1]

So far as the vocabulary and style are concerned, it is pointed out that the Epistle has thirty-nine words or expressions not found in the Gospel, and that of the words used in the Gospel some thirty are not employed in the Epistle.[2] The Gospel is much richer in prepositions, adverbial particles, and conjunctive and other particles; it has nearly ten times as many compound verbs, and contains 'Aramaisms' which are either non-existent or doubtfully represented in the Epistle. On the other hand, the Epistle uses idioms which are either absent from, or are rare in, the Gospel, including the use of the rhetorical question, definitions of the type: 'This is the message which we have heard from him' (i. 5), and looser forms of the conditional sentence. The linguistic and stylistic facts certainly confirm the impression that 'the style of the Epistle is more monotonous and less flexible', but they do not leave the common authorship of the two works 'in grave doubt'.[3] On this question J. H. Moulton held that, 'on every consideration of style', the Johannine Epistles form with the Fourth Gospel 'a literary unity'.[4] The argument from 'Aramaisms' is too uncertain to be pressed, and the difference between the Gospel and the Epistle in this respect can be explained without resorting to the theory of diverse authorship, either by the possible use of Aramaic sources or tradition or the effect of time in the interval between the two writings. The determinative considerations, however, are the fact that the Gospel is nearly seven times as long as the Epistle, that it is a carefully executed literary work, while the Epistle is a tractate or homily, and the unusually long list of common phrases and expressions which the industry of commentators has collected.[5] As against these facts the objections to the identity of authorship, while not unimpressive, are hardly convincing.

---

[1] See the article of C. H. Dodd referred to on p. 131.

[2] From Dodd's list of thirty-three words, θέλημα should be omitted (cf. ii. 17 and v. 14) and probably also κρίσις and γράφω. Φιλεῖν is a mere synonym for ἀγαπᾶν. It is also doubtful if such lists should contain words used less than five times in the Gospel, in view of the relative lengths of the two writings.

[3] Cf. Dodd, op. cit., pp. 132, 141.

[4] Grammar of New Testament Greek, ii, p. 31. In Peake's Commentary, p. 592, Moulton speaks still more trenchantly. See also Peake, Introduction, p. 170; Streeter, The Four Gospels, p. 460; Denney, The Death of Christ, p. 242.

[5] Cf. A. E. Brooke, I.C.C., The Johannine Epistles, pp. ii–iv; B. F. Westcott, The Epistles of St. John, pp. xli–iii.

The objections based upon doctrinal differences raise more difficult questions, but are in no way decisive against the theory of common authorship. To a considerable extent the differences are real; their significance is the point at issue.

In the Epistle the eschatological hope is certainly fully alive (cf. ii. 28 iii. 2, iv. 17), but while in the Gospel it is largely replaced by the promise of the Spirit, it is by no means absent as v. 28 f., vi. 40, 44, 54 show. Moreover, eschatological beliefs are notoriously affected by existing conditions like those of Europe to-day; and there does not seem to be any sound reason why the same writer who had previously seen the great Adversary in Satan himself, the Prince of this world (John xii. 31, xiv. 30 xvi. 11), should not afterwards stigmatize as 'antichrists' the false prophets who did not confess Jesus (1 John ii. 18, iv. 3).

Again, there is undoubtedly a greater emphasis upon the expiatory aspect of Christ's death and its relation to sin in the Epistle than in the Gospel (cf. 1 John i. 7, ii. 1 f., iii. 5, iv. 10). Nevertheless John i. 29: 'Behold, the Lamb of God, which taketh away the sin of the world!', stands in the Gospel, and its essential similarity to 1 John iii. 5 (cf. also ii. 2, iv. 10) is not disposed of by the fact that there is no agreed opinion regarding the origin of the phrase 'the Lamb of God'.[1] Without doubt the idea that the death of Christ is that by which He is 'glorified' or 'exalted' (xii. 23 32, xiii. 31) is replaced in the Epistle by thoughts which are in closer harmony with the beliefs of St. Paul and the writer of the Epistle to the Hebrews, but in a popular and later homily this is a fact which is neither impossible nor remarkable. Must we accept the principle that theologians are to be judged by their sermons, or the view that a brilliant teacher never returns to older and more traditional beliefs?

The same considerations also apply to the treatment of the doctrine of the Spirit in the two writings; and especially as regards the passages in which the Spirit is represented as the *alter ego* of Christ, it must be remembered that their presence within the Gospel itself raises a problem of no little difficulty.[2] Too much should not be made of the fact that Christ, and not the Spirit, is described as the παράκλητος (ii. 1) in the Epistle, since His ministry for men is directed Godwards, whereas the work of the

---

[1] The one point in connexion with the passage which Dodd, 145 f., considers.

[2] Cf. H. Windisch, *Die fünf johanneischen Paralketsprüche* (*Festgabe für Adolf Jülicher*), 1927, pp. 110–37.

Spirit as the Paraclete (John xiv. 16 f., 26, xv. 26, xvi. 7 ff.) is wrought upon men. Such divergences ought not to 'raise serious doubts about unity of authorship',[1] unless views once committed to writing represent an author's last word.

The claim that the Epistle 'stands closer than the Gospel to the "Gnosticism" against which both writings are directed', in support of which Professor Dodd cites interesting and important evidence,[2] is intelligible if the Epistle is the later writing; and it cannot be thought strange if he really is 'more unguarded' in turning the weapons of the false teachers against themselves than he is in the Gospel. The truth is that the difference in the character of the two writings is the clue to not a few of the differences of thought and expression which seem so significant to the critical investigator. Equally important is the lapse of time and the possibility that the brilliant writer of the Gospel was now an older man and possibly more conservative in thought and tendency.

In much that has been said above it is assumed that the Epistle is the later work; and in view of the signs of dependence on the Fourth Gospel, to which Dodd[3] points and which A. E. Brooke[4] has worked out in greater detail, this is much the best view to take. It may well be that an interval of ten or twenty years separates the composition of the two writings. The Epistle is almost certainly the work of an old man, but the Gospel leaves upon the mind the impression that it is the work of a writer in the full possession of his intellectual powers. If this suggestion has any force, it is by no means 'simpler to conclude that the two works are by different authors',[5] since it is neither unknown nor unusual for a gifted theologian to turn with the passing of years to older and more traditional ways of thinking.[6] If these possibilities are open to us, there is good reason to think that, in view of the remarkable similarity of language and thought between the Gospel and 1 John, including as it does characteristic teaching on love, life, the Fatherhood of God, and mystical union with Christ, the two writings are the

---

[1] Cf. Dodd, op. cit., p. 148.
[2] Op. cit., pp. 148–54.
[3] Ibid., p. 155.
[4] I.C.C., The Johannine Epistles, pp. xix–xxvi.
[5] Cf. Dodd, op. cit., p. 155.
[6] Dodd, on the contrary, argues that the Epistle reveals 'a mind inferior to that of the Evangelist in spiritual quality, in intellectual power and in literary artistry', that to speak of him as a religious genius or as a philosophical thinker 'would be flattery', whereas 'no description short of this would fit the author of the Fourth Gospel' (156). To this I would reply that, even if the relative descriptions were justified, the argument is a case of non sequitur.

product of one and the same mind. Such, at least, is the view taken in the present discussion.

(b) The Use made of Primitive Christian Tradition in the Fourth Gospel and in the First Epistle of St. John

As before the simplest way of treating this question will be to use the list of primitive Christian ideas which we have already found of value in studying the teaching of St. Paul and that of the writer of the Epistle to the Hebrews. It may be repeated that it is not suggested that the ideas in question were universally present in the various centres of early Christianity, or that we can give a true account of primitive Christian thought by simply adding them together: they are the ideas which in varying degrees belong to the first three or four decades of Christianity.

	The Fourth Gospel.	*1 John.*
1. The idea of the divine purpose.	iii. 14, vii. 30, viii. 20, x. 17 *f.*, xii. 23, 27, xvii. 1.	iv. 14.
2. Messianic character.	iii. 14, viii. 28, xii. 23, xiii. 31 (n. 1).	
3. Vicarious nature.	x. 11, 15, xi. 50 *f.*, xv. 13, xviii. 14.	iii. 16.
4. Representative aspect.	i. 29, 36.	ii. 1 *f.*
5. Relation to sin.	i. 29, xii. 31.	i. 7, ii. 1 *f.*, 12, iii. 5, iv. 10.
6. Sacrificial significance.	i. 29, 36, xii. 24 *f.*, xvii. 19.	i. 7, ii. 1 *f.*, iv. 10.
7. Servant-conception.	i. 29 (n. 2).	
8. The Resurrection.	(n. 3.)	
9. Idea of a faith-relationship.	(n. 4.)	
10. Eucharistic teaching.	vi. 51, 53–8.	
11. Suffering with Christ.	(xv. 12 *f.*, 20) (n. 5).	(iii. 16.)
12. Relation to the Love of God.	iii. 16.	iv. 9 *f.*
13. Ethical and spiritual ends.	iii. 15, 16, vi. 51, 53–8.	i. 7, ii. 12.
14. Universality.	iv. 42, vi. 51, x. 16, xi. 51 *f.*, xii. 32, xvii. 2.	ii. 2, iv. 14.

NOTES

1. In the passages cited, the Messianic title is associated with suffering (and glorification) as in Mark.

2. The influence of Isaiah liii appears to be reflected in the use of the term 'Lamb' in i. 29, 36 and (ultimately) in the references to the Son of Man noted above.

3. While the importance of the Resurrection is fully recognized in the Gospel, it is not closely related to the meaning of the Cross. The reality of the Exalted Lord is the assumption of both the Gospel and the Epistle.

4. Faith is related to the person of Christ, but not directly to His redemptive ministry.

5. In the Johannine Writings this teaching is practical rather than mystical,

(1) *The Idea of the Divine Purpose.* This idea is strongly emphasized both in the Gospel and the Epistle. The Son of Man, it is declared, 'must be lifted up' (John iii. 14). This inner necessity is grounded in human need in the words: 'that whosoever believeth may in him have eternal life' (iii. 15), and it is related to the purpose of God in the sublime passage which immediately follows: 'God so loved the world, that he gave his only begotten Son' (iii. 16). Oneness of purpose is also indicated when Jesus says: 'Therefore doth my Father love me, because I lay down my life, that I may take it again' (x. 17), and in his declaration: 'This commandment received I from my Father' (x. 18). This dual reference is also to be found in the allusions to the 'hour' of Jesus, both those of the Evangelist (vii. 30, viii. 20) and those of Jesus Himself (xii. 23, xvii. 1). The hour is one in which the Son of Man is to be 'glorified' by the Father (xvii. 1). In St. John's usage the idea is distinctive, but it is deeply rooted in primitive Christian belief. It reappears in 1 John iv. 14 in the form: 'And we have beheld and bear witness that the Father hath sent the Son to be the Saviour of the world.'

(2) *The Messianic Character of Christ's Death.* This thought, as we might expect, recedes into the background in the Fourth Gospel and disappears in 1 John, in consequence of the writer's fuller apprehension of the Person of Christ as the Word of God. All the more interesting is his retention of the term 'Son of Man' in John iii. 14 and in the Passion-sayings of viii. 28, xii. 23, and xvii. 1. The titles 'Son' and 'Son of God', so frequent in both writings, are also in origin Messianic, however rich may be the content the writer gives to them.

(3) *The Vicarious Aspect of the Death of Christ.* This traditional idea is well represented in both works, especially in the Gospel. 'The good shepherd layeth down his life for (ὑπέρ) the sheep' (x. 11; cf. 15). 'Greater love hath no man than this, that a man lay down his life for (ὑπέρ) his friends' (xv. 13). The words of Caiaphas: 'It is expedient for you that one man should die for (ὑπέρ) for the people' (xi. 50; cf. xviii. 14), are doubtless a counsel of worldly prudence, yet at the same time the Evangelist's pointed repetition of the saying indicates how profoundly it expresses his personal belief. In unforgettable words he has expressed it in 1 John iii. 16: 'Hereby know we love, because he laid down his life for (ὑπέρ) us.'

(4) *The Representative Element in Christ's Work.* This element is

not prominent in the Gospel, but it is by no means absent. However we interpret the phrase 'the Lamb of God' (i. 29, 36), it designates One who acts for men in a representative manner, and possibly this is also true of the title 'the good shepherd', since the term 'Shepherd' is used in the Old Testament of the Messiah (cf. Micah v. 4, Ezekiel xxxiv. 23 f., xxxvii. 24) and was used throughout the East to designate the bringer of salvation.[1] Moreover, a representative function is implicit in the words of Caiaphas, already quoted, in the reference to one man dying for the people, 'that the whole nation perish not' (xi. 50; cf. 52). A clearer indication of the idea of expiation appears in the description of the work of the Lamb of God as that of 'taking away' the sin of the world (i. 29). It cannot be said, however, that this aspect of the work of Christ is present to the degree in which it is found in the teaching of St. Paul (cf. Romans iii. 25), much less in the Epistle to the Hebrews (*passim*). It is overshadowed by other teaching which is distinctive of the Gospel. None the less, the signs of its presence are important, since they prepare the way for the clearer doctrine of the Epistle. Here, as we have seen, Jesus is 'the Paraclete with the Father' and is the 'expiation' (ἱλασμός)[2] 'for our sins', and, the writer continues, 'not for ours only, but also for the whole world' (ii. 1 f.; cf. iv. 10). It is characteristic of Biblical teaching in general, and of the New Testament in particular, that it is not said that Jesus by His death propitiates God, or causes Him to become gracious. Jesus Himself is the expiation in the eyes of God. This statement is epigrammatic, and therefore requires more than lexical information about the meaning of ἱλασμός for its interpretation. It clearly marks an advance in the way of reflection upon the traditional data, and in consequence can be appreciated only in connexion with a fuller study of the writer's teaching about God, sin, and the work of Christ as 'the Paraclete with the Father'.[3]

(5) *The Relation of the Death of Christ to Sin.* Already in the previous section it is manifest that this aspect of primitive Christian belief is an important element in the Johannine theology. It is much more prominent, however, in the Epistle than in the Gospel. The saying of the Baptist about the Lamb of God (i. 29) who takes away 'the sin of the world' is not the only passage to con-

---

[1] Cf. J. Jeremias, *Jesus als Weltvollender*, pp. 32 f.
[2] Cf. C. H. Dodd, *The Bible and the Greeks*, pp. 94 f.
[3] See pp. 142–52.

sider in the Gospel. The Passion-saying of xii. 31: 'Now is the
judgment of this world: now shall the prince of this world
[cf. xiv. 30, xvi. 11] be cast out', raises a different aspect of the
problem of sin and recalls both the saying of Jesus: 'This is your
hour, and the power of darkness' (Luke xxii. 53), and the Pauline
conception of the death of Christ as a victorious encounter with
'the principalities and powers' (Colossians ii. 15).[1] A similar
thought emerges in the Epistle in the statement that the Son of
God was manifested 'that he might destroy the works of the
devil' (iii. 8). In the Epistle, however, other aspects of the work
of Christ in relation to sin are emphasized. Thus, His blood
'cleanses us from all sin' (i. 7); He is the expiation for the sins of
'the whole world' (ii. 2; cf. iv. 10); sins are forgiven 'for his
name's sake' (ii. 12); the purpose of His manifestation was 'to
take away sins' (iii. 5). These are the relevant passages which
must be considered in connexion with the problem of expiation
mentioned in the previous paragraph. Once more reflection
upon the primitive data is obvious.

(6) *The Sacrificial Significance of the Death of Christ.* This aspect
also is markedly present in the Johannine theology; in the Gospel
in the designation of Jesus as 'the Lamb of God' (i. 29, 36), in the
eucharistic sayings of vi. 53–8, in the reference to the grain of
wheat which falls into the earth and dies (xii. 24), and in the
prayer of self-dedication: 'And for their sakes I sanctify myself,
that they themselves also may be sanctified in truth' (xvii. 19);
in the Epistle in the reference to the cleansing blood (i. 7), and
the expiatory passages mentioned above (ii. 1 *f.*, iv. 10). Jesus
Christ, the writer insists, is 'he that came by water and blood', a
statement which he repeats with solemn emphasis in the words:
'not with the water only, but with the water and with the blood'
(v. 6). Of the strength of this sacrificial emphasis there can be no
question.

(7) *The Use of the Servant-Conception.* In line with the claim that
the ideas of Isaiah liii, so vital for the thought of Jesus Himself,
exercise a decreasing influence in the later New Testament
writings, is the isolated example of this teaching in John i. 29 and
its total disappearance in 1 John. Many commentators deny
its presence in the Baptist's saying, but of the various interpretations of the phrase 'the Lamb of God' there is most to be said for
the opinion that the Evangelist is thinking of Isaiah liii. 7 and

---

[1] See pp. 62 *f.*, 81 *f.*

10.[1] The difficulties of this view are that he does not use the term 'Servant', that he is not influenced by the Hebrew text,[2] and speaks of the 'taking away' rather than of the 'bearing' of sin. On the whole, it is best to conclude that, while he is indebted to the Servant-conception, it is only to a small degree that he is influenced by it, and that the broad sacrificial idea in the passage has many sources which cannot be separated with certainty. It is disappointing not to be able to speak with greater precision, but the facts do not warrant a more definite interpretation; while the one offered is supported by the fact that elsewhere the Servant-conception is wanting in the Johannine Writings.

(8) *The Resurrection and the Death of Christ.* While in the historical sections of the Gospel the greatest importance is assigned to the resurrection, its doctrinal significance for the death of Christ is replaced by the emphasis laid upon the death as itself His 'glorifying' (vii. 39, xii. 16, 23, 28, xvii. 1) and 'exaltation' (iii. 14, viii. 28, xii. 32, 34). The necessity of the resurrection is affirmed in xx. 9, but more characteristic of the Evangelist's theology is the saying of Jesus: 'I am the resurrection, and the life' (xi. 25). These ideas are not found in 1 John and the resurrection is not mentioned in that writing. As in the Pauline Epistle and the Epistle to the Hebrews, the reality of the Living and Exalted Christ is assumed.

(9) *Faith-union with the Crucified.* It is a striking feature of the Johannine theology that while, both in the Gospel and in 1 John, the ideas of 'believing in Christ', 'abiding in Him', and 'being in Him' are characteristic and constant features, this act of faith is nowhere related to Christ as the Crucified Lord. The Pauline conception of 'dying with Christ' is also absent. Faith, in the Johannine sense, is much more than loyalty and reliance upon the unseen ministry of Christ as in the Epistle to the Hebrews; it is mystical union with Christ, fellowship with Him, and, in 1 John, fellowship also with God or with the Father (ii. 24, iv. 15, 16). As we shall see, there is a marked similarity between this conception of faith and the kind of eucharistic teaching characteristic of the Gospel, and the explanation of both will be

---

[1] Cf. Bernard, *I.C.C., St. John*, p. 44. Other interpretations refer to the lamb offered at the morning and evening sacrifice (Exodus xxix. 38–46), to Jeremiah xi. 19, to the Paschal lamb (Exodus xii), or to the horned lamb or young ram of apocalyptic imagery (cf. Dodd, in the article previously cited, p. 146). I have discussed the passage in *Jesus and His Sacrifice*, pp. 226 f.

[2] Cf. Dodd, *op. cit.*, p. 146.

found to lie in the Evangelist's distinctive teaching concerning the death of Christ. In form at least the Johannine conception of faith is more like that attitude of personal attachment to Himself for which Jesus looked in His relationships with His disciples; and this fact must of necessity raise in the most pointed fashion the relative merits of Pauline and Johannine teaching. This important question will obviously require further consideration at a later stage.

(10) *The Eucharist and the Death of Christ.* Eucharistic teaching is a characteristic feature of the Fourth Gospel. As such, it necessarily includes terms which call to mind the sacrifice and death of Christ, as, for example, the phrases 'my flesh' and 'my blood' repeatedly found in the section vi. 53-8 and the references to 'eating 'and 'drinking'. The source of this teaching is the Synoptic sayings: 'This is my body', 'This is my blood of the covenant, which is shed for many' (Mark xiv. 22, 24); but the fact that it is given in a Galilean discourse, and in a Gospel which does not record the story of the institution of the Eucharist in the account of the Last Supper, raises the most difficult, historical and doctrinal questions. On the historical side it may be suggested that, if the Last Supper was preceded by communion-meals anticipatory of the great Messianic Feast, the Evangelist may have preferred to introduce the polemical discourse of chapter vi. at the point where it appears rather than in xiii–xvii, where a different tone prevails. If this suggestion has force, it is supported by doctrinal considerations, since his eucharistic teaching, like his conception of faith, centres in the idea of communion with the Living Lord rather than, as in St. Paul's teaching, the thought of participation in His Sacrifice.

(11) *The Idea of Suffering with Christ.* In the mystical Pauline sense, this idea is not found in the Johannine Writings, and this fact is entirely in harmony with the Evangelist's teaching concerning faith and sacramental communion. On the side of Christian life and practice his teaching about the loyalty which inevitably involves suffering and the mutual love of believers inspired by the example of Christ, is rich and full. 'A servant', the disciples are reminded, 'is not greater than his lord. If they persecuted me, they will also persecute you' (xv. 20), while the saying about 'Greater love' immediately follows the words: 'This is my commandment, that ye love one another, even as I have loved you' (xv. 12 f.). In the Epistle this teaching is repeated

more fully still, and in 1 John iii. 16 a direct relation between the sacrifice of Jesus and the life of believers is expressed in the words: 'Hereby know we love, because he laid down his life for us: and we ought to lay down our lives for the brethren.'

(12) *The Love of God in the Death of Christ.* It is to St. John and St. Paul more than to all others that we owe the expression of this great truth, probably assumed but so little emphasized in the earliest preaching. The great words of John iii. 16 are among the best known sayings of the New Testament: 'God so loved the world, that he gave his only begotten Son, that whosoever believeth on him should not perish, but have eternal life'; and parallel to them is the statement of 1 John iv. 9 *f.*: 'Herein was the love of God manifested in us, that God sent his only begotten Son into the world, that we might live through Him. Herein is love, not that we loved God, but that he loved us, and sent his Son to be the expiation for our sins.' Less often quoted than the former passage, the latter is the greater utterance in that it presents the startling thought that the expiation in the Son is the expression of the love of God. In the light of both passages any opposition between the Father and the Son in the ministry of redemption is seen to be entirely false to the spirit and teaching of the New Testament.

(13) *The Ethical and Spiritual Purpose of the Death of Christ.* Already in the last three sections ethical and spiritual ends made possible by the death of Christ have been noted, especially the begetting of love within the hearts of believers. In the Gospel also the gift of life is closely related to His death. The bread which Christ gives is His flesh 'for the life of the world' (vi. 51; cf. 54, 57, xvii. 2), and the consequence of the spiritual acts of the eating of His flesh and the drinking of His blood is fellowship with Him and His abiding presence (vi. 56). The purpose of God in the lifting up of the Son of Man is that men may have 'eternal life' in Him through believing (iii. 14 *f.*; cf. 16). Life and eternal life are also frequently mentioned in 1 John, but here, as in the Gospel also, in connexion with Christ Himself. Besides the removal of sin, of which as we have seen both writings speak, the Epistle also mentions cleansing from sin (i. 7) and the remission of sins (ii. 12) as spiritual blessings, the former by reason of His blood, the latter 'for his name's sake'.

(14) *The Universality of Christ's Work.* In the Johannine Writings this truth is stated more emphatically than anywhere else in the

New Testament. In the Gospel Christ is described as 'the Saviour of the world' (iv. 42); His flesh is for the world's life (vi. 51); He dies to gather into one the scattered children of God (xi. 51; cf. x. 16); and His lifting up draws all men to Himself (xii. 32). 1 John adds that He is the expiation 'for the whole world' (ii. 2) and repeats the phrase 'the Saviour of the world' (iv. 14).

(c) St. John's Distinctive Teaching

The preceding analysis shows to what a surprising extent the teaching of the Johannine Writings is rooted in the traditional beliefs of the Church. On very few points is there complete silence, and in most cases the beliefs either receive a new emphasis or are developed in new ways. The comparison also throws into relief the distinctive teaching of St. John. This teaching must now receive attention. It consists of a number of rich and striking ideas, each perfect in itself, which are woven into a connected whole or pattern of thought. It is this fact which goes far to explain why there are those, as Dr. Temple has reminded us, who pay visits to St. John as to a fascinating foreign country, but come home to St. Paul, and others who find St. Paul the exciting, and also rather bewildering, adventure, but with St. John are at home.[1] The beauty and the grandeur of Johannine thought offer liberty to the mind and scope for meditation. St. Paul covers a wider range of religious experience, challenges his readers at every point, and gives no rest or peace of mind in his startling claims about the ways of God with sinful men.

In this section, in seeking to understand the teaching of St. John about the death of Christ, it will serve no useful purpose if we limit ourselves to the study of his direct statements taken out of their context; rather must we set these statements against the background of his theology as a whole, if full justice is to be done to them. For this reason, even if the treatment is brief, it is necessary to consider such Johannine themes as the Purpose and Love of God for men, the Nature of Sin, the Incarnation of the Son of God, the Glorifying and Exaltation of Christ, the Sacrifice of Christ, and the Appropriation of Life in Christ. In treating these themes our present interest must be one of exposition; we require to know what St. John actually says, how he relates one theme to another, and what place the death of Christ occupies in his

[1] *Readings in St. John's Gospel* (1939), p. v.

theology. The questions which must necessarily arise will be considered separately in the concluding summary.

(1) *The Purpose and Love of God for Men.* The fundamental truth in the teaching of St. John concerning God is that He is Spirit and Love. In 1 John it is added that He is Light (i. 5). Through His eternal Word He has revealed Himself to men, and His purpose is that through faith in His Son men should know Him, receive at His hands the gift of eternal life, and enter into fellowship with Him as His sons. All these ideas are characteristic. Life in particular is a cardinal theme[1] both of the Gospel and the Epistle, and its highest expression is eternal life which is defined in the Gospel as consisting in the knowledge of God and of His Son Jesus Christ (xvii. 3). Fellowship with God is also a foundation conception. 'Our fellowship', writes St. John, 'is with the Father, and with his Son Jesus Christ' (1 John i. 3). Especially is God represented as the Father, but not, it should be noted, the Father of all men apart from and independent of faith in Christ. Pre-eminently He is the Father of Jesus Christ His Son, and it is not by natural right, but in consequence of believing in Christ, that men receive from Him the right to become His children. To as many as received the Word, St. John says, 'to them gave he the right to become children of God, even to them that believe on his name' (John i. 12). These were 'born', not by human generation nor by the will of man, 'but of God' (i. 13). The fellowship, which is the ideal relationship between God and man, is an experience of mutual indwelling. 'God is love', it is said, 'and he that abideth in love abideth in God, and God abideth in him' (1 John iv. 16). Both in the Gospel and the Epistle parallel statements are made of 'abiding in' or 'being in' Christ or the Son. In the closest agreement with this teaching is the Johannine emphasis upon the gift of the Son, and His work as the expiation for sins, as grounded in the love of God. Both in John iii. 16 and 1 John iv. 9 the divine purpose is expressed in terms of life, 'eternal life' in the former passage, life through the Son in the latter.

(2) *The Nature of Sin.* That which prevents the gift of sonship and the entrance into the enjoyment of eternal life is sin: such is the Johannine teaching. In the Epistle sin is defined as 'lawlessness' (iii. 4); it is the deliberate choice of evil and self-centred ways of living out of harmony with the will of God. 'All un-

[1] Cf. R. N. Flew, *The Idea of Perfection in Christian Theology* (1934), p. 94; W. F. Howard, *The Fourth Gospel in Recent Criticism and Interpretation* (1931), p. 96.

righteousness', says the writer, 'is sin' (v. 17). As is natural in a homily, the evil of sin is treated to a greater extent in the Epistle than in the Gospel. In the Gospel, however, the noun is used seventeen times and the verb three times, a total greater than in any of the Synoptic Gospels, and than in Matthew and Mark taken together. If the instances of the use of the verb seem few, it must be remembered that St. John uses the noun in striking verbal phrases, as, for example, 'doing sin' (viii. 34; cf. 1 John iii. 4 8, 9), 'having sin' (ix. 41, xv. 22, 24, xix. 11; cf. 1 John i. 8), 'being born in sins' (ix. 34), and 'dying in sin' or sins' (viii. 21, 24 (*bis*)). He also speaks once in the Gospel of the 'taking away' of sin (i. 29; cf. 1 John iii. 5) and once of the remission of sins (xx. 23; cf. 1 John i. 9, ii. 12). Sin, as he sees it, exercises despotic power, since 'every one that doeth sin is the slave of sin' (viii. 34); nevertheless, men may not be conscious of their servitude, and it is the work of the Spirit to 'convict the world in respect of sin' (xvi. 8 *f.*). Many of these ideas reappear in the Epistle, but in addition St. John there speaks of cleansing from all sin (i. 7), of confessing sins (i. 9), of Christ as the expiation for sins (ii. 2, iv. 10), of a sin 'unto death' (v. 16). The certainty and universality of sin are expressed in the most uncompromising terms, and with reference both to actions and to sin as a state. 'If we say that we have not sinned, we make him a liar, and his word is not in us' (i. 10). 'If we say that we have no sin, we deceive ourselves, and the truth is not in us' (i. 8). Only those who abide in Christ do not sin (iii. 6) or those who have been 'begotten of God' (iii. 9, v. 18). It is not too much to say that from these statements we can construct 'a whole theology of sin',[1] except that no light is thrown on its origin, not even in the statement that 'the devil sinneth from the beginning' (iii. 8).

Instructive, however, as these passages are, they do not convey an adequate impression of the teaching of St. John concerning sin. Behind all that he writes he has the conception of a kingdom of evil ruled over by the Evil One, the Prince of this world (xii. 31, xiv. 30, xvi. 11). The coming of the Word is a conflict with darkness (i. 5), which threatens to overtake men unless they believe on the light (xii. 35 *f.*). The Evil One is the power from whom Jesus prays that His own should be preserved (xvii. 15). This idea does not fade from his mind with the passing of years as passages like 1 John ii. 13 *f.*, iii. 12, and v. 18 show. Indeed, as he writes

---

[1] W. F. Lofthouse, *The Father and the Son*, p. 158.

the Epistle and surveys the conditions of his day, he writes: 'We know that we are of God, and the whole world lieth in the Evil One' (1 John v. 19.) Parallel with this conception is his use of the term 'Devil'. The Jews are of their father, the Devil, who was a murderer from the beginning (John viii. 44). It was the Devil who put it into the heart of Judas Iscariot to deliver up Jesus (John xiii. 2). Men are either the children of God or the children of the Devil (1 John iii. 10), and the Son of God was manifested that He might destroy the works of the Devil (1 John iii. 8). However challenging these thoughts may be to the modern mind, it is impossible to explain them away from the Johannine Writings as metaphorical expressions. Evil, as a kingdom with its supreme Lord, is a terrible reality to the mind of St. John.

(3) *The Incarnation of the Son of God.* It is against this background of belief concerning God, sin, and evil, that we shall understand best St. John's teaching about the Incarnation. To him it is essential that men should know God and enter into fellowship with Him. . . 'No man', however, 'hath seen God at any time' (John i. 18; cf. v. 37, vi. 46; 1 John iv. 12, 20). Hence the Prologue to his Gospel ends with the emphatic claim: 'The only begotten Son, which is in the bosom of the Father, he hath declared him' (i. 18). So, too, his Epistle opens with the announcement: 'And the life was manifested, and we have seen, and bear witness, and declare unto you the life, the eternal life, which was with the Father, and was manifested unto us' (i. 2). Equally necessary is it that the coming of the Son should be a real coming in flesh. Accordingly, he emphasizes the fact that 'the Word became flesh, and tabernacled among us', so that men saw His glory, 'glory as of the only begotten from the Father, full of grace and truth' (John i. 14). Throughout both writings it is insisted that the humanity of Christ was real; it was no appearance, but a veritable coming under the conditions of flesh. A further point cardinal to St. John's theology is that Christ should be recognized as embodying the light and life of God, and as being in Himself the one and only way to the Father. For this reason the great 'I am' passages are essential to his purpose. Christ declares Himself to be 'the bread of life' (vi. 35), 'the light of the world' (viii. 12), 'the door of the sheep' (x. 7), 'the good shepherd' (x. 11), 'the resurrection and the life' (xi. 25), 'the true vine' (xv. 1), 'the way, the truth, and the life' (xiv. 6). No desire to make extravagant claims accounts for these utterances in the Gospel; they are the deepest

K

convictions of the Evangelist, the foundations of his theology. Fully germane to his purpose also is the attitude of the Johannine Christ to unbelief and to the menace of the powers of darkness, headed by 'the Prince of this world'. When the voice out of heaven declares that the Father has glorified the name of His Son, and will glorify it again, Jesus cries: 'Now is the judgment of this world: now shall the Prince of this world be cast out' (xii. 31); as He faces death He declares that the Prince of the world cometh and hath nothing in Him (xiv. 30); when He speaks of the Paraclete, one of the reasons given for His mission is that 'the Prince of this world hath been judged' (xvi. 11). The very passion with which St. John asks: 'Who is the liar but he that denieth that Jesus is the Christ?' (1 John ii. 22), and stigmatizes as 'antichrist' the one who denies the Father and the Son (1 John iv. 3), is born of the conviction that God has manifested His love and has sent His Son into the world that men might live through Him (1 John iv. 9).

(4) *The Glorifying and Exaltation of Christ.* Where, then, in this theology lies the significance of the death of Christ? It is of vital importance in St. John's teaching, but its meaning is so closely integrated with all that he has to say of God and of the Incarnation that reflection is needed to perceive its true place in his theology. The life of God, he maintains, is manifested in the Son, who is the living way to fellowship with the Father. The Incarnation, therefore, was necessary to the attainment of this fellowship. It was of essential importance that the Son of God should come in flesh that men might see with their eyes 'the Word of life' (1 John i. 1). St. John, however, clearly recognizes the limitations which the Incarnation imposed upon the Son of God. Thus it is, that in his Gospel Christ 'groans in spirit' and is 'troubled' in the world of men (xi. 33, 38); that He declares it to be 'expedient' that He should go away, in order to come again in His Spirit (xvi. 7); that upon the Cross He cries: 'It is finished' (xix. 30); and that, after His resurrection, He says to Mary in tones of victory: 'I ascend unto my Father and your Father, and my God and your God' (xx. 17). The Evangelist's belief is that, freed from the limitations of the Incarnate life, Christ is for ever accessible as the Living and Exalted Lord, with whom men can have fellowship by faith, on whom they can feed, and thus obtain the gift of eternal life, which is knowledge of, and communion with, the Father.

St. John is far from thinking of the death of Christ as incidental to the fulfilment of this divine purpose. On the contrary, the death constitutes His glorifying or exaltation; it is that through which, and in which, He becomes the Living Lord. It is for this reason that the word 'glorify' is used so frequently in the Gospel with reference to the death of Christ. The Evangelist explains that 'the Spirit was not yet', because 'Jesus was not yet glorified' (vii. 39), and that 'when Jesus was glorified' His disciples remembered what was written of Him (xii. 16). When Jesus sees the Greeks, He cries: 'The hour is come, that the Son of man should be glorified' (xii. 23). At the departure of Judas into the night He exults: 'Now is the Son of man glorified, and God is glorified in him' (xiii. 31 *f.*). In the high priestly prayer He says: 'Father, glorify thy Son, that the Son may glorify thee' (xvii. 1). To the same order of thought belong the passages which speak of the exaltation of the Son in death: 'Even so must the Son of man be lifted up' (iii. 14); 'When ye have lifted up the Son of man, then shall ye know that I am he' (viii. 28); and, greatest of all: 'I, if I be lifted up from the earth, will draw all men unto myself' (xii. 32). There could be no vainer controversy than the dispute whether in these passages the crucifixion or the exaltation is meant. The death *is* the exaltation, the liberation of the Son from the self-imposed conditions of mortality into the freedom of the Spirit. The total absence of this teaching from the Epistle is one of the strongest arguments in favour of its separate authorship. It would be folly to pretend that we can completely explain the omission, except in so far as it is true to say that this teaching is integral to the finely wrought conception of the significance of Christ in the Gospel, and not indispensable in a homiletical writing which deals with a concrete situation in which the presence of false teaching is of supreme importance. Moreover, as we shall see in the next section, the teaching concerning Christ as the ἱλασμός, which is characteristic of the Epistle, owes its distinctive form to the same Johannine theology of which the doctrine of the glorifying of the Son is a conspicuous example.

It remains for us to consider how the teaching under discussion is related to the judgment of the world and to the downfall of the Evil One, the Prince of this world. At first sight they appear to have no connexion at all. What has the uplifting of the Son of Man to do with the eschatological idea of the casting out of the Prince of Evil? The answer is, of course, that the Evangelist's eschatology is 'realized eschatology'; he uses traditional language, but is far removed from the thought of the author of the Apocalypse when he depicts Michael and his angels hurling down the great dragon from heaven (Apocalypse xii. 7–9). His belief is rather that the glorifying of the Son by the Father is *ipso facto* the judgment of the world[1] and the defeat of the Prince of Evil; that the judgment does not belong to the End-time, but is implicit in the crowning of the Son, the giver of life and the living way to the Father. For all its Johannine colour, this thought is closely analogous to that of Jesus, who in the height of the Galilean Mission cried: 'I beheld Satan fall as lightning from heaven' (Luke x. 18). In the Fourth Gospel, however, the humiliation of the Cross has practically disappeared; it is no longer a σκάνδαλον, but a shining stairway by which the Son of God ascends to His Father. The story of Gethsemane is replaced by an allusion to the possibility that the Father should save Him 'from this hour', which Jesus faces only immediately to reject (xii. 27).[2] The 'hour' is not one of dereliction, but of judgment and of victory.

(5) *The Sacrifice of Christ.* How far does St. John think of the death of Christ as a sacrifice for sin, and what place does he give to this idea in his theology? The answer to this question is not easy, especially in view of the differences of emphasis in the Gospel and in the Epistle.

As we have already seen, there can be no doubt that sacrificial ideas are present in both writings. For the Gospel no other conclusion is possible in view of the saying about the Lamb of God (i. 29), the phrase 'my blood' in vi. 54–6, the imagery of the grain of wheat (xii. 24), the reference to the sanctifying of Jesus (xvii. 19) the allusion to the Paschal lamb in the quotation of xix. 36;[3] and still more is this inference valid for the Epistle, in view of the description of Christ as the Advocate with the Father (ii. 1), the use of ἱλασμός (ii. 2, iv. 10), and the words about cleansing blood (i. 7) and the taking away of sins (iii. 5), all of which, directly or indirectly, are ideas associated with sacrifice. The distribution of this evidence is of great interest; it shows that a greater use is made of sacrificial ideas in the Epistle than in the Gospel.

The Gospel references are allusive rather than direct. The Baptist's saying lies solitary and undeveloped; the phrase 'my

[1] The idea of the κρίσις as 'a testing of men' (cf. Bernard, *I.C.C.*, *St. John* p. 441) does not appear to be the Evangelist's thought. Cf. Lagrange, *Evangile selon Saint Jean*, p. 334.

[2] In xviii. 11 the reference to the cup suggests the thought of obedience to the Father's will.

[3] Cf. Bernard, *op. cit.*, p. 651; Lagrange, *op. cit.*, p. 501.

blood' suggests the opportunity of life open to the appropriation of the believer; the reference to the grain of wheat is at most a sacrificial analogy; the words about sanctification bring to the mind the thought of priestly dedication; the allusion to the Paschal lamb is left to be appreciated by the reader. These allusions are significant, but they do not permit us to say that the obedience of Jesus is presented as the One great Sacrifice. No use is made of analogies in the sin-offering and the covenant-sacrifices as in the Epistle to the Hebrews, and there is no reference to an offering which man may make the vehicle of his approach to God. All that we can say is that the materials out of which this conception can be formulated are present in the Gospel, but still unshaped and awaiting the builder's hand.

Both facts, the absence of the idea of the One Sacrifice for men and the presence of the thoughts out of which it can be shaped, are important. On the one hand, there is reason to think that the emergence of a definite sacrificial theory is restrained by the Evangelist's preoccupation with the thought of the death of Christ as His glorifying, as the release for man's taking of that eternal life of which He is the perfect embodiment. On the other hand, it should be observed, this thought of life released to be received is itself the vital concept without which no sacrificial theory can ever be adequately presented. It is reasonable then to claim that in a later writing, compiled on a different plan, the idea of the Sacrifice of Christ, so far from being alien to the writer's mind, was likely to receive fuller development. The presence, therefore, of sacrificial ideas to a greater and richer degree in the Epistle is not a difficulty to be overcome; it is a step to be expected.

Of the distinctive ideas of the Epistle those of Christ as the Advocate with the Father and as the ἱλασμός for the sins of the world are by far the most important, and they must now be considered. Both in different ways are influenced by the teaching of the Gospel. In the farewell discourse of John xiv–xvi, Jesus promises to send[1] the Spirit or Paraclete (xiv. 16, 26, xv. 26, xvi. 7). The word describes 'one who is called in to help', 'a friend of the accused person, called to speak to his character, or otherwise enlist the sympathy of the judges',[2] and is thus best

---

[1] Cf. xv. 26, xvi. 7. In xiv. 16, 26 the Father gives or sends the Paraclete.

[2] Field, *Notes*, p. 102. Cf. Moulton and Milligan, *The Vocabulary of the Greek Testament*, p. 485; Bernard, *op. cit.*, pp. 496–8; Deissmann, *Light from the Ancient East*, pp. 336 f.

rendered by 'Helper' or 'Advocate'. His work is to teach the disciples and to guide them into all the truth, and to convict the world in respect of sin, of righteousness, and of judgment; and while He is the gift of Jesus and of the Father, He is also closely identified with Jesus Himself (cf. xiv. 18). In xiv. 16 He is spoken of as 'another Paraclete', with the suggestion that Jesus also is a Paraclete, and this is supported by the promise of xiv. 14: 'If ye shall ask me anything in my name, that will I do'. Can it then be thought strange, much less improbable, that in a later pastoral writing the same writer should definitely employ this word as a designation of Christ and, since He is the Exalted Lord, of His ministry in heaven for men. The word itself was worthy to be used in this connexion. G. G. Findlay well observed that 'the παράκλητος of the old jurisprudence, in the best times of antiquity, was no hired pleader connected with his client for the occasion by his brief and his fee; he was his patron and standing counsel, the head of the order or of the clan to which both belonged, bound by the claims of honour and family association to stand by his humble dependent and to see him through when his legal standing was imperilled; he was the client's natural protector and the appointed captain of his salvation'.[1] As used, however, of the Exalted Christ the word necessarily gains a richer meaning. While in the Gospel it means 'Strengthener' or 'Helper', in 1 John ii. 1 it means 'Advocate' or 'Intercessor';[2] it describes the work of the Son of Man exalted on high who speaks for men with the Father. In such a context of thought the legal associations of the word have fallen away, and the work of Christ is akin to that of 'the high priest after the order of Melchizedek' in the Epistle to the Hebrews. That, for St. John, it has a sacrificial meaning is indicated when he immediately adds: 'and he is the expiation for our sins'. In his usage the meanings of παράκλητος and ἱλασμός are manifestly connected, and to the consideration of the latter we now turn.

We have already accepted the view, so conclusively argued by C. H. Dodd, that the meaning of ἱλασμός is not 'propitiation' but 'expiation'. One must feel more hesitant, I think, about his further suggestion, 'i.e. a means of removing guilt, or forgive-

---

[1] *Fellowship in the Life Eternal* (1909), p. 117.

[2] W. Bauer renders it *Helfer* in the Gospel (cf. Moffatt), but *Fürsprecher* ('intercessor', 'advocate') in 1 John. Cf. *H.Z.N.T., Das Johannesevangelium*, p. 177; Bauer, *Griechisch-Deutsches Wörterbuch*, 3rd. ed., cols. 1330 f.

ness',[1] unless 'guilt' here means the sinner's 'standing with God' rather than his 'consciousness of guilt'. Although St. John speaks in i. 7 of the cleansing power of the blood of Christ, there is no indication in ii. 1 *f.* that he is thinking primarily of the moral and spiritual effects which are wrought by Christ in the consciousness of sinners. In a context in which he speaks of Christ as our Advocate with the Father, the meaning of ἱλασμός must be that in Him sins are annulled so that they no longer stand between ourselves and God. At this point, however, we must note the absolutely new and unparalleled sense in which St. John uses the Greek word, so much so that lexical studies can be no more than a preparatory discipline to the work of exegesis. St. John does not say that Christ provides a means of expiation, but that He is Himself the expiation, the cancelling or annulling of sins, thus giving to the word an application which it bears nowhere else in the Greek Bible.[2] We cannot affirm that he is commenting on the Pauline use of ἱλαστήριον in Romans iii. 25, but the situation presupposed by 1 John ii. 2 is exactly as if he had been asked to explain the Pauline passage. 'Yes', he says in effect, 'but our Advocate with the Father, Jesus Christ the righteous, is Himself the Expiation.' It cannot escape our notice how closely this usage is in harmony with Johannine theology as a whole, in which all the emphasis lies, not so much upon what Christ does, as on what He is in Himself, the Word of God, the Way, the Truth, and the Life, the immediate object of faith, the spiritual food and drink of believers who enjoy eucharistic fellowship with Him. So far from thinking it improbable that the Fourth Evangelist who speaks of the glorifying of Jesus should describe Him as the Expiation, it is difficult to think that any one else would have been more likely than he to use the word in this highly characteristic sense.

In the use of the two words we are considering there is certainly a development in Johannine thought, but it is one that is both natural and intelligible if we allow for the originality of the Gospel, the homiletical character of the Epistle, and the time interval between the two writings. The meaning of the two words must be understood in the light of the Johannine theology.

---

[1] *Bulletin of the John Rylands Library*, vol. 21, no. 1, April, 1937, p. 145 *n.*

[2] It is for this reason that a study of the examples of the use of ἱλασμός in the Septuagint (Leviticus xxv. 9, Numbers v. 8, 1 Chronicles xxviii. 20, Psalms cxxix (cxxx) 4, Sir. xviii. 20, xxxii (xxxv) 3, Amos viii. 14, Ezekiel xliv. 27, Daniel ix. 9, 2 Maccabees iii. 33), absolutely indispensable to the study of the word, yields so limited a harvest.

The work of Christ as the Advocate does not imply any unwillingness on the part of the Father to receive men into fellowship with Himself. On the contrary, it is a ministry directed to that very end; it is the presentation by Christ of the totality of His work for men, in His Incarnation and death, and of their response to Him in faith and love. Such a ministry of Christ becomes Him as the Son of Man and is of inexpressible blessing to men in their relationships with God. To say that Christ is the Expiation for the sins of the world is only to express the same thought more directly in the language of sacrifice. In the Johannine epigram: 'He is the ἱλασμός', the pronoun ·describes not only Christ in Himself, but Christ as He is found to be in the experience of the believer. The act of covering is not conceived as an external event, but as a fact which corresponds to spiritual realities. United with Christ by faith, men find that their sin is annulled in the sense that its guilt is purged, its might broken, and its estranging power dissolved. Since, however, it is not their faith in itself, but their faith *in Him*, which accomplishes this result, and therefore the experience of fellowship with God, it is right to say that *He* is the ἱλασμός. Such appears to be the Johannine teaching. On the positive side it corresponds to the affirmation that the glorifying of the Son is the casting out of Satan. Each truth is implicit in the other, and each becomes actual in Christ. A unity in the Johannine theology is thus disclosed which comes to light in the fuller use of sacrificial ideas which are nascent in the Gospel and emergent, though still in part, in the Epistle.

In answer, then, to the question raised at the beginning of the present section, we conclude that, while the idea of the Sacrifice of Christ is not the central thought of the Gospel, and is not represented fully even in the Epistle, the Johannine theology is always steadily moving to a spiritualized expression of the sacrificial principles of life through death and access to God through a mediatorial ministry, in a characteristic manner in which all the emphasis falls upon the Person of Christ as the Word of God, the Giver of Life, and the Way to the Father. Why this formulation does not find an even fuller expression is one of the questions to be considered in the concluding Summary.

(6) *The Appropriation of Life in Christ.* The roots of the Johannine teaching on this theme and its distinctive character have already been indicated in the attempt to trace St. John's debt to the primitive Christian tradition; and all that remains for us to

do now is to show how intimately his teaching about faith-union and sacramental communion is related to his doctrine of the work of Christ.

While he studiously avoids the noun 'faith',[1] perhaps because of its place in Gnostic teaching, he uses πιστεύειν, 'to believe' about 100 times in the Gospel and nine times in the Epistle. Especially striking are the thirty-seven instances,[2] out of a total of forty-five in the entire New Testament, in which he uses the verb with εἰς and the accusative case, a construction which, as Moulton says, 'recalls at once the bringing of the soul *into* that mystical union which Paul loved to express by ἐν Χριστῷ'.[3] In addition must be mentioned his use of the ideas of 'abiding in' and 'being in' Christ. The former is used in the Gospel in vi. 56, xv. 4, 5, 6, 7, and even more frequently in the Epistle, in ii. 6, 24, 27, 28, iii. 6, 24, while in 1 John iv. 12–16 it is used of 'abiding in God' (cf. ii. 24: 'in the Son, and in the Father') and of His 'abiding' in the believer (iv. 12, 15 *f.*). The latter describes the same mystical relationships in John xiv. 10, 20, xvii. 21, 23, 26, and 1 John ii. 5, v. 20. A careful study of these passages shows how characteristic this teaching is and how consistently it is related to the Person of Christ without any direct reference to His death. Our investigation, however, has shown that it is quite mistaken to infer from this fact that the death of Christ has little significance for St. John; it is because the death is itself a part, and indeed the crowning moment, in the revelation in the Son that the faith-union of the believer is mystical fellowship with Christ Himself, in the totality of His Person, rather than with Him as Redeemer and Saviour. What the believer receives is Life in Christ glorified and exalted through death.

Sacramental communion as it is conceived by the Evangelist is of the same character, as the eucharistic sayings in John vi. 51, 53–8 clearly show. These sayings are as follows:

John vi. 51: 'I am the living bread which came down out of heaven: if any man eat of this bread, he shall live for ever: yea and the bread which I will give is my flesh, for the life of the world.'
John vi. 53: 'Verily, verily, say unto you, Except ye eat the flesh of the Son of man and drink his blood, ye have not life in yourselves.'
John vi. 54: 'He that eateth my flesh and drinketh my blood hath eternal life; and I will raise him up at the last day.'
John vi. 55: 'For my flesh is meat indeed, and my blood is drink indeed.'

[1] The one instance is 1 John v. 4.
[2] Including three in 1 John.
[3] *Grammar of New Testament Greek, Prolegomena*, p. 68.

John vi. 56: 'He that eateth my flesh and drinketh my blood abideth in me, and I in him.'

John vi. 57: 'As the living Father sent me, and I live because of the Father; so he that eateth me, he also shall live because of me.'

John vi. 58: 'This is the bread which came down out of heaven: not as the fathers did eat, and died: he that eateth this bread shall live for ever.'

Some reference has already been made to the difficult historical problems which are raised by these sayings,[1] and our present interest is in their doctrinal significance. The elements are not mentioned, just as in the Gospel the institution of the Eucharist itself is not described; but, in view of the references to 'flesh'[2] and 'blood' and to the acts of eating and drinking, the allusions to the manna in the wilderness, and the explanatory statement: 'the bread which I will give is my flesh', it is almost certain that the Evangelist is unfolding his teaching concerning the meaning of sacramental communion. And for him, it is clear, the communion is a communion with Christ Himself. In a sense strongly guarded against materialistic associations by the words: 'It is the spirit that quickeneth; the flesh profiteth nothing: the words that I have spoken unto you are spirit, and are life' (vi. 63), he teaches that the believer eats Christ's flesh and drinks His blood. If nothing more were said in the section it would be apparent from vi. 63 that by these strong metaphorical expressions the idea of a mystical fellowship with Christ is meant; but, as it is, this inference is confirmed by the fact that the same spiritual blessings are mentioned as in the case of faith-union, namely, 'life', 'eternal life', the experience of abiding in Christ and of His abiding in us, and to these is added the gift of victory over death. As before, the Evangelist's thought is centred in the Incarnation and in Christ's death as included therein. In this respect there is a marked difference between his apprehension of the Eucharist and that of St. Paul who, as we have seen,[3] interprets it rather as the opportunity of sharing in the redemptive power of Christ's Sacrifice. Both ideas are necessary to a full doctrine of the Eucharist, and each is determined by the place assigned to the work of Christ. In the case of the Evangelist the emphasis lies upon the reception of life through communion with the Living and Exalted Christ.

The same ideas are implicit in the allegory of the Vine (John

---

[1] See earlier, p. 140.

[2] The use of 'flesh' rather than 'body' is probably due to the Evangelist's anti-docetic interests. Cf. Bernard, *op. cit.*, p. clxx.

[3] See earlier, pp. 70, 96 *f.*

xv. 1–8),[1] and especially in the words: 'Abide in me, and I in you. As the branch cannot bear fruit of itself, except it abide in the vine; so neither can ye, except ye abide in me' (xv. 4). The underlying conception is the thought of life communicated to believers through union with Christ. Without this union, they are cast forth as a branch, and are withered and burned (xv. 6), whereas in bearing much fruit, they are truly Christ's disciples and the Father is glorified (xv. 8).

Throughout the whole of St. John's writings it is apparent how constantly the idea of life in Christ conditions his teaching. Whether his immediate theme is the revelation of God, the Incarnation, the death of Christ, or the experience of believers, this thought of life appears and reappears. It determines all that he has to say about the person and death of Jesus, and, even in 1 John where there is a closer approximation to traditional beliefs, the same emphasis is to be seen. His teaching as a whole is well summed up in the words of 1 John v. 11 f.: 'And the witness is this, that God gave unto us eternal life, and this life is in his Son. He that hath the Son hath the life; he that hath not the Son of God hath not the life.'

(d) Summary

In the Johannine teaching as a whole with reference to the death of Christ two features, at first sight incompatible, stand out with startling clarity—the great extent to which it is rooted in the primitive faith of the Church and at the same time its highly distinctive character. The individuality of the teaching is so obvious that its traditional basis can easily be overlooked, and it is not surprising that the attempts to explain it by over-estimating the influence of Philonic, Hermetic, and even Mandæan parallels have commanded sympathy and support. Only by a close and careful study is it revealed that almost all the ideas for which a primitive basis can be claimed are represented at some point or other, some it is true faintly and others more markedly, in the Johannine teaching; and where, as in the case of the idea of a faith-relationship with the Crucified extending to His redemptive work, a primitive idea is wholly wanting, there is actually a return to the conditions of pre-Pauline Christianity as illustrated in the

---

[1] Some commentators not unreasonably argue that the allegory is suggested by the words of institution at the Last Supper. Cf. Bernard, *op. cit.*, pp. clxxiii–vi; Hoskyns and Davey, *The Fourth Gospel*, pp. 555 f.

sayings of Jesus and the early chapters of the Acts, balanced, however, by a new and overwhelming emphasis on a faith-relationship with Christ Himself as the Risen and Exalted Lord.

The question arises whether this agreement of the Johannine teaching in respect of faith with the primitive tradition proves its superiority over the Pauline teaching. The answer must be that the agreement is not decisive. It is natural that before His death Jesus should have sought from men an attitude of personal attachment to Himself rather than faith in Himself as the Crucified Saviour; and it can occasion no surprise that the earliest preaching followed His example in this respect. It is fitting also that St. Paul, as well as St. John, should repeatedly speak of faith in Christ quite apart from His redemptive ministry; and indeed the necessity of this faith is a permanent element in the Christian Gospel, yesterday, to-day, and for ever. Nevertheless, St. Paul, St. John, and the preacher of to-day, all stand on the other side of the Cross, not facing it as an event of the future, as Jesus faced it, but looking back upon it both as an accomplished fact of history and as an act of supreme moment for the religious experience of men. When, therefore, St. Paul speaks both of faith in Christ Himself as Lord and of faith in Him as the Crucified, including in this experience reliance upon all that He has accomplished in His death for men, he is following a necessary and inevitable line of development. But if this is so, with equal justice we must conclude that, since St. John does not take this step, as manifestly he does not, he fails to take account of this development, remaining still upon traditional soil. The explanation can only be that, despite the sublimity of his positive teaching, his apprehension of the meaning of the Cross is much less profound than that of St. Paul. In his conception of faith and of faith-union with Christ St. Paul accepts the logic of history; St. John still lingers in Galilee, in spite of all the insight he has gained into the significance of the Person of Christ through long experience and reflection in Ephesus. We thus reach the paradoxical conclusion that while as a whole his theology is highly distinctive and of marked originality, at certain points St. John stands so close to primitive beliefs and ways of thinking that in some respects his teaching bears the marks of arrested development. There is no writing in the New Testament which can be compared with the Fourth Gospel in respect of the strange and unexpected manner in which the traditional is combined and intertwined with the original; and in this fact lie its perennial fascination and its undoubted power to meet the religious needs of all kinds and conditions of men.

The grandeur of the Johannine teaching is in no need of defence. Indeed, without fear of contradiction it may be claimed that he who cannot recognize its worth is a 'profane person' for whom it is hard to find a place of repentance. The danger, in fact, for the New Testament scholar is not want of appreciation, but rather exaggeration. Many examples, which perhaps it would be invidious to cite, could be given of the confident claim that the Johannine theology represents the crown and climax of New Testament teaching. So long as we look at this theology in itself there is much to be said in support of this claim; it is certainly the perfect flowering of important developments which have their origin in the mind and teaching of Jesus Himself. If, however, we accept it as the very essence of New Testament teaching, and as complete in itself, we are compelled to regard other aspects of that teaching, and in particular some of the most distinctive Pauline doctrines, as of secondary, if not merely academic, importance. It is for this reason that many who find their spiritual home in the Fourth Gospel pass somewhat lightly over the ideas of Romans iii. 25, are distinctly apprehensive about the Pauline teaching that Christ was 'made sin on our behalf', and prefer to interpret the Eucharist along the lines of a 'Christ-mysticism' rather than as a sharing in the redemptive power of Christ's Sacrifice. We may indeed go further than this and affirm that an almost exclusive reliance upon the limited teaching of the Fourth Gospel in respect of the death of Christ is in no small degree responsible for the widespread, but rapidly disintegrating, conviction that we have said all that is important about the Atonement when we declare that Christ died in order to embody and make known the love of God for men. The true use of the Fourth Gospel is that of the Interpreter's House in which we stay for a while, and to which we often return, in order to survey with new eyes the greater wealth of New Testament teaching as a whole.

To some it will appear almost treason to suggest that there are serious limitations in the Johannine theology; the facts, however, are stubborn, and the neglect of them is certain to lead to an unbalanced judgment. In the first place, it is significant that repentance is never mentioned in the Johannine writings, and that the verb 'to forgive' is used once only in the Gospel (John xx. 23) and once in the Epistle (1 John ii. 12). Love, moreover, in these writings is always love for Christ or for believers, never love for sinners, except so far as they are included in the phrase 'the world' (cf. John iii. 16). In the great high-priestly prayer the Johannine Christ expressly declares that He prays 'not for the world', but for those whom God has given to Him (John xvii. 9). In John vii–ix the Jews are constantly assailed with bitter invective; no appeal is made to their better nature, and in John xii. 40 a climax is reached in the application of the terrible words of Isaiah vi. 9 f.:

> 'He hath blinded their eyes, and he hardened their heart;
> Lest they should see with their eyes, and perceive with their heart,
> And should turn,
> And I should heal them.'

The skilled exegete knows how to explain these chapters, but significantly enough by referring to the attitude of the Jews to the Church in the Evangelist's day, or by assembling the severer sayings of Jesus like the Woes upon Chorazin and Bethsaida (Luke x. 13–5) which, however, in the Synoptics, are accompanied by more tender sayings like the Lament over Jerusalem (Luke xiii. 34). Again, there is a notable difference between the Johannine interviews of Jesus with sinners and those in Luke (cf. John iv. 1–42 and Luke vii. 36–50, xix. 1–10), while by its subject-matter alone the story of the Woman taken in Adultery (John vii. 53–viii. 11) is seen to be an alien element in the Fourth Gospel.[1] These and other features are closely connected with the Evangelist's delineation of Jesus. The sublimity of His figure and the tenderness of His relationships with His own are known to every reader of the Gospel. None the less one must agree with the opinion of R. N. Flew that 'the shadow of a Stoic ἀπάθεια is already falling on the supreme figure'.[2] 'For Him there is no Gethsemane. He goes out of the Upper Room to face no desolation. There are no words in the Fourth Gospel with the horror of ἐκθαμβεῖσθαι, καὶ ἀδημονεῖν (Mark xiv. 33) crying in them. Even if Jesus weeps, the story of the tears reads more like a refutation of Docetism than the sob of a wounded heart. Serene and confident, He has no unexpected problems to face. He knows no surprise, for He sees every step of the pathway in front of Him to the very end.'[3]

---

[1] The textual evidence, of course, is decisive that this genuine story did not originally belong to the Gospel.

[2] *The Idea of Perfection in Christian Theology*, p. 117.   [3] *ibid.*, p. 117.

These facts are recalled because they explain the notable limitations of the Evangelist's doctrine of the death of Christ. In the light of them it cannot surprise us that he never represents Christ as dying for sinners, as bearing their sins, falling under their curse, offering Himself in sacrifice on their behalf, inviting them to trust in His redemptive ministry and share in the power of His self-offering. These ideas are not present because they belong to another world of thought and experience. Herein is explained his halting use of the Servant-conception which lies behind i. 29 but never really comes to the surface here or in any part of his writings. In i. 29 he describes the Lamb of God, not as 'bearing' the sin of the world, in the sense of enduring or sharing in its consequences, but as 'taking it away', a phrase which in the Johannine theology can only mean that in some way He removes or annuls it; while in xii. 38, the one passage in which he directly quotes Isaiah liii, he uses the quotation, not to interpret the meaning of Christ's death, but to expose the unbelief of the Jews in its darkest colours. It cannot be said, therefore, that the Servant-conception exercises a controlling influence upon the Evangelist's theology. Full and rich as it is, his doctrine of the Incarnation differs from Pauline teaching in that it does not include the idea of the self-identification of Christ with sinners and of His voluntary participation in the consequences of their sin. His death is vicarious, but it is in no sense penal.

The results of this aspect of the Johannine theology are very far-reaching. It is a direct consequence of the character of his doctrine of the Person of Christ that, while his thought moves in sacrificial channels, and is thus a valuable witness to the prevalence of sacrificial ideas in the primitive Church, the Evangelist never gives expression to the idea of the One great Sacrifice in the form in which it appears in the Epistle to the Hebrews. For the same reason his eucharistic teaching does not extend the idea of Christ-mysticism by the suggestion of participation in a sacrificial meal. More important, because more fundamental, there is no description of a self-offering of Christ for sinners with which they can identify themselves in their approach to God for pardon, reconciliation, and peace, other than the statement that He sanctifies Himself for His own that they too may be sanctified in truth (xvii. 19). No mediatorial bridge spans the gulf which separates the sinner from that sublime revelation of God as Life, Spirit, and Love, which it is the supreme merit of the Gospel to describe. So little does the atoning work of Christ, as the Evangelist presents it, provide in itself a means of access to God, that the recovery of the sinner is attributed rather to a regeneration accomplished by the Spirit in the waters of baptism (iii. 5); and only in the Epistle, in the declaration that the blood of Jesus cleanses men from sin (i. 7) and that He is our Advocate and ἱλασμός (ii. 1 *f.*), is there a closer approximation to distinctively sacrificial doctrine. Drawn by the spectacle of the uplifting of the Son of Man upon the Cross (xii. 32), the believer is born from above rather than saved through reliance upon a redemption wrought there by Christ on his behalf. These aspects of the Johannine theology are not isolated phenomena, without inner connexion; they are the direct results of a sublimation or spiritualization of sacrificial ideas which is carried to such a degree that, when expiation is mentioned at all, it is represented as implicit in His Person glorified in the act of death. A mediatorial ministry in heaven is certainly attributed to Christ in the statement that He is our Advocate with the Father, but in what sense He fulfils this function, and what it entails, remain the writer's secret, if indeed in using this bold expression he had arrived at any clearly defined conception of His work of intercession.

The considerations mentioned above are of great value to the theologian because they reveal how profoundly the doctrine of the Atonement is affected by the views we take of the Person of Christ and of His relation to sinners. From the negative point of view the Johannine Writings are an impressive warning of the attenuated conceptions of the significance of the death of Christ which inevitably follow when the Incarnation is thought of predominantly in terms of revelation, of life, and of knowledge. The distinctive Pauline emphasis upon the coming of Christ as the voluntary acceptance of a 'poverty' whereby we may become 'rich' (2 Corinthians viii. 9), and upon a self-emptying which issues in humility and obedience, even 'unto death, yea, the death of the cross' (Philippians ii. 5–11), is seen to be a necessary supplement to the greatness of Johannine teaching. This truth may be recognized without in any way diminishing our appreciation of the positive contribution of this teaching to the doctrine of the Atonement, a contribution which, in presenting so fully the work of Christ as the purpose of God, the proof of His love, the crown of the Incarnation, the source of eternal life ever at the disposal of the believer, has bequeathed to the Church a treasure she cannot measure and dare not lose. The true lesson which emerges from our inquiry, as from our investigation of New Testament teaching as a whole, is that we cannot afford to limit our attention to the message of any one Gospel, Epistle, or group of Epistles, since they are all organic members in a living body of truth wherein each has its function but is not the whole body. The explanation of this singularly vital character of the New Testament revelation is that its fount and origin is the life, death, and resurrection of Jesus Christ Himself, interpreted by Him in His sayings, worked out in the life and experience of the primitive Church, and elucidated in its various aspects by St. Paul, the author of the Epistle to the Hebrews, and St. John. The New Testament is not a fortuitous collection of separate writings, but a medium in which the significance of Christ, as the Word of God and the Saviour of men, emerges clearly into the light of day.

DETACHED NOTE ON THE EUCHARIST IN THE PRIMITIVE COMMUNITIES

In the preceding investigation it has been seen that the question of the place of the Eucharist in the earliest Christian communities is one of great complexity, and it will be of advantage to discuss this question in greater detail.

Perhaps the least serious difficulty is the claim, that the eucharistic teaching of the New Testament is due to the infusion of alien ideas derived from the Mystery-religions; for a generation of inquiry has shown that, however deeply these influences affected later Christian thought and practice, their effects within the period A.D. 30–60, and even later, are negligible.[1] The more important difficulties are two: a reluctance to believe that Jesus can have attached much significance to rites, and the silence of a considerable part of the New Testament regarding the Eucharist.

That Jesus saw any compelling value in rites *per se* does not merit serious discussion, but that He disdained them as means to spiritual ends is contradicted by the value He attached to table-fellowship and to the communal meals which anticipated the joys of the future Messianic Banquet. Such meals are visible behind the stories of miraculous feeding in Mark vi. 35–44, viii. 1–9, and the Last Supper, in which eschatological expectations still survive, is itself a communion-meal re-interpreted and charged with a new significance in view of His swiftly approaching Messianic suffering and sacrifice.

[1] Cf. *Jesus and His Sacrifice*, pp. 117, 124, 131 *f.*, 216 *f.*

L

The more serious difficulty is the second. How can we account for the silence of so large a part of the New Testament regarding the meaning and importance of the Christian Eucharist?[1] Found in the sayings of Institution in St. Mark and St. Matthew, in the teaching of St. Paul in 1 Corinthians x and xi, and in the Johannine discourses of John vi, why is this teaching wanting in St. Luke, the Acts, and 1 Peter,[2] and in later writings like the Pastoral Epistles, Hebrews, and the Apocalypse? In facing this question, the gap in the witness of the New Testament records must be frankly recognized. Our own investigation has made it plain, for the references to 'the breaking of bread' in the Acts, bare as they admittedly are, hardly suggest more than fellowship-meals different in character from the accounts of the Supper in Mark xiv. 22–5 and 1 Corinthians xi. 23–5. The explanation would seem to be that the earlier eschatological character of the Galilean fellowship-meals was more easily understood, and therefore more readily remembered and observed; whereas the deeper content which Jesus had given to the Last Supper was difficult to apprehend, apart from the light thrown upon it by the Cross itself. In consequence, during the period immediately following the death of Christ, it did not everywhere and always become a central feature in the life and worship of the primitive communities. Parallel situations to these circumstances can be seen in the Galilean Ministry of Jesus. Jesus did not always aim at being immediately understood. He preferred to sqw seed thoughts which, in His Father's time, and with greater knowledge and experience on the part of His disciples, would germinate in their minds and ultimately determine their action. His teaching concerning His Messiahship is a case in point. He waits until the great day near Cæsarea Philippi before even asking the vital question: 'Who say ye that I am?' 'Thou art the Messiah', Peter replies, and forthwith, after declaring that this revelation has been made to him, not by flesh and blood, but by the Father, Jesus begins to teach His disciples a new conception of Messiahship. 'The Son of man', He says, 'must suffer'; His Messianic task is to die and to rise again, to give Himself a ransom for the many.

[1] 'If, however, the disciples had learnt on that last evening to attach so much importance to the rite, we should surely have expected to hear more of it in the epistles' (W. F. Lofthouse, *The London Quarterly and Holborn Review*, April, 1938, p. 238, in an extended review of *Jesus and His Sacrifice*).

[2] Windisch, *H.Z.N.T.*, p. 59, rejects the view that the Eucharist is referred to in 1 Peter ii. 3. Lohmeyer, *Theol. Rundschau* (1937), p. 296, treats the suggestion with greater sympathy on the ground that ii. 1–10 is full of cult pictures and ideas.

Jesus makes repeated efforts to impart this teaching, but the disciples do not understand. This representation is not the schematization of Mark; it is the realism of history. Preoccupied with Messianic dreams, they could not assimilate the thought of a Suffering Messiah. There is no sign that they ever understood until after the resurrection; and even then in the course of time they lost the key to the thoughts of Jesus when during the Gentile Mission they gave an ever decreasing attention to the Servant-ideas of Isaiah liii. Less anxious than many teachers to win immediate results, Jesus was content to leave it so. He knew that once again the Father, and not flesh and blood, would make known the truth to His own. Precisely the same features are to be observed in His teaching concerning the New Israel, the community which He founded and which came to be known as the Church. In the case, then, of His teaching regarding the Supper the circumstances under which it was given, and the method of Jesus as a teacher, account for the facts revealed in the New Testament; and all the more is this so because the sayings at the Supper, 'This is my body', 'This is my blood of the covenant, which is shed for many', are the climax of His revelation concerning the meaning of His death. The supposition that these words can have been luminous to the disciples on the night of the Supper, is devoid of historical foundation. All the probabilities are against it. Yet Jesus knew that in the Father's time they would understand. It is against reason to think that the revelation would come immediately and to all even after the death of Christ. Just as Peter saw that Jesus was the Messiah first, and then only in part, so the meaning of the words of Institution would be understood first by the few, gradually by the rest, and still later by the scattered Christian communities. The presence, therefore, of circles within the Church, in which the breaking of bread was a fellowship-meal pointing to the Parousia, and little more, is precisely what we have every reason to expect. Equally intelligible is the existence of the community, probably at Cæsarea, from which was derived the account of the Supper preserved for us in Luke xxii. 14–18, an account which does not include the Markan sayings quoted above, although later, in composing the Third Gospel, St. Luke added the saying regarding the bread in xxii. 19 *a* and later still an unknown hand appended the words of Institution in xxii. 19 *b*–20. The view that Luke xxii. 14–18 is the only primitive and historical narrative, and that Mark xiv. 22–5 is a late legend coloured by doctrinal interests, is a critical construction due to an unwarranted scepticism and a neglect of the methods of Jesus as a teacher. The original tradition is that of Mark xiv. 22–5, countersigned by 1 Corinthians xi. 23–5. Luke xxii. 14–18 is of the things that pass because they are partial and incomplete. The true process to be discerned, in the materials presented by critical analysis, is not one of corruption, but of integration, as the pregnant teaching of Jesus was understood in the life and experience of the Church. It is this process which accounts for the gap evident enough in the witness of the New Testament to the Christian Eucharist. The references are not present because the meaning of the Supper was appreciated gradually throughout the New Testament period.

Two considerations, one historical and the other doctrinal, confirm the historical reconstruction presented above.

In 1 Corinthians xi. 20–34, and in the narrative of 1 Corinthians xi. 23–5 in particular, St. Paul implies that he is handing on valid tradition, 'that which I received', and that he is recalling what he had taught to the Corinthian Church, 'I delivered unto you'. At the same time it is equally plain that he is imparting teaching which is new, when he declares that the cup of blessing is 'a communion of the blood of Christ', and the broken bread 'a communion of the body of Christ' (1 Corinthians x. 16). We cannot infer from the narrative that the Corinthians had received a tradition resembling that found in Luke xxii. 14–18. On the contrary, the implication of St. Paul's words is that the tradition which he had imparted to them, and which he repeats in 1 Corinthians xi. 23–5, was substantially like that of Mark xiv. 22–5. It was a story in which Jesus said of the bread: 'This is my body, which is for you', and of the cup: 'This cup is the new covenant in my blood.' Nevertheless, it is clear that the Corinthians had not really understood this teaching, and that St. Paul felt it necessary to give them further instructions. The evil of eating unworthily (1 Corinthians xi. 27) hardly seems to have occurred to them. If these inferences are justified, we actually possess in the case of the Corinthian Church a definite example of the failure of a community to appreciate the meaning of the Supper, and of an Apostolic attempt to give a truer interpretation of its significance. The suggestion, therefore, that other communities may have followed partial and imperfect traditions, is reasonable enough.

Whatever the character of the tradition they knew may have been, instruction and experience, covering an appreciable period of time, were needed before the intention of Jesus could be intelligently apprehended.

The second consideration is doctrinal. Our investigation has shown that the failure to perceive the importance of the Eucharist in relation to the death of Christ was not an isolated phenomenon; it was accompanied by a want of emphasis upon the faith-relationship of the believer to Christ as Redeemer and Saviour, and, in some cases, by a feeble perception of the relation of the resurrection to the work of Christ upon the Cross. These deficiencies of primitive belief go together; the records which disclose one reveal two, or even more. Acts knows nothing of eucharistic communion; it also knows nothing of faith-union with the Saviour, unless we are to find it in the words of St. Paul and Silas to the Philippian jailor: 'Believe on the Lord Jesus, and thou shalt be saved' (Acts xvi. 31). The Apocalypse knows a Living Christ, but does not mention the Eucharist or faith in the Crucified. 1 Peter nowhere relates the resurrection to the Cross, does not refer to the Eucharist, and describes faith as faith in God rather than in Christ. These facts are not recalled to the disparagement of the primitive Christian communities, but as evidence of forms of early belief which were not integrated, but which existed in the inchoate form they might be expected to assume.

It is difficult to believe that the deficiencies to which we have referred were merely synchronous and without inner connexion. The inference is strongly suggested that the relationship between them was *causal*. It was because in the first communities many Christians had not yet perceived that the death, resurrection, and session on high were indissoluble elements in Christ's work of sacrifice and atonement that they were strangers to the thought of faith-union with Him; and it was because, while believing in Christ, they knew so little of faith-union, that their communion-meals remained almost exclusively eschatological in character. If these are valid inferences, the silence of the New Testament regarding the Eucharist in so many of its writings is eloquent indeed; but it is eloquent, not of the secondary importance of the rite, but of the significant fact that the Eucharist is seen in the fulness of its meaning only as richer conceptions of the work of the Living Christ are attained, and only as faith-union with Him is a deep and dominating experience.

We may conclude, therefore, that St. Paul's handling of the situation as it existed at Corinth, and the nature of primitive Christian belief and experience, validate our account of the way in which the meaning of the Last Supper came to be appreciated in the Church. The process is not one of accretion, but of gradual integration, as the original intention of Jesus fulfilled itself in Christian experience and history.

One question still remains to be considered. Why does St. Paul not refer more frequently to the Eucharist in his Epistles? In point of fact, his contribution to this theme is greater in extent than is often recognized, since it includes, not only the narrative of 1 Corinthians xi. 23–5, but the whole of 1 Corinthians x. 14–22 and xi. 17–34. Nevertheless, it cannot be compared in range with his teaching concerning the Living Christ and faith-union with Him. The former is everywhere the presupposition of his arguments and appeals; and for every reference to the Supper he has a score or more to faith-union with the Redeemer. The answer to the question can only be that the order in which he thought of these vital experiences of the Christian life was: knowledge of the Living Christ, faith-union with Him, and sacramental communion with His Body and Blood. This is the order which corresponded with his personal experience, as it has represented the experience of countless Christian men and women in the centuries which have followed. The order is that of attainment, and because St. Paul is the practical missionary-preacher he emphasizes what he believes to be fundamental and determinative. We cannot, however, infer from the relative infrequency of his references to the Eucharist that he thought it of minor importance; on the contrary, his words in 1 Corinthians x and xi show that he held it in the highest esteem. We may therefore believe, even though we cannot support the opinion by his words, that he would also have recognized the validity of the experience of those who, by the avenue of sacramental communion, come to know more perfectly the reality of faith-union with Christ, and so enter more deeply into saving fellowship with the Living Lord who gave Himself in redemptive love for men. The vital factors are the knowledge of Christ and living faith in Him.[1]

[1] In addition to the works mentioned on p. 29, the following treat the question of the place of the Eucharist in primitive Christianity: A. Arnold, *Der Ursprung des christlichen Abendmahls* (1937); the three important articles of E. Lohmeyer, 'Von urchristlichen Abendmahl' in the *Theologische Rundschau* (1937), pp. 168–94, 195–227, 273–312; F. L. Cirlot, *The Early Eucharist* (1939).

PART THREE

THE DOCTRINE OF THE ATONEMENT IN THE LIGHT OF THE NEW TESTAMENT

INTRODUCTION

THE purpose of Part III is to provide for the New Testament as a whole the kind of Summary which has been attempted in each of the three sections of Part II in respect of the teaching of St. Paul, the author of the Epistle to the Hebrews, and St. John. The best method of procedure will be to consider, first, the immediate inferences which may be drawn from the New Testament evidence, and secondly, the more ultimate problems which are involved and the theory of the Atonement most in harmony with its witness.

I. THE IMMEDIATE IMPLICATIONS OF NEW TESTAMENT TEACHING

To a considerable extent, although not entirely, it is possible to separate the immediate inferences which may be drawn from the teaching of the New Testament with reference to the Atonement, and it is undoubtedly a great gain for the study of the more ultimate problems and the formulation of doctrine if this task can be accomplished. From our earlier discussions it is clear from the outset that these inferences will be connected with the nature of the Atonement, the relationship of God thereto, the work of Christ, and man's appropriation of the blessings of Christ's atoning ministry, or, alternatively expressed, his entrance upon the life of abiding fellowship with God.

(a) The Nature of the Atonement

The teaching of the New Testament clearly implies that the Atonement is a work of God upon the greatest and grandest scale; it is nothing less than the doctrine of how man, feeble in his purpose and separated from God by his sins, can be brought into a relationship of true and abiding fellowship with Him, and thus can be enabled to fulfil his divine destiny, both as an individual, and as a member of the community to which he belongs. From beginning to end it is a doctrine of reconciliation and of fulfilment, which concerns not only man as an individual but the world itself in all its corporate relationships. It is natural, and inevitable, that the New Testament should be supremely concerned with this work as it is related to the moral and spiritual needs of individuals, but its scope is unduly narrowed and injuriously affected if this wider reference is lost. Man is redeemed in order that he may know the power of the Kingdom of God in his inner life and in all his complex relationships with men. Such is the impressive witness of the New Testament. Indeed, in the thought of St. Paul reconciliation extends to the universe itself, for in the Epistle to the Colossians he declares that it was the good pleasure of God, through Christ, to reconcile all things unto Himself 'whether things upon the earth, or things in the heavens' (i. 19 f.), and in the Epistle to the Romans he speaks of the hope 'that the creation itself also shall be delivered from the bondage of corruption into the liberty of the glory of the children of God' (viii. 21). Whenever Christian teaching narrows the idea of the Atonement to a prospect less dazzling than this, it is untrue to the New Testament. The Atonement is the reconciliation of man and of the world to God.

The scope of the New Testament teaching as it relates to the needs of man is both negative and positive; the Atonement concerns his sins and his blessedness; it is both deliverance and attainment because it cannot be the one without being the other. Directly or indirectly, and more often directly than indirectly, every part of its teaching treats the problem of sin. The reason is that, as a state in which man finds himself and as a principle determining his actions, sin stands in the way of his blessedness, not only making fellowship with God impossible, but also darkening his very awareness of God and thwarting the spiritual possibilities of his being. It is natural that the work of Christ in relation to sin should receive ever-increasing attention in the later stages of New Testament thought, and especially in the writings of its greatest teachers, since the redemptive power of the Cross, as it is seen and known, reveals the evil of sin in its darkest outlines. From the beginning, however, the connexion of the death of Christ with sin is implicit in its teaching, in the saying of Jesus concerning His covenant-blood (Mark xiv. 24), and in the new emphasis of the earliest preaching upon the forgiveness of sins (Acts ii. 38, iii. 19, 26, xiii. 38 f.), whilst the phrase 'Christ died for our sins' speedily becomes a primitive Christian formula. How deeply rooted in New Testament belief is the idea of the Atone-

ment as salvation from sin, has been shown by our study of the
common faith of the Church as it is reflected in 1 Peter, the
Apocalypse, and the Pastoral Epistles, and by our investigation
of the distinctive teaching of St. Paul, the author of the Epistle
to the Hebrews, and St. John.

Not always appreciated to the same extent, at least in the
variety of its expression, is the primitive conviction that the
Atonement is a work of God directed to the highest moral and
spiritual ends. From the sayings which have come down to us in
the Gospel tradition we can infer this connexion in the mind of
Jesus, in His constant pre-occupation with the thought of the
Rule of God and in His belief that by His death He would establish a new covenant-relationship of men with God. The Acts
also speaks of the gift of 'seasons of refreshing from the presence of
the Lord' (iii. 19) and of believers as the sons of God's ancient
covenant (iii. 25). In 1 Peter it is explicitly asserted that Christ
died 'that he might bring us to God' (iii. 18) and that He bore our
sins that we 'might live unto righteousness' (ii. 24); in the
Apocalypse the seer exults in the fact that by the blood of Christ
a kingdom is established and priests who already 'reign upon the
earth' (v. 10); in the Pastorals the purpose of the self-giving of
Jesus is not only that He may redeem us from all iniquity, but
also that He may purify unto Himself 'a people for his own possession, zealous of good works' (Titus ii. 14), while the prospect
opened out by the appearance of 'the kindness of God our Saviour'
is that 'we might be made heirs according to the hope of eternal
life' (Titus iii. 4–7). It is not possible here to repeat in detail the
wealth of St. Paul's teaching concerning the ethical and spiritual
purposes fulfilled in the death of Christ, or to dwell at greater
length upon that gift of life which is so distinctively emphasized
in the teaching of the Fourth Evangelist. Even in the Epistle to
the Hebrews, where the main emphasis lies upon the thought of
deliverance from sin, among the results traced to Christ's Sacrifice
are freedom from the fear of death (ii. 15), the service of the living
God (ix. 14), and, above all, the mediation of a new covenant
(vii. 22, viii. 6, ix. 15, xii. 24). From a purely general knowledge
of New Testament teaching it ought to be difficult to miss this
almost universal interest in the positive aspects of the Atonement,
but careful and prolonged study of its pages brings it home to the
mind to an overwhelming degree. Reconciliation, peace, fellowship with God, ethical and religious fruits of every kind, are themes

integral to the statement of the doctrine. If in later theological reconstructions the sense of this positive interest is sometimes lost, it is restored abundantly whenever we return to the fountain of New Testament teaching.

Perhaps the most comprehensive phrase in which we can express this positive aspect of the Atonement is fellowship with God, provided we remember that the New Testament knows nothing of a fellowship with God which fails to find outward expression in the practical life, in common duties and relationships, in the contacts of family and social life. So controlling is this idea of fellowship with God in all that concerns the Atonement that the meaning of sin is determined by it. Sin is that which makes fellowship impossible; and if so much of New Testament teaching is concerned with sin, this pre-occupation is due to the fact that only by annulling sin, destroying its roots, and removing its stain, can communion with God be attained and perfected. 'Christ died for our sins' does not, as a confession, mean that His work begins and ends with sin; it is a negative way of declaring what is also expressed positively in New Testament teaching, namely, that He died to 'bring us to God' (1 Peter iii. 18). The determinative conception is the intention that we should 'know God and enjoy Him for ever'.

A further pronounced element in the teaching of the New Testament is its emphasis upon the universality of the Atonement; both its deliverance and its blessings are for all men. Here again it is entirely natural that this truth should be emphasized by the great New Testament teachers and should find expression in the later rather than the earlier records of the common faith of the Church. The absence of a direct statement in the sayings of Jesus that the Son of Man would die for all mankind, and the declaration that He came to give Himself a ransom 'for many' (Mark x. 45), do not mean that the universality of the Atonement was a later addition to the primitive Christian creed; on the contrary, this belief was implicit from the first. Only as the Gentile Mission developed was any problem raised, and here the problem was not whether Gentiles might enter into covenant-relationships with God, but whether their entrance must be through the gate of circumcision. In the mind of St. Paul the universality of redemption is assumed; indeed, it is for him a conspicuous achievement of the work of Christ that He reconciles both Jew and Gentile 'in one body unto God through the cross', that 'through him we both have our access in one Spirit unto the Father' (Ephesians ii. 13–22). In Hebrews, with a definiteness which leaves nothing to be desired, it is asserted that by the suffering of death Christ was crowned with glory and honour, 'that by the grace of God he should taste death for every man' (ii. 9). In the Johannine Writings, as we have seen, this same truth is expressed repeatedly, especially in John iii. 16, iv. 42, vi. 51, xi. 52, xii. 32 and in 1 John ii. 2 and iv. 14.

While the New Testament teaches that all men may be reconciled to God, it is no less insistent that men should be reconciled one to another. Its testimony is that 'God is not a God of confusion, but of peace' (1 Corinthians xiv. 33), and its protest is unremitting against faction[1] and strife.[2] War, oppression, and injustice are so alien to its spirit that the Atonement cannot be said to be fully consummated until the decisive victory of the Cross over the powers of evil is extended to all the fierce ravages of a beaten foe, and God is all in all. No world vision less than this can satisfy the statements and implications of New Testament teaching, and it is no wonder that so often this hope has been the inspiration of Christian poets and hymn-writers. Yet here, as always, the New Testament never loses the practical in the speculative, the individual in the process. Without for a moment relaxing its insistence upon the uniqueness and finality of the work of Christ, it calls men to the fellowship of His sufferings, to cross-bearing, and the drinking of the cup, in order that the Rule of God may be established in the earth. Such is the nature of the Atonement, the dream in which all dreams are included, but founded as many dreams are not, on the deed of God in Christ.

(b) The Relationship of God to the Atonement

The testimony of the New Testament to the belief that the Atonement is the realization of the purpose of God is as full as it is conclusive. He wills the reconciliation of men to Himself, makes it possible, and consummates it in Christ. Such is the teaching of Jesus,[3] the witness of the earliest preaching, the affirmation of the greatest of the New Testament teachers. Jesus goes to His Cross confident that He is doing the will of His Father. 'Not what I

---

[1] Romans ii. 8; 2 Corinthians xii. 20; Galatians v. 20; Philippians, i. 17, ii. 3; James iii. 14, 16.

[2] Romans i. 29, xiii. 13; 1 Corinthians i. 11, iii. 3; 2 Corinthians xii. 20; Galatians v. 20; Philippians i. 15; 1 Timothy vi. 4; Titus iii. 9.

[3] Cf. *Jesus and His Sacrifice*, pp. 255 f.

will, but what thou wilt' is His prayer in Gethsemane after His request for the removal of the cup of suffering (Mark xiv. 36), and if on the cross He endures desolation (Mark xv. 34), He commends His spirit to the Father's keeping in perfect obedience and trust (Luke xxiii. 46). In all the writings we have examined, with fainter echoes in 1 Peter, the Apocalypse and the Pastoral Epistles, and silence only in the few Epistles which do not mention the death of Christ, this note is clearly sounded, especially by St. Paul, the writer of Hebrews, and St. John.[1] In the belief of St. Paul, God sent His Son to condemn sin in the flesh (Romans viii. 3); in the theology of Hebrews, it is by the grace of God that Christ tastes death for every man (Hebrews ii. 9); in the teaching of St. John, the proof of the love of God is that He sent His Son to be the expiation for our sins (1 John iv. 10). This truth of the undying purpose of God to redeem men and reconcile them to Himself is the foundation principle of the doctrine of the Atonement, the touchstone by which erroneous theories are revealed, the heart of the preacher's message, and the religious basis for Christian worship and devotion.

Equally fundamental is the New Testament teaching that the death of Christ is the revelation and expression of the love of God. We have seen that the passages in which this truth is decisively stated, Romans v. 8, Hebrews ii. 9, John iii. 16, 1 John iv. 10, are comparatively few in number; but apart altogether from the many passages in which the grace of God is associated with the gift of Christ,[2] and in spite of the want of statements which connect the divine love with the death of Christ in the sayings of Jesus and the records of primitive preaching, the idea is a fundamental assumption of the New Testament. The Atonement is the purpose of God and the proof of His great love. No inferences are more certain than these, even if it is also clear that to limit ourselves to them, and to fail to do justice to other elements in its witness, is to be wanting in loyalty to much of its most distinctive teaching.

In considering the history of the doctrine one cannot but see how many unsatisfactory and unethical theories we might have been spared if the New Testament emphasis upon the Atonement as the work of God and the sign-manual of His love had been fully appreciated. How can it be said that Christ, the merciful Son, was punished by the Father, that He died as man's substi-

[1] See earlier, pp. 57, 75 f., 103, 136, 143.   [2] See earlier, p. 72.

tute, or offered compensation to God for sin, if in all that He does for man, God is the moving cause of redemption and in it gives free course to His love? These views are either unethical or opposed to the unity of the Godhead. Perhaps every theory of the Atonement, except those which are purely immanental, is exposed to the danger of *appearing* to divide the Godhead, since the work of God in Christ is wrought in time upon the plane of history; but we need not, and in the light of New Testament teaching ought not, to add to the speculative problem ethical difficulties which the teaching of Scripture clearly excludes. In our investigation we have seen how closely the doctrine of the Incarnation is connected with that of the Atonement, both as regards the ministry of Christ for man and the work of God in Him. Nothing less than the Catholic doctrine of Christ's Person is the necessary foundation for the message of the Cross.

(c) The Work of Christ for Men

Our study of New Testament teaching has shown that the work of Christ for men is regarded as vicarious, as representative, and as sacrificial. Each of these aspects must be considered separately.

(1) *As Vicarious.* On this point there is not even room for doubt. Almost every strand of New Testament evidence reveals the existence of the primitive belief that Christ died 'for us' or 'on our behalf'. Our inquiry, however, has also shown that this confession does not always mean the same thing. Can we, for example say that 'Christ died for us' has precisely the same meaning for St. Paul, the writer of Hebrews, and St. John? There is, of course, a common element in the affirmations of all these teachers, but the tone of each is sensibly affected by the degree to which they find a representative function in the ministry of Christ and the extent to which they think of the death of Christ in sacrificial terms. When we read the words: 'The good shepherd layeth down his life *for the sheep*', we tend to think of them in the light of the common faith of the Church; but when we read them against the background of the Evangelist's view of the death of Christ as His glorifying and exaltation, we see that they cannot have the same meaning, and I would add, the same depth of meaning, as when St. Paul exults in the love of the Son of God who, he says, 'gave himself up *for me*'. Nor indeed can the Johannine endorsement of the belief that 'Christ died for us' have the meaning which it bears when the writer of Hebrews speaks of the entrance of Christ

into heaven itself, 'now to appear before the face of God *for us*'. We may even claim that this confession as it appears in the Fourth Gospel falls short of the significance which it has in the Epistle, when St. John declares: 'Hereby know we love, because he laid down his life *for us*'. In short, to say that Christ died for us is to use a symbol or mould into which we pour all the meaning we have found in the suffering and death of Christ. Who could claim that the advocate of the Moral Influence Theory, the adherent of the doctrine of Penal Substitution, and the exponent of the Sacrificial Theory express the same truth when they use the same words? We must therefore conclude that, while we truly represent the teaching of the New Testament when we think of the death of Christ as vicarious, we are allowing ourselves to be content with an ambiguous expression if we do not go further and seek to understand more fully all that it affirms. We have still to face the question: *In what sense* did Christ die *for us*?

(2) *As Representative*. New Testament teaching upon this theme cannot justly be regarded as other than impressive. It begins with the teaching of Jesus Himself, for when He reinterpreted the idea of the Son of Man in terms of the doctrine of the Suffering Servant, and used the Messianic title of Himself in the Passion-sayings, He implied that His ministry for men has a representative aspect.[1] No kind of justice, I would claim, can be done to His words: 'The Son of man came . . . to give himself a ransom for many', unless in some positive sense they are held to mean that, in dying, He represents the many; and the same inference is also valid for His description of His blood as 'blood of the covenant'. With few signs of dependence on Pauline teaching the idea of representative action is implied by the reference to 'sin-bearing' in 1 Peter ii. 24 (cf. iii. 18)[2] and the description of Christ as the 'mediator between God and men' in 1 Timothy ii. 5,[3] while in St. Paul's Epistles[4] it is unmistakable in Romans v. 18, 19, vi. 10 *f.*, 2 Corinthians v. 14, 21, Galatians iii. 13. To cite a single example, the least that can be said of the statement that He was made 'sin on our behalf' (2 Corinthians v. 21) is that He suffered in the name of men. In Hebrews,[5] as we have seen, the idea is fundamental to the writer's theology, as the numerous references to Christ as our 'high priest', and as the 'surety' and 'mediator' of a new covenant, conclusively prove; and, while it is not distinctive of the theology

---

[1] Cf. *Jesus and His Sacrifice*, pp. 281–5.   [2] Pp. 28 *f.*

[3] P. 45 *f.*   [4] Pp. 84–92.   [5] Pp. 119 *f.*

of the Fourth Evangelist, it is implicit in John i. 29, 36, xi. 50–2, and strikingly presented in the Epistle in the claim that He is our Advocate with the Father and is Himself the Expiation for the sin of the world (ii. 1 f.; cf. iv. 10).

As in the case of the vicarious aspect of Christ's death, although by no means to the same extent, the representative character of His ministry can be variously interpreted, and its closer definition is a question for further consideration; but that, in some reputable sense of the word, Christ represents men in the eyes of His Father, is undeniably the teaching of the New Testament. This teaching is not merely the testimony of a few isolated 'proof-texts'; it is the thought of Jesus Himself, the faith of the primitive Church, and with differing degrees of emphasis the belief of St. Paul, the writer of Hebrews, and St. John. So much is this true that, unless this idea finds a place in our theology, we are out of line with New Testament teaching.

Can the idea of Christ's representative ministry be more closely interpreted? In the first place, it may be described as a representative act of obedience. St. Paul, in Romans v. 18, contrasts the 'one trespass' of Adam with the 'one act of righteousness' of Christ, and in the following verse refers to 'the obedience of the one' through which 'the many' shall be constituted righteous. Obedience also is seen to be a distinctive characteristic of Christ's work in the statement of Hebrews v. 8, that He 'learned obedience by the things which he suffered', and in the saying of Mark xiv. 36: 'Not what I will, but what thou wilt.' Secondly, it is an act of submission to the judgment of God, a voluntary endurance of the consequences of human sin. This idea is present, as we have seen, in 1 Peter, when it is said that Christ 'bore our sins in his body' (ii. 24; cf. Hebrews ix. 28) and that He 'suffered for sins once, the righteous for the unrighteous' (iii. 18). In the Pauline Epistles, it is implied when it is said Christ 'gave himself for our sins' (Galatians i. 4) or 'was delivered up for our trespasses' (Romans iv. 25), that 'one died for all' (2 Corinthians v. 14), was 'made sin on our behalf' (2 Corinthians v. 21), and became 'a curse for us' (Galatians iii. 13). The idea is also implicit in the Pastorals in the statement that He 'gave himself a ransom for all' (1 Timothy ii. 5), and in Hebrews ii. 17 and 1 John ii. 1 f, and iv. 10. Theology has not been mistaken in finding this kind of suffering in the Gospel Story, in the account of the Agony (Mark xiv. 32–42) and in the cry of desolation upon the Cross (Mark xv. 34) for the opinion that these incidents are doctrinally coloured legends is an unsupported assumption.

From the evidence cited above it is clear that Christ's ministry for men was one of obedience to the Father's will and of self-identification with sinners. The witness of the New Testament is that in perfect obedience to the Father's will He bore upon His heart the burden of human sin. The representative character of this experience appears not only in the manner in which it is described, but also in the fact that it was *His* experience as the Christ, the Son of Man, the high priest and mediator of the new covenant with God. His Person gives a unique character to His work, since He fulfils this obedience and endures this suffering, not as an individual within the race, but as the Incarnate Son of God. M'Leod Campbell describes the representative ministry of Christ as 'a perfect confession of our sins', and R. C. Moberly as 'the sacrifice of supreme penitence'. These descriptions have no direct support in New Testament teaching, but depend for their justification on the view that the work of Christ was sacrificial as well as representative. If His ministry has this nature these further descriptions of its representative character are permissible, provided they are not otherwise open to objection, but as doctrinal inferences, not as explicit New Testament teaching.

The fact that Christ's work is that of a representative has been shown to be the teaching of the New Testament, but in none of the passages we have examined is it described as that of a substitute. His obedience is not rendered instead of ours, and our punishment is not transferred to Him. Nowhere have we found any support for such views. We must therefore conclude that the representative ministry of Christ cannot be explained by legal categories, but is fully ethical and completely religious. In this fact a problem of an ultimate kind is raised which it is the task of the theologian to consider, but which cannot usefully be treated except in the light of the New Testament teaching as a whole. One reason why it has so often proved intractable is that very frequently it has been faced almost exclusively in the light of the New Testament evidence assembled in the present section. This evidence is indispensable to a true solution, but there are other aspects of the death of Christ which must be considered if we are to see its representative character in proper perspective. Of these one of the most important is its sacrificial significance, to which we now turn.

(3) *As Sacrificial.* In view of our investigation in Parts I and II it is difficult to understand the opinion that the sacrificial character of Christ's death is a matter of secondary importance, for in every field of the inquiry, in the sayings of Jesus, the Acts,[1] 1 Peter, the Apocalypse, the Pastoral Epistles, the correspondence of St. Paul, and the Johannine Writings, sacrificial terms and ideas are found on a wide scale. In fact, as the Tables previously given show, the sacrificial aspect of the Atonement is one of the most widely attested ideas in New Testament teaching. The 'blood'[2] of Christ is mentioned nearly three times as often as 'the Cross',[3] and five times as frequently as 'the death' of Christ.[4] Especially notable in 1 Peter (cf. i. 2, 18 *f.*, ii. 24) and the Apocalypse,[5] and important in the Pastoral Epistles (cf. 1 Timothy ii. 5 *f.*; Titus ii. 14), this sacrificial interest pervades the Pauline Epistles,[6] assumes the most remarkable proportions in the Epistle to the Hebrews,[7] and is present also in the Fourth Gospel and to a more marked degree in 1 John.[8] The theological importance of this interest must be considered in the next chapter; and for the present it is enough to observe its characteristic features. (1) In the first place, the extent to which sacrificial ideas are present varies in the New Testament writings and is affected by other theological interests. (2) Only a limited use is made of analogies based on the various Old Testament sacrifices. The covenant-sacrifices are in mind in the sayings of Mark xiv. 24 and 1 Corinthians xi. 25, and in the theology of the Epistle to the Hebrews, the Passover in the Synoptic accounts of the Passion, in 1 Corinthians v. 7, and John xix. 36, the sin-offering in Hebrews xiii. 11 *f.*, if not in Romans viii. 3; but none of these is adopted as the New Testament analogue *par excellence* to the death of Christ, while a use is made of ideas which, strictly speaking, take us outside the sacrificial system in parallels in John i. 29 and 1 John iii. 5 to the thought of the scapegoat. (3) Apart from specific references to the Old Testament sacrifices, the influence of sacrificial ideas is also to be seen in the use of the ideas of 'cleansing', 'washing', 'redeeming', and 'expiation'. (4) A significant use is made of the idea of the Suffering Servant, a conception which in Isaiah

---

[1] In the Acts, however, only in the striking passage, xx. 28: 'the church of God, which he rescued by the blood of his Own' (Lake).

[2] The distribution is as follows: Matthew (1); Mark (1); John (4), cf. xix. 34; Acts (1); Pauline Epistles (8); Hebrews (6); 1 Peter (2); 1 John (3); Apocalypse (4).

[3] Pauline Epistles (10); Hebrews (1).   [4] Pauline Epistles (6).

[5] Pp. 36 *ff.*   [6] Pp. 63 *ff.*   [7] Pp. 120 *ff.*   [8] Pp. 148 *ff.*

M

liii. 10 is associated with the sin-offering, and is sacrificial in its origins and expression. Profoundly influential for the thought and teaching of Jesus Himself, it is echoed in the primitive preaching as described by the Acts, colours the language and teaching of 1 Peter, the Apocalypse and to a limited extent the Pauline Epistles, but as a controlling influence is almost spent in the Epistles to the Hebrews and the Johannine Writings. (5) The Eucharist, in the sayings of Jesus and the teaching of St. Paul, has marked sacrificial associations, but in the Fourth Gospel is more directly related to the experience of faith-union with Christ.

The foregoing summary obviously raises the most difficult questions, and all the more because the problem for discussion is not merely the meaning of the several points mentioned, but also their mutual relationships and their importance as a whole. The alternatives we shall need to consider are (1) whether the use of sacrificial terms and ideas in the New Testament is simply a matter of language and expression, or (2) whether the death of Christ is to be regarded as essentially sacrificial in its significance. Stated in this way, the two alternatives seem sharply separated. It may be doubted, however, whether the difference is radical, unless the former is interpreted as a matter of verbal usages and nothing more. The more reputable form of this alternative would compel us to ask what are the religious *values* which the terminology expresses; and if we face this question, it may well be that the answer is not very different from that which is implied in the claim that the foundation principle of the doctrine of the Atonement, as it appears in New Testament teaching, is sacrificial in character. Everything depends, of course, upon what we mean by the word 'sacrificial'. The whole problem calls for further discussion in the following chapter among the ultimate issues raised by the doctrine of the Atonement. Meantime, we may reasonably conclude that, like the vicarious and representative aspects of the work of Christ, its sacrificial character is a most important element in New Testament teaching, and that full account of its bearings must be taken in the formulation of doctrine.

Before closing this section, two further considerations must be mentioned. (1) Each of the three aspects of the work of Christ noted above has been treated separately, but it is clear that they are interrelated and must ultimately be considered as a whole. The history of the doctrine shows how unsatisfactory it is to isolate the vicarious, the representative, and the sacrificial aspects of the

THE LIGHT OF THE NEW TESTAMENT 179

work of Christ. The content of the word 'vicarious', as it is applied to the ministry of Christ, is determined by the sense in which His death is representative, and there is good reason to suppose that its representative character is closely connected with its sacrificial significance. These are points for further inquiry, but already it is clear that, however helpful it may be for purposes of exposition to separate these elements, a point is reached when it is necessary to study them in combination one with another. (2) A further matter of the greatest importance is that, even when the suggestion just made is carried out, a still more vital process of articulation is necessary. Our investigations have abundantly shown how intimately the appropriation of the work of Christ by the believer is related to the understanding of the doctrine of the Atonement. For purposes of thought it is most useful to isolate Christ's deed and man's response, but in practice without both there is no 'at-one-ment' and, in consequence, no satisfactory statement of the doctrine. Many popular objections to the Atonement are due to this fatal separation between the deed and the response. The deed is seen in itself, apart from the response it is intended to sustain, with the result that it is viewed as the work of a substitute and as a 'transaction' accomplished on man's behalf. So powerful in their effect are these objections that, although the theories of the Atonement on which they rest belong to the past, theological reconstruction is impeded by them to this day. What is required is a category of representative action which, far from suggesting a purely external work of Christ passively accepted, includes within itself both a transcendent deed of Christ on which redemption rests, and, at the same time, a human response so intimately related to it that, with no claim to personal merit, man can find true reconciliation with God.

(d) Man's Appropriation of the Blessings of Christ's Work

The wealth of New Testament teaching upon this theme has already been fully described,[1] and all that is necessary at this stage is to summarize the facts of its distribution and variety of expression. As in the case of other truths associated with the Atonement, it ought not to surprise us that faith-union with Christ, sacramental communion, and suffering with the Crucified, are more fully emphasized by some New Testament teachers than by

[1] See pp. 92-7, 152-5.

others and in the later rather than the earlier stages of New Testament revelation. The actual appropriation of the blessings of Christ's atoning ministry must necessarily precede forceful and intelligible teaching upon these themes. It is natural, therefore, that in the earliest preaching faith should be regarded as belief, or confident reliance upon the truth of the Apostolic message, and that in the hands of St. Paul its richer character as union with the Living Lord should receive powerful expression. Time, however, and even the virility of the Christian experience, are not the only factors which lead to fuller teaching. Our study of the Epistle to the Hebrews shows how dependent the apprehension of the possibilities of faith-union is upon the recognition of the amazing love of God for sinners, and the interpretation of the love of Christ as a love which shares in the consequences of sin. The Fourth Gospel also, so rich in its teaching concerning 'abiding' and 'being' in Christ, illustrates the manner in which this relationship is coloured by the interpretation given to Christ's death. No more instructive example, indeed, can be found of the bearing of theology upon the form and description of the Christian experience. Just for this reason opinions will always differ upon the question of the relative merits of the Johannine and the Pauline teaching about union with Christ; and, only as a personal estimate can the present writer claim that the Pauline account is the profounder teaching because it rests upon a deeper and more penetrating analysis of the meaning of the death of Christ. Including the experience of communion with the Living and Exalted Lord, it extends the range of this fellowship so that it embraces His sufferings, involving a baptism and dying with Him which call to mind the words of Jesus about the cup and baptism in Mark x. 38 f.

The eucharistic teaching of the New Testament is similarly conditioned. Where faith is pre-eminently faith in God, as in 1 Peter, or response to the Apostolic message, as in the Acts, or fidelity to Christ and confidence in the reality of the unseen, as in Hebrews, eucharistic teaching is in abeyance; but where the idea of faith-union is prominent, as in the Fourth Gospel and the Pauline Epistles, this teaching is explicit, with an emphasis upon the idea of communion with the Living Christ and that of participation in the power of His sacrifice, according as the Incarnation or the doctrine of the Cross is the dominating theological interest. If this is a true summary of New Testament teaching, the import-

THE LIGHT OF THE NEW TESTAMENT

ance of the Eucharist in relation to the Atonement is to be recognized, not only where eucharistic teaching is present in the New Testament, but also where it is wanting, since its absence is associated with, and is probably occasioned by, limited presentations of the meaning of the death of Christ. Moreover, the close association of the Supper with His death, revealed by the sayings of Jesus in Mark xiv. 24 and 1 Corinthians xi. 25, is best explained, not as an example of later accretion, but as a striking and original element in His teaching, apprehended gradually in New Testament times and endorsed in the subsequent experience of the Church. In the Eucharist, as in personal faith and trust in Christ, we enter into the meaning of His death and appropriate the blessings of His atoning ministry. Such is the teaching of the New Testament and the witness of Christian experience.

Already in what has been said of faith-union reference has been made to the idea of suffering with Christ. Here again we cannot fail to be impressed with the variety of New Testament teaching, in which it appears both as a mystical and a practical experience, and in both cases intimately connected with the thought of His death. The words of Jesus about cross-bearing and the drinking of His cup and His command to follow Him were an imperishable legacy to the primitive Church; but it is His dying even more than His teaching which has made it a self-evident demand upon the Christian consciousness that, as He laid down His life for us, 'we ought to lay down our lives for the brethren' (1 John iii. 16). Moreover, the contemplation of His Passion has developed a type of mystical experience which does not lose itself in idle dreams, but is the constant inspiration of service and of deathless hope for the world.

The student of the New Testament is not unnaturally impressed with the variety of its teaching concerning faith-union, sacramental communion, and sacrificial living, and must of necessity have his own preferences for some aspects rather than for others. What he cannot fail to observe, with the Gospels and the Epistles open before him, is the vital connexion of this varied teaching with the suffering and death of Christ. He is compelled, therefore, to include it in his apprehension of the meaning of the Atonement. He cannot isolate the death from the appropriation of its blessings. For this reason he can never be satisfied with a doctrinal statement of the Atonement which concentrates so exclusively upon the significance of the work of Christ that teaching about man's response follows as an addendum. As we have argued at the close of the last section, a category is needed which by its very nature finds room for man's appropriation of the blessings of Christ's redemptive work. It must, in fact, be more inclusive still, since, as we have seen, the Atonement is the work of God which concerns man both as an individual and as a member of the race, and which meets his needs both as a sinner and as a potential citizen of the Realm of God. It will be argued subsequently that the category capable above all others of including all these elements and relationships is that of sacrifice.

In concluding this chapter, we may with advantage attempt to summarize both the direct implications of New Testament teaching and the more ultimate problems that are involved. Among the immediate implications we have included the following: (1) The Atonement is the work of God in restoring sinners to fellowship with Himself and establishing His Kingdom in the world; it is the reconciliation of man and of the world to God. (2) It is the fulfilment of His purpose for man and the final proof of the greatness of His love, both revealing that love and expressing it for time and eternity. (3) The Atonement is accomplished in the work of Christ, whose suffering is vicarious, representative, and sacrificial in character; it is on behalf of men, in their name, and for the purpose of their approach to God. (4) The vicarious nature of Christ's ministry is one of the clearest elements in New Testament teaching, but its true content can be discerned only as its representative and sacrificial aspects are more closely defined. (5) The representative character of His death is disclosed by the fact that, in the greatness of His love for men, He identified Himself with sinners and in their service was completely obedient to the will of the Father, entering into and enduring in His own person the consequences of sin and the rejection and gainsaying of men. (6) The sacrificial significance of His death is suggested by the frequent use of the term 'blood', by a limited use of analogies found in the ancient sacrificial system, by references to cleansing, redemption, and expiation, by allusions to the idea of the Suffering Servant, and by eucharistic teaching sacrificial in character. (7) The Atonement is consummated in the experience of men through faith-union with Christ, through sacramental communion with Him, and in sacrificial living and suffering.

No theory of the Atonement is presented in the New Testament, but the material upon which theories are based is present in great abundance. The outlines of various theories are present in the teaching of St. Paul, the writer of Hebrews, and St. John, but by none of these writers is the theology of the Atonement presented in its fulness, while their combined witness has presented to the Church a living body of truth which in the subsequent history of the doctrine has too often been grasped in part rather than assimilated as a whole. The difficulty of theological construction is the magnitude of the problem which is such that the best efforts of theologians and teachers must always prove inadequate and incomplete. It is also due to the fact that New Testament teaching exposes a vista of unsolved ultimate problems, which happily do not foreclose ventures of reasoned faith, but by their nature admit only of tentative and provisional solutions.

Among these ultimate problems the following may be noted. (1) First, there is the difficulty of apprehending how the Atonement as the purpose of God is fulfilled in the work of Christ, without accepting an immanental view of His Person, which is less than the witness of the New Testament, and without dividing the unity of the Godhead by setting the representative ministry of the Son over against the love, justice, and mercy of God. (2) A second problem is that of relating the death of Christ, as a fact of history, to an eternal reconciling purpose of God related to the needs of men at all times, in all ages, and in all circumstances. (3) A third question, raised by New Testament teaching, concerns the representative ministry of Christ, which if it is to be the basis of man's approach to God must be more than an act of obedience and of submission to the divine judgment upon sin, and yet is not described with greater fulness in the Gospels and the Epistles. (4) Lastly, the sacrificial allusions must either be explained as of merely verbal, and therefore of secondary, importance, or must be regarded as indicating the need of a sacrificial category in which room can be found for the reconciling purpose of God, the representative ministry of Christ, and the approach and return of sinners. This alternative, as well as the third question noted above, compels us to ask how far we are justified in going beyond what is directly taught in Scripture, and whether the answers offered give practical expression to its witness and a sufficient basis for the needs of worship, of the devotional life, and the service of the Kingdom of God.

2. ULTIMATE PROBLEMS AND THE DOCTRINE OF THE ATONEMENT

Now that we have examined the beliefs of the primitive Christian communities, the teaching of St. Paul, the author of the Epistle to the Hebrews, and St. John, and have considered the inferences which may be drawn from the evidence of the New Testament as a whole, it is necessary in this final chapter to face the ultimate problems which are involved and to discuss their bearings upon the statement of the doctrine of the Atonement.

(a) The Representative and Sacrificial Aspects of the Work of Christ

Of the ultimate problems mentioned at the end of the preceding chapter, the representative and sacrificial aspects of the work of Christ claim attention first, because they are closely connected, and because the conclusions we reach upon these questions vitally affect our opinions on the still more ultimate issues.

One of the most conspicuous results we have gained from our investigation is the intimate manner in which one aspect of the Atonement is affected by another. The doctrine is an organic whole, one part of which cannot be neglected without serious injury to others, or understood except in relation to the whole. This fact is especially true of the representative character of the work of Christ. We have seen that His work is a ministry accomplished on our behalf, but not in our stead; it is perfected in our name, but this is true only in so far as we enter into its significance, and find it to be the means by which we approach God and in which He comes to us in the wonder of His redeeming grace. The representative nature of such a ministry, as we have seen, is unique. It cannot be embraced by legal categories, as a work of substitution or satisfaction, although in these ideas there are important truths which may be missed by a simple attitude of denial which is not followed by a constructive presentation. The category we require must be ethical and religious, and sufficiently inclusive to embrace the purpose and love of God, the distinctive work of Christ, and the appropriation by man, guided and directed by the Spirit, of all that God has accomplished in Christ on our behalf.

In the strict sense of the term there is no such category as the one described, since no general conception is sufficiently wide to include a doctrine so unique as the doctrine of the Atonement. The best category of this inclusive kind, at once ethical and religious, which excludes pretences to human merit and opens the way for God to man and man to God, is the sacrificial category, provided it is rightly understood, and provided it is freed from all unworthy and pagan associations. In order to support this claim it will be necessary to examine further the use which is made of this category in Scripture, not so much in isolated passages as in its theology as a whole.

(b) *The Sacrificial Category*

Elsewhere, in *Jesus and His Sacrifice*, I have discussed in detail the idea of sacrifice, its significance in the Old Testament cultus, the attitude of the prophets thereto, and the teaching of Jesus in relation to the sacrificial aspect of His Messianic suffering. A further consideration of these subjects in the same detail is not possible in this work, but I should like to take the opportunity of saying that further study and reflection have not suggested to me the need of altering the conclusions already reached in the earlier investigation in any important particular. It is, however, essential for our immediate purpose to describe in general terms what is meant by a sacrificial interpretation of the ministry of Jesus and of the doctrine of the Atonement. In order that it may be used for such a purpose the idea of sacrifice must be purged of all un-ethical and degrading associations, and especially of the idea of propitiating God in the pagan sense, and so of winning His favour and of causing Him to be gracious towards men. Apart from all other considerations, the fundamental character of the Atonement as the proof and expression of the love of God, imposes this necessity upon us.

Already in the Old Testament, a higher stage of religious development had been attained, apart from a few stories of a primitive character and examples of the infiltration of heathen ideas easily perceived by the careful reader. Here sacrifice is a recognized means of expiation, that is, of the covering or annulling of sins, not because God is bribed by gifts, but because the worshipper identifies himself with the purity of his offering, making it the vehicle of his approach to God. Increasingly in rabbinic teaching down to the time of Christ and in the early Christian centuries emphasis was laid on the ethical aspects of sacrifice, with a correspondingly decreased insistence upon its material accompaniments; so much so that, when the Temple worship ceased, Judaism continued to live, for ever indebted to the cultus it could no longer maintain. A similar point of view, but with a deeper apprehension of the worth of sacrificial ideas, is one that we have every right to attribute to Jesus Himself, and to the first Christians who from the Cross looked with new eyes on the faith of their fathers. If the great unknown prophet of the Exile could use sacrificial ideas in the construction of the immortal conception of the Suffering Servant, all the more might Jesus, with His matchless spiritual insight, use these ideas as the thought-moulds of His teaching concerning His Messianic suffering. There is strong evidence in the Gospels that Isaiah liii influenced His thought, but it may well be that it was independently of that Scripture that He surpassed the prophet's originality, as perhaps the allusive character of his Old Testament references indicates. His followers also, especially if His teaching about His death was of the kind we believe it to have been, could not fail to use the ideas and analogies ready to hand in the sacrificial system of their day. Unlike ourselves, they did not make use of ideas derived from books, but of the familiar religious beliefs of their time, as natural to them as the accepted ideas of to-day are to ourselves. The use therefore, both by Jesus and the first Christians, of sacrificial ideas was as natural as it was inevitable.

The very fact that this sacrificial approach was natural in New Testament times provokes the question whether it is desirable still as an aid in the presentation of the doctrine of the Atonement. This question must receive careful attention, but in order to answer it intelligently it is necessary first to examine more closely the use of this principle in the New Testament itself.

In our study of the New Testament we have noted the comparatively small extent to which the meaning of the death of Christ is assimilated to that of the sacrifices of the Levitical cultus. Suggestive allusions are made to the sin-offering, to the Passover, and most of all to the covenant-sacrifices; but even in the Epistle to the Hebrews it is not claimed outright that His death is to be explained pre-eminently as any one of these sacrifices. The nearest approach to such a claim is the statement of St. Paul: 'Our passover also hath been sacrificed, even Christ' (1 Corinthians v. 7), but no one would suppose that in these words he is making a formal and exact identification. The significant fact in the New Testament teaching is not the confronting of type and antitype, but rather the use of such expressions as 'blood', 'covenant', 'expiation', 'means of expiation', the presence of the ideas of cleansing, redeeming, sanctifying, offering, eating and drinking, participating, believing, and in close association with this literary usage, the tremendous emphasis upon a deed of Christ which is vicarious and representative, and in which all man's hopes of reconciliation and peace are centred. These facts suggest that the true significance of the sacrificial element undeniably present in New Testament teaching is to be found, not so much in the specific rites of the cultus, as in the underlying ideas of sacrifice, the idea of the drawing near of the worshipper to God in humility and contrition, the thought of an offering with which he can identify himself in penitence and faith, the conception of sharing in the cleansing power of life which has been released in death, dedicated, and presented to God. It is not simply a matter of separate ideas, but of a religious standpoint, a group of religious assumptions bearing upon the problem of the renewal of a fellowship broken by sin. In the New Testament these ideas are not deliberately selected or even consciously employed; they belong to the texture of Jewish-Christian thought and provide it with the necessary means of expression. So little is the usage deliberate that sacrificial terms, while the most frequent, are freely combined with words reminiscent of the market and the law court, without the latter exercising a dominating influence except in the Pauline teaching concerning justification and adoption. Powerful, however, as these ideas and assumptions are in shaping New Testament teaching, they do not come to the surface to such a degree as to constitute an articulated framework of thought, except in a measure in the Epistle to the Hebrews, where, nevertheless, elements essential to the frame are wanting. In the Fourth Gospel, as we have seen, the ideas are spiritualized to such a point of refinement that, while the great truths of the Incarnation find in it classical expression, important aspects of the Atonement are either but faintly delineated or are faultlessly expressed in isolated sayings, like the word of the Baptist about the Lamb of God and the matchless utterance: 'God so loved the world that he gave his only begotten Son.' Perhaps the profoundest use of sacrificial ideas is to be found in the Epistles of St. Paul, but they are less obvious in these than in other New Testament writings because they are associated with legal and even commercial ideas which strike the reader's attention, and because the Apostle has made but a limited use of the thought of the Suffering Servant, nowhere presenting his burning thoughts as a connected whole. The field, therefore, is open to the theologian to use the sacrificial category if he will. In using it, he will be compelled to go beyond the actual witness of the New Testament, as any work of theological construction must, but with this category as a frame he can incorporate its teaching concerning the Atonement, and not only the fragments which appeal to his individual taste, in a living body of truth satisfying to the mind and soul, fruitful for the devotional life, and inspirational for service and endeavour.

In making a bold use of the sacrificial category the theologian is compelled to make a statement of doctrine which, in its entirety, is not presented within the New Testament itself, and, in consequence, his results will have a definiteness strange to its pages. This fact is inevitable in all theological construction, whatever may be the category employed, and the justification and the usefulness of the sacrificial category will be shown if it finds room for a greater range of New Testament teaching and experience than any other.

The use which has been made of sacrificial ideas in the history of the doctrine hardly encourages this hope, although many important aspects of its truth have been emphasized by this method of approach. Clement of Rome, for example, bids us gaze upon the blood of Christ and recognize 'how precious it is to God His Father, because it was shed for our salvation and obtained for all the world the grace of repentance'.[1] Origen argues that 'since sin entered into this world, whilst the necessity of sin requires a propitiation, and a propitiation is not made but by a victim, it was necessary that a victim should be provided for sin'.[2] Augustine explains that Christ is Himself called sin 'from having to be sacrificed to wash away sin',[3] and Ambrose asks: 'What greater mercy was there than that He offered Himself to be sacrificed for our crimes, that He might wash with His blood the world, whose sin could be blotted out in no other way?'[4] John of Damascus also speaks of Christ offering Himself as a sacrifice to God.[5] In the Middle Ages Aquinas explains sacrifice as any-

---

[1] *1 Clem.*, vii, 4. Cf. Clement of Alexandria: 'And being about to be offered, and giving Himself as a ransom, He leaves us a new covenant: "My love I give unto you." . . . For the sake of each of us He laid down His life—worth no less than the universe,' *Quis dives salvetur*, c. 37.

[2] '*In Num.*', xxiv. 1.   [3] '*Ench.*', 41.

[4] *In Ps.* xlvii, *exp.* 17.   [5] '*Exp. Orth. Fid.*', 3, 27.

thing done towards the honour properly owed to God, to placate Him, and expounds the passion of Christ in terms of this conception,[1] quoting Ephesians v. 2. Among the Reformers Melanchthon speaks of Christ as given to us and made a sacrifice, 'that for His sake we might certainly conclude that we please the Father',[2] and, in exalting Christ's priestly office, Calvin describes Him as a priest employed to appease the wrath of God, and says: 'By the sacrifice of His death He wiped away our guilt, and made satisfaction for sin'.[3]

From these brief quotations it will be seen that, while the thought of sacrifice is freely used, it is not worked out as the foundation of a comprehensive theory, and that all too frequently it is presented as propitiatory or placatory. In large measure these two features explain each other. The accepted conceptions of sacrifice were pagan, and the want of a scientific exegesis concealed from the minds of the great theologians of the Church that the Old Testament ideas of sacrifice are mainly eucharistic and representative in character. The consequence was an unethical presentation of the idea of God, falling far beneath the standards of New Testament teaching and the foreclosure of successful attempts to supply a constructive doctrine of the Atonement, in which full justice is done to the representative ministry of Christ for men, and to the believer's appropriation of that work in his penitent approach to a reconciling God. It was necessary to show that the attitude of God had been changed by the sacrifice of Christ, with all the risks of introducing division within the Godhead, and to assert that, since His sovereign rights had been satisfied and His just demands met, men might rest in the merits of Christ secured through the sacraments and within the penitential system of the Church. Patently inadequate as a doctrine of the Cross, this misuse of sacrificial ideas not only issued in failure, but has also tended to provoke sympathy for opposite extremes of teaching, and especially for Abailardian views, in which the ethical conditions of reconciliation receive inadequate, if not superficial, attention. Only in comparatively modern times, thanks to the researches of students of comparative religion,[4] and the work of many Old Testament scholars,[5] has it been possible

---

[1] *Summa*, qu. 48, art. 3. [2] '*Loci*', p. 166.

[3] '*Instit.*', ii, 15, 6. For Luther's views, see H. Rashdall, *The Idea of Atonement*, pp. 398 *ff.*; R. S. Franks, *A History of the Doctrine of the Work of Christ*, i, 353 *ff.*

[4] W. Robertson Smith, J. G. Frazer, and many others.

[5] Notably G. Buchanan Gray, *Sacrifice in the Old Testament*, and G. F. Moore, *Encyclopædia Biblica* (article on 'Sacrifice'), iv, cols. 4183–233.

to use sacrificial ideas to better purpose, by showing that the conditions of reconciliation, grounded in the Love of God, are met through His gift in the self-offering of Christ, the medium and the vehicle by which sinners can enter into fellowship with Himself.[1]

NOTE ON THE SUFFERING SERVANT OF THE LORD

For the examination of the Servant-conception I must refer to my treatment of this subject in *Jesus and His Sacrifice*, pp. 39–48, 281. While the Servant is not represented as an offering made by the people, the entire conception seems to me to be influenced by sacrificial ideas, and would not have been possible apart from them. Thus, the idea of 'sin-bearing', closely connected with sacrificial doctrine, is integral to the representation. The Servant bears sins (Isaiah liii. 6, 12), and is spoken of in verse 10 in terms of the 'guilt-offering' ('*āshām*). However uncertain the Hebrew text may be in this verse, the idea of the 'sin-offering' (περὶ ἀμαρτίας) appears in the Septuagint, the Bible of Early Christianity. A further point of importance is that the relation of the onlookers to the Servant is just that which was characteristic of sacrificial worship at its best (cf. verses 4–6). The delineation represents a spiritualized sublimated idea of sacrifice which expresses the highest values of Hebrew religion. On the subject of the Servant, see the important articles of R. S. Cripps, 'The Prophets and the Atonement', reprinted from *The Atonement in History and Life* (S.P.C.K., 1929), and of O. Eissfeldt, 'The Ebed-Jahweh in Isaiah, 40–55', *The Expository Times*, xliv, pp. 261–8.

(c) *The Doctrine of the Atonement*

In the space at our disposal it is quite impossible to give a full treatment of the doctrine of the Atonement, but it would be most unsatisfactory to treat the New Testament evidence without indicating, even if only in outline, the kind of theory which is most in harmony with its witness. In the preceding section we have argued that the ideas which interpret its teaching best are sacrificial, but we have also recognized that there is no category, not even the sacrificial category, which is sufficiently inclusive to include all the aspects of the doctrine. The Atonement can be elucidated by human analogies, but ultimately it can be compared with nothing else; in the last resort it is *sui generis*.

In accordance with this view, it will be best not to use the sacrificial category as a fixed mould within which to present New Testament teaching, but to state broadly the doctrinal implications and to show the vital points in which they are interpreted by sacrificial ideas, since no other ideas can assist us to the same degree.

[1] In the Early Church sacrificial teaching, of course, was combined with other ideas. Athanasius, for example, emphasizes the representative character of Christ's death. Cf. J. Bethune-Baker, *Early Christian Doctrine*, pp. 346, 351 *f.*

The best New Testament word to describe the purpose of the Atonement is *Reconciliation*. It is true that this word is used only by St. Paul, but in the teaching of Jesus its essential content is expressed in the Parable of the Prodigal Son and in the idea of a New Covenant established by the death of Christ between God and men. Redemption is an important New Testament word, but is of more restricted content, since it concentrates attention more especially upon the thought of deliverance from evil and from sin, both in the present and in the future. Forgiveness, in modern usage, is almost a synonym for reconciliation, but in Scripture, I believe, its meaning is much more restricted; it signifies the annulling, or removal, of the barriers to reconciliation.[1] If this is so, reconciliation has the advantage of including in its meaning all that is covered by the words 'redemption' and 'forgiveness', and, at the same time, of emphasizing the thought of the restoration of personal relationships, which have become distorted and broken, and of their permanent security in an ever deepening fellowship between God and men. This end is the purpose of God, and, as a statement of the Gospel, it is perfectly expressed by St. Paul when he declares that, in Christ, God was reconciling the world unto Himself.

The effective barrier to reconciliation is *sin*. It is because of sin that the need for a restored fellowship exists, and only when sin is renounced and annulled is the fellowship possible. It is unnecessary to repeat the New Testament teaching upon this point, for everywhere we have found its witness to be full and undeviating. Whatever may be said of the origin of sin, its existence, both as an activity and a state, is firmly attested by conscience and by history alike. St. Paul's question: 'Who shall deliver me from the body of this death?', has in it the note of universality; it is the voice of every man when he has awakened to the truth about himself.

How serious an obstacle to reconciliation sin is, will be seen best if we consider the problem both from the side of man and from the side of God.

Sin has the most serious effect upon man's knowledge of God. Because of it he cannot know God, love Him, and serve Him with an undivided heart. Its presence in his life is the cause of his remoteness from God, his failure to apprehend His reality; and its

[1] For a fuller discussion of this question, see my article on 'Forgiveness' in the Series on 'Constructive Theology', *Expository Times*, li, pp. 16–21.

final penalty would be the loss of all living knowledge of Him. So long as he is in bondage to sin anything like fellowship with God is an impossibility. Upon this point New Testament teaching and Christian opinion are agreed. The conviction of all who seek to interpret the doctrine of the Atonement is that the problem of reconciliation is the problem that is thus created. How is sin, which sunders fellowship with God, to be set aside and annulled?

This problem, however, has its divine as well as its human side. Sin affects both sides of the relationship which it breaks. It is not only a barrier to our fellowship with God; it also prevents Him from entering into fellowship with ourselves. It has this consequence, not of course from any want or weakness in His love, but for the very opposite reason of its strength and depth. Love moves God to see us as we are, and thus to judge and condemn us in our sin. The common belief, that 'God hates the sin, but loves the sinner', has the strength and the weakness of such popular opinions. We cannot separate the two in this simple manner, since the sin does not exist, either as a state or an act, apart from the sinner. We are not thereby driven to conclude that God hates the sinner. The true view is that, by reason of the strength and reality of His love, He condemns both the sin and the sinner with a mercy that explores the hidden motive, a compassion that marks the hidden struggle, but with a certainty that will not compromise with truth.

A situation, then, of the utmost complexity is created by the fact of sin, as may be seen by the questions which it raises. How can man, in spite of his sin, enter into fellowship with God? In what way can God's judgment be replaced by His forgiveness? How can the relationship, broken by sin, be re-established, renewed, and consummated? In what manner can reconciliation be brought to pass?

In considering these questions it is not safe to assume that reconciliation is wholly a human problem, and that the only thing necessary is a change on the part of man. Sin, as we have seen, affects the relationships of both God and man; and for this reason, reconciliation will have its divine as well as its human side. Since this *divine* aspect of the problem is of greater difficulty, we may with advantage consider it first, and all the more because in reconciliation the initiative is, and must be, with God.

In what way, then, does God seek to reconcile men to Himself?

If our account of the relation of God to sin is true, it follows that reconciliation involves a new relationship with sinners. Instead of resting under His judgment, in reconciliation men come to know the joy of His forgiveness. We cannot, therefore, avoid the question, in what sense reconciliation involves a change in the attitude of God to man. We ought to consider this question with care, for swift answers are likely to be wrong.

. The problem cannot be solved by observing that in the New Testament God is described as reconciling men to Himself, but not as being reconciled to them, since it is not a question of hostility being replaced by love, or of law by grace. The only change that is conceivable in respect of God is in the different manifestations of His unchangeable love. Such a change, however, is not only conceivable, but is necessary in the relationships of the Loving Father with men.[1] In these relationships His attitude to saints and to sinners cannot be the same. He cannot look upon the evil and the utterly contrite with the same eyes, and think of them alike. Otherwise, His attitude to men would be void of ethical content, since no account would be taken of their actual moral and spiritual condition. It follows therefore that, in reconciling men to Himself, His attitude to sinners is transformed in consequence of a vital change in their relationship to Himself. This change, however, is not a change from hostility to love, but from the love which judges and condemns to a love which welcomes and receives men into fellowship with Himself.

It is only so long as we think of God in legal terms, contrasting His wrath as a Judge with His love as a Father, that we are tempted to fall back upon the dogma that He knows no change, with serious consequences to the doctrine of reconciliation. Once we intelligently believe that first, last, and always He is Love, and that Fatherhood is the highest category under which we can conceive or think of Him, we restore freedom to the Godhead, and are mentally prepared to appreciate at its true value that amazing outburst of restoring love which comes to us in the Crucified, when God sees us, no longer in the category of the godless, but in the company of penitent and obedient men. In this question a religious, and not only a philosophical, issue is at stake. Doubtless, the word 'change' is misleading, since it tends to suggest that which is arbitrary and fickle, but to reject it, without sup-

---

[1] This necessity, it need hardly be said, is not imposed upon God by an ethical standard external to Himself, but by the quality of His own nature, as the God of righteousness, truth, and love.

N

plying a better alternative, is more misleading still, since, in doing so, we may easily miss the transformed face which in reconciliation the Father turns to sinners. To miss this vision is to dim for ourselves and for others the very spirit of Christianity; to see it, and to make it known to men, is to present the Gospel in its richest colours.

We return, then, to the question of the part of God in reconciliation.

We have already claimed that God's restoring grace welcomes and responds to a changed attitude on the part of sinners. This statement is true, and it is a very precious element in the Gospel; but it is not by any means the whole truth concerning God's part in reconciliation. It cannot be consistent with the nature of the God of love that He should simply await a change in the disposition of sinners, much less that He should stand aloof until that change is visible. His grace demands that, along with His judgments, His restoring love should swiftly anticipate the penitence of the ungodly, calling it into being and making it possible for their response to be all that love requires. As the Creator also, who has set man in a world of trial, in which exposure to evil and the possibility of sin are essential to growth in freedom and in sonship, love requires that His reconciling work should be active, complete, and decisive. What form, then, will it assume? At this point we move in regions where sinful man cannot make claims upon a holy God. None the less, we may describe, not as man's right, but as grounded in God's love, two movements of His grace as essential to reconciliation: first, such a triumphant disclosure of His redeeming love that man can be in no doubt of His willingness to receive repentant sinners into fellowship with Himself; and, secondly, such an effective expression of this love, that the response of men, without which reconciliation cannot be achieved, will in kind and in degree be all that is demanded by His holiness and His love.

Beyond the dreams of men, the first of these requirements is fulfilled in the glory of the Incarnation, culminating in the Cross, the Resurrection, and the Session of the Son on high. The second, as we shall subsequently maintain, is met in the representative ministry of Christ, in His obedience, suffering, and sacrifice, in dependence upon which man turns from his evil ways to the joy of fellowship with God.

Modern Christianity has fully grasped the belief that the Cross is the commendation of the love of God. It is, indeed, the supreme service of all Moral Theories of the Atonement, set forth so frequently and with such variety of expression throughout the last two or three generations, that they have impressed this truth so deeply upon the Christian consciousness. Gone for ever are feudal and merely legal conceptions of God, except in quarters where the modern spirit finds it difficult to enter. In fact, our danger is that of being content with this great truth, deepened by a growing emphasis upon the suffering of God Himself, and by the claim that the love is objectively manifested.

The second truth, that the love of God is expressed in the representative ministry of Christ, has not received the same wholehearted recognition, largely because of the fear that it entails the acceptance of a doctrinal of penal substitution. This fear is groundless. In the submission of the present writer the doctrine of the Atonement will always suffer from grave understatement until this truth finds its rightful place in theology, as God's part in reconciliation and man's requisite for fellowship with Him.

We turn now to the *human* side of the problem of reconciliation, to the conditions which are necessary if man is to be reconciled and brought into fellowship with God.

No serious doubt obtains among Christian thinkers as regards these conditions. They are repentance, obedience, and submission to the will of God. Only when, in the power of the Spirit, man hates his sin and resolves to have done with it, only when he makes a filial response to the Father's love and accepts those judgments upon sin which not even forgiveness can remove, is reconciliation possible. 'I will arise and go to my father, and will say unto him, Father, I have sinned against heaven, and in thy sight: I am no more worthy to be called thy son; make me as one of thy hired servants'. These words are the perfect description of the filial response of man. It is the work of Christian preaching to make these conditions known, to explain their meaning and implications, without adding to them or making them more difficult, but also without representing them as simple, easy, or meritorious.

If man is to make this response, he must be certain of the reconciling love of God. He must not merely hear of it, or read of it; he must see it in terms of flesh and blood and upon the stage of history. In this fact lies the importance of the story of the Cross, contained in the Gospels, and interpreted in the New

Testament as the proof of the love of God, the manifestation of His will to receive men into His heart. Further, this response must, in a true sense, be that of man himself. A substituted repentance is a fiction; a vicarious obedience, in which he does not participate, is a contradiction; a submission made in his stead has neither power nor meaning. The reconciliation he needs is between God and himself, and no one, not even Christ, can impart it to him as an external gift.

So far there is general agreement, but not general recognition how tragic these conditions are if more cannot be said. It does not follow that, because man must make this threefold response, he must make it within the limits of his personality, in the more limited sense of that term. He can respond to the appeal of the love of God in virtue of his relationship to Christ, by entering into the significance of, and relying upon, His representative service and ministry for men.

In point of fact, in our own person and power we are not able to make the response to any adequate or complete degree. As I have pointed out elsewhere,[1] our penitence is fitful, limited, and often individualistic in the narrow sense of the word. Our obedience is restricted by our ignorance, waywardness, and frailty; our submission by the uprisings of rebellious nature and the presence of a clouded judgment. With any deep sense of the majesty of God, the purity of His judgments, and the wonder of His love, how can we suppose that, in themselves, our penitence, obedience, and submission enable us to enter into abiding fellowship with God? The supposition that this 'impossibility' might none the less be true, can be supported only by pleading the grace of God to such a degree that we represent Him as ready to accept the imperfect, the best response of which we are capable in our human frailty. Such a plea introduces complacency into the idea of God, dims our apprehension of His holiness, and weakens our grasp upon the truth of His infinite love. On all grounds it is surely much more probable that He will meet our need by providing wings for our penitence, a vehicle for our obedience, and a medium for our submission to His holy will.

We are brought back once more to the representative ministry of Christ for men. Our claim is that the fulfilment of the human conditions necessary to reconciliation depends on the work of Christ wrought on our behalf. By His death, as the Son of God

[1] *Jesus and His Sacrifice*, pp. 301*f.*

and the Son of Man, He brings to us a matchless revelation of the
love of God, and also accomplishes for us a saving work and service directed Godwards, into which, in the power of the Spirit,
we can enter through faith-union, sacramental communion, and
sacrificial living. Not only does this ministry meet our human
need, it also gives effect to the purpose of God in reconciling men
to Himself. In it God triumphantly makes known His will to
redeem and makes possible man's penitent and believing response
to His love.

Of necessity, the claim we have just made compels us to consider
the work of Christ in relation to reconciliation in greater detail. We
must now take up our earlier contention that His work is interpreted best by the aid of the sacrificial category, both as regards
its character and the manner in which its blessings are appropriated by men.

Now that we have examined more closely the nature of sacrificial ideas, and have set the idea of the representative ministry
of Jesus against the background of the doctrine of reconciliation,
we are able to do greater justice to this claim. Perhaps the most
striking feature of New Testament teaching concerning the representative work of Christ is the fact that it comes so near, without
actually crossing, the bounds of substitutionary doctrine. Paulinism, in particular, is within a hair's breadth[1] of substitution. If,
moreover, we read Mark x. 45 by itself ('a ransom for many'[2]),
apart from Mark xiv. 24 ('my blood of the covenant'), a similar
claim, although with less justice, can be made for certain aspects
of the teaching of Jesus, and, indeed, for not a little of New Testament doctrine concerning redemption, purchase, and mediatorial
action. In fact, a theologian who retires to a doctrinal fortress
guarded by such ordnance as Mark x. 45, Romans vi. 10 *f.*,
2 Corinthians v. 14, 21, Galatians iii. 13, and 1 Timothy ii. 5 *f.*, is
more difficult to dislodge than many New Testament students
imagine. Now this argument is not intended as a defence of substitution. On the contrary, in the earlier discussions we have
given reasons, which we believe to be conclusive, for rejecting
such teaching. The fortress can be outflanked, captured, and
dismantled. The point of our argument is the *significance* of the
fact that New Testament teaching about the representative work

---

[1] John Wesley uses this phrase of the relation of the Gospel both to Calvinism and
Antinomianism. Cf. G. C. Cell, *The Rediscovery of John Wesley*, p. 249.

[2] Cf. F. Büchsel's discussion of ἀντί, *Theol. Wort.*, i, p. 373.

of Christ is almost, but not quite, substitutionary. What is the explanation of this fact? How is it that it is incorrect to describe all that He does for men as accomplished 'in their stead', and yet inadequate, because ambiguous or wanting in precision, to say that it is wrought 'on their behalf'? This question cannot be said to have received sufficient discussion in studies of New Testament theology. Too often we are content to deny substitution without replacing it with any clear conception which can serve as a doctrinal basis for theology and for worship alike. None the less the nature of the explanation we require is sufficiently evident. We need a category of representative action, which describes a work of Christ for men so altogether great and inclusive that they cannot accomplish it for themselves, but which, far from being external to themselves, and therefore substitutionary, is a vital factor in their approach to God, because in it they can participate both by personal faith and in corporate worship. Our submission is that such a category actually exists, implicit in the sacrificial ideas which are so notably present in New Testament teaching. The work of Christ is vicarious because it is representative; it is representative because it is sacrificial.

In claiming that the work of Christ is sacrificial we are far removed from propitiatory ideas which are sub-Christian in their character and implications. We are, however, certainly in the realm of expiatory ideas, if we use this adjective, as the New Testament encourages us to use it, of the covering, cancelling, or annulling of sins which stand between ourselves and the blessedness of fellowship with God. Only when sins are annulled are the joys of forgiveness, justification, and reconciliation with God open to us as the amazing gifts of God's reconciling grace. These gifts are ours because of our repentance, our filial response to the love of God, and our readiness to accept His will for ourselves; but happily, not through these experiences as they are circumscribed within the poor confines of our individual life, but as they are enriched, transfigured, and glorified through our response to the self-offering of Christ for the world. The sacrificial category is peculiarly suitable for this doctrinal presentation because, in the use of the term 'blood', it suggests the thought of life, dedicated, offered, transformed, and open to our spiritual appropriation, and because in its basal suggestion of an offering which the worshipper may make his own, it supplies a religious pattern for the needs of thought, devotional culture, worship, and service.

We have already recognised that the sacrificial interpretation of the work of Christ carries us beyond the letter of New Testament teaching. This is notably true of its account of the representative aspect of that ministry, and the step is justified only if sacrificial ideas serve to interpret it more adequately.

We have seen that in the New Testament Christ's representative work is one of obedience to the Father's will and of self-identification with sinners, and that the emphasis laid upon His person, as the Son of Man and the Son of God, gives to His work a universal character. His ministry is not simply that of an individual within the race, but the service of the high priest of our humanity, the mediator of the new covenant between God and men. These are great and moving truths, essential to any worthy doctrine of the Atonement; but a prolonged study of the New Testament leaves one with the feeling that more remains to be said. It was at this point that we were conscious most of a gap in Pauline teaching. With clear eyes St. Paul marks 'the one act of righteousness' in the obedience of Christ (Romans v. 18 f.) and the fact that He was 'made to be sin on our behalf' (2 Corinthians v. 21); but he nowhere speaks of Him as voicing the sorrow and contrition of men in the presence of His Father. At one point only does he come within the range of this teaching, when he speaks of Christ 'at the right hand of God, who also *maketh intercession for us*' (Romans viii. 34). This truth, however, remains undeveloped, and elsewhere in his writings the work of intercession is attributed to the Spirit (Romans viii. 26). Our earlier suggestion was that the facts might have been otherwise if he had made a greater use of sacrificial ideas. In the Epistle to the Hebrews this development is arrested by the small attention given to the love of Christ, and in the Fourth Gospel by the extent to which sacrificial ideas are sublimated. In 1 John the thought of Christ as our Advocate with the Father emerges, but receives no further treatment. It follows, therefore, that if we are to give a fuller description of the representative ministry of Jesus, we must do so by developing its sacrificial implications. This, as we have seen, is the step taken by Campbell and Moberly, by the former in the claim that Christ made 'a perfect confession of our sins' and by the latter in the view that He offered 'the sacrifice of supreme penitence'. The psychological aspects of this teaching cannot be discussed here,[1] but the strongest protest must be made against the habit

---

[1] Cf. *Jesus and His Sacrifice*, pp. 310–12.

of dismissing the views of these theologians by objections[1] of which they were fully aware and which they met by anticipation. In Campbell's teaching the 'deep, multiform, all-embracing harmonious Amen of humanity, in the person of the Son of God, to the mind and heart of the Father in relation to man', is meant to be accepted by 'the Amen of our individual spirits'; it is not offered as a substitute for our own repentance.[2] In the case of Moberly, apart from his treatment of the doctrine of the Holy Spirit and his view of the Church and the Sacraments, the fact that he speaks of 'the *sacrifice* of supreme penitence' ought to be enough, for all who understand the meaning of sacrificial worship, to show that he means an offering in which we are to participate. Moreover, his position is perfectly clear in the following passage:

'We are now hundreds of miles from the thought of vicarious punishment. . . . Even if, in a sense, we may consent to speak of vicarious *penitence*; yet it is not exactly vicarious. He indeed consummated penitence in Himself, before the eyes, and before the hearts, of men who were not penitent themselves. But He did so, not in the sense that they were not to repent, or that His penitence was a substitute for theirs. He did so, not as a substitute, not even as a delegated representative, but as that inclusive total of true Humanity, of which they were potentially, and were to learn to become, a part. He consummated penitence, not that they might be excused from the need of repenting, but that they might learn, in Him, their own true possibility of penitence.'[3]

No doubt, in a realm where so much is obscure, and where direct New Testament teaching is wanting, there is need for further study and reflection, but there is every reason to claim that the sacrificial interpretation of the Atonement supplies the key, both for theology and for practical religion, to a fuller understanding of the representative ministry of Christ for men.

The sacrificial approach, however, has more to contribute to the statement of doctrine than the explanation it affords of the character of Christ's work; it also gives a new meaning to the believer's appropriation of that work in the life of the Christian Society; and it links together the ministry itself and the reception of its blessings within the bounds of a uniform conception.

The wealth of New Testament teaching on the subject of the appropriation of the blessings of Christ's redemptive work is astonishingly full even for those who know it best. The most distinctive feature of this teaching is the intimate manner in

[1] One is left with the impression that the knowledge of *The Nature of the Atonement* and *Atonement and Personality* revealed by these criticisms is neither recent nor profound.
[2] Cf. *The Nature of the Atonement* (4th ed.), p. 340. See also the whole of chap. vii.
[3] *Atonement and Personality*, pp. 283*f*.

which faith, sacramental communion, and sacrificial service are connected with the death of Christ. Faith, in the New Testament sense, is not only faith in Christ, but in Christ who died, and in its richest expression it becomes faith-union with the Crucified. In like manner, sacramental communion is a sharing in all that He has accomplished in His death, as well as fellowship with Himself. Even service in the most practical relationships of the Christian life is both personal loyalty to Christ as Master and Lord and the expression of a mystical fellowship with Him in His sufferings. We ought not, of course, to set the dual aspects in which these vital Christian experiences are described in opposition to each other, but equally we must take account of their distinctive reference to what Christ has accomplished for the believer. Too often, in the statement of doctrine, the experiences and the work of Christ have been sharply separated, and the Atonement has been identified almost exclusively with the latter, with results injurious to theology and to religion.

The deepest cause of the close relationship we have described must lie in the work of Christ itself, which inevitably evoked the kind of faith-union and communion in question. It may be claimed, however, that it was because that work was essentially sacrificial in character, and was apprehended as such, that the relationship assumed its most distinctive form. Otherwise, it might have remained exclusively a fellowship with Christ's person. We have maintained that the Fourth Gospel offers some evidence on this point, and we suggest that the claim is supported by the character of the Christian experience when the Atonement is interpreted mainly, or altogether, as a revelation of the divine love.

The reason why a sacrificial interpretation of the work of Christ relates faith to all that He does, as well as all that He is, is simple. It is due to the essential character of a sacrifice. A sacrifice is not simply an offering; it is an offering presented by a worshipper. Without an offering and a worshipper the sacrifice does not exist. The relative value of the two factors cannot be assessed; it depends altogether upon the character of the offering and the spirit of the worshipper. Nevertheless, even when the offering is as inexpressibly precious as the self-offering of Christ, the relationship of the individual to His ministry is an element of vital importance. The greatness of the opportunity of entering into the meaning of all that Christ has done cannot be exaggerated and there is no temptation to estimate His service as that of a substitute.

All the various aspects in which the relationship is expressed owe much to sacrificial ideas and practices. This is true of faith in particular.[1] Without any desire to minimize the enormous importance of the teaching of prophets[2] and psalmists, one cannot fail to see the deep impress which must have been left by centuries of Hebrew worship; so much so that the idea of faith-union with Christ may have been more intelligible to the first believers than it is to Christians of to-day. The same also may be said of sacramental communion.[3] St. Paul does not seem conscious of saying anything novel when he asks: 'Have not they which eat the sacrifices communion with the altar?' (1 Corinthians x. 18). Eating and drinking are associated with sacrifice the world over, and, as the ministry of Christ was understood, must have offered, in the Eucharist, a communal opportunity of sharing in its spiritual power. In like manner also the ideas of dying with Christ and suffering with Him in missionary toil and service present few difficulties to minds familiar with sacrificial worship. Finally, the idea of the Church, as the community of the redeemed, the New Israel of God, in which the individual enjoys in fellowship with others the experiences we have described, is most closely connected with a sacrificial interpretation of the work of Christ. To those who think of the Atonement from this point of view it appears entirely natural that such emphasis should be laid on the idea of a 'new covenant' in the teaching of Jesus (Mark xiv. 24; 1 Corinthians xi. 25), the earliest preaching (Acts iii. 25), and the theology of the Epistle to the Hebrews; that, in connexion with the death of Christ, the New Testament should speak of 'a people for God's own possession' (1 Peter ii. 9; cf. Titus ii. 14), 'a kingdom, and priests' from 'every tribe, and tongue, and people, and nation' (Apocalypse v. 9 f.), an *Ecclesia* which Christ loved, and for which He 'gave himself up' (Ephesians v. 25; cf. Acts xx. 28). The Church, in short, is the home of reconciliation, the highest expression it has received, the visible form and prophecy

[1] The resting of the hands upon the head of the sacrificial lamb may often have been a merely ritual act, but to the sincere and enlightened worshipper it would mean self-identification with the purity of the offering made to God.

[2] The relationship between the prophet and the priest was much closer than we have often been led to believe. Cf. A. C. Welch, *Prophet and Priest in Old Israel, passim.*

[3] In Hebrew religion, with the exception of the sin- and the guilt-offerings, the sacrifices ended in a religious meal. The meal was part of the sacrifice, not merely an appendage to it.

of the perfected Kingdom, when things on earth and things in heaven move harmoniously, obedient to the will of God. It would be idle to pretend that this splendid vision is for none save those who read the Atonement in terms of sacrifice. Our submission is the humbler claim that for those who see the Cross in this light no vision less sublime is possible.

In themselves, the experiences we have described are manifestly deeply ethical and spiritual, and thus reveal the worth of that apprehension of the Atonement with which they are so closely connected. When we contemplate the One great Sacrifice, we can do no other than repent. The idea that any one should do it in our stead is intolerable. Our penitence, however, is caught up into something greater and grander, because more perfect and universal, even the sorrow of Christ Himself for a world He bears upon His heart. So, too, our obedience, ours indeed, but not limited to the compass of our powers, is immeasurably enriched because it becomes one with the obedience of the Son of Man. And finally, our submission to the judgment of God, whereby we are able to say: 'Righteous art thou, O Lord, and upright are thy judgments',[1] is robbed of every sting of bitterness as we see His suffering; so that judgment is transformed into discipline, and discipline into growth in perfect love.

This enlargement of our spiritual powers comes to pass through no merits of our own, but through faith-union with the Crucified and dependence upon His sacrificial ministry. It is deepened through every act of eucharistic fellowship, and through daily experiences of self-denial in which we enter into the meaning of His sufferings. Always a theme for wonder, it cannot be a claim that needs defence that reliance upon such a ministry should be the living way to reconciliation with God. In this way God Himself draws near, revealing His love in the pierced hands of Christ and using them to raise us from sin to abiding fellowship with Himself. The spiritual possibilities of such an interpretation match the extent to which it meets the obstinate questions of the mind, while the wealth of its demand for adoration and worship equals its challenge to sacrificial service in the conflicts of daily life.

Now that we have set forth the doctrine of the Atonement in the light of sacrificial principles, we may return to the question raised at an earlier stage, whether this particular approach is

[1] Psalm cxix. 137.

still necessary as an aid in the presentation of doctrine. Granted that sacrificial ideas have deeply influenced the New Testament data, are they still necessary to the preservation of the New Testament witness? Cannot the doctrine be presented without the use of beliefs which are strange to the modern mind, however familiar they may have been in ancient times?

This demand, it seems to me, is sound in principle, and ought not to be resisted. It cannot be maintained that so rich and so living a doctrine as that of the Atonement is inextricably bound up with any particular vehicle or mode of presentation. The time may come when, without such a theory as the one presented in these pages, the doctrine will be set forth in terms more familiar to the modern mind. The only thing we have the right to ask, and it is a condition of the greatest importance, is that the *values* essential to the sacrificial theory shall be adequately preserved in any modern restatement. Christ must be presented as achieving a work of vital significance for us in our approach to God. Our relationship to Him must be of such an intimate character, in its personal, communal, and social aspects, that we can receive that living revelation of God which He brings to us, and at the same time, through Him and His service on our behalf, enter into the peace and blessedness of fellowship with God.

It is the very greatness of this task, as well as the many perils to which it is exposed, which leads us to doubt whether its fulfilment is likely, or even desirable, for some time to come. The failure of modern efforts to attain a simplicity of statement, combined with depth of perception, is a sufficient warning in this matter. It is no part of our intention in this work to attack other theories of the Atonement, and we have recognized to the full the positive value of what is known as the Moral Theory, especially in some of its most recent forms. Yet can it be other than disquieting that the view that the Cross is the crowning revelation and expression of the love of God should be all that so many theologians and preachers can say concerning the Atonement? Unless such a theory is extended, and brought into fuller accord with New Testament teaching, it is no more than an Ark of Refuge from which the theologian looks wistfully for a green leaf of hope in a world of cataclysm. It is the prolegomena to the doctrine of the Atonement, not the doctrine itself.

Why should we, moreover, in our efforts after restatement, look askance at strong words like 'blood', 'sacrifice', 'offering', 'covenant', when simple explanations can remove any misconceptions to which they are exposed. 'Propitiation' is certainly a word with which we may well dispense, and it may be that we shall find an equivalent for 'expiation' which will preserve the Old Testament ideas it has to serve. It is even possible that those to whom the word 'penal' is such a ground of offence may yet propose a term less menacing, but equally capable of describing those consequences of the sins of others into which the innocent do enter in the world as it is constituted, and in which the holy and the loving *must* participate if they are to minister to the saving of the guilty. In all these terminological changes, however, we must take care lest, in divesting ourselves of a traditional vocabulary, we find ourselves without a language and to all intents and purposes dumb. Even more important is it to observe sympathetically the ends which traditional theories sought to fulfil, and not to content ourselves with the recital of their patent deficiencies. These ends are precisely the objects for which we must provide in the restatement of doctrine, and the difficulty of meeting them will make us less confident of our powers and more appreciative of splendid attempts which failed. Finally, in these endeavours we shall always need to go back to the classical expressions of early Christian belief which we find in the New Testament, and we may be sure that if the most promising and imposing theological construction is not faithful to its witness, we have missed essential elements in the doctrine.

The more one considers the proposal to replace the sacrificial theory of the Atonement with a presentation more in harmony with modern ideas and ways of thinking, the less confident can we feel that the time is ripe for carrying it into effect. Our confidence also will probably be still further reduced if we reflect that so many of these ideas and ways of thinking are reactions to rejected beliefs rather than positive and creative modes of thought. Can we find, for example, in all our modern thought a better vehicle of expression for the exposition of the doctrine of the Atonement than the idea, fundamental to a sacrifice, of an offering which in humble faith we make our own? It is possible, too, that in any success we may attain, we shall discover that, instead of replacing the sacrificial theory, we have succeeded only in expressing it in other terms, that we have merely transposed it into another key, or translated its language into another tongue.

Some justification of this claim will be found if we observe that the sacrificial theory already contains within itself, or can easily be harmonized with, the positive merits of other theories. It is not possible to enter into that full discussion of the history of the doctrine which alone would completely substantiate this claim; yet even a survey of the leading ideas which have obtained in the great historical theories is sufficient to indicate its truth.

The idea of *deification*, which appears in some of the Greek Fathers, is a case in point. The words of Irenæus, for example, 'Jesus Christ because of His immeasurable love was made what we are, that He might make us completely what He is',[1] or the claim of Athanasius, 'He was made man that we might be made God',[2] express an idea by no means conditional upon the acceptance of a realistic philosophy. All that is vital to them is secured in that pursuit of the ideal of perfect love which cannot be avoided by those who take the sacrificial theory seriously in union and fellowship with the Crucified.

Again, the idea of a *ransom*, which appears and reappears in Greek and Latin theology for a thousand years, is preserved in the idea of a redemption from sin which is one side of the doctrine of reconciliation, without the necessity of asking to whom the ransom is paid; while the thought of *satisfaction*, freed from less than Christian conceptions of God, has its counterpart in the emphasis laid upon the necessity of meeting the ethical conditions of love in the work of reconciliation.

The thought of *substitution* is one we have perhaps been more anxious to reject than to assess; yet the immeasurable sense of gratitude with which it is associated in the religion of those who take small account of its intellectual difficulties, is too great a thing to be wanting in a worthy theory of the Atonement. In the sacrificial theory this sense of gratitude has its fitting basis, not only in the truth of love revealed and sin disclosed, but in the representative ministry of One who does for us a work we cannot do for ourselves, and yet invites us to share therein that so we may know reconciliation, peace, and sonship.

Least of all perhaps is the idea of *imputation*, so prominent in many forms of Reformation teaching, harmonious with a sacrificial theory; and yet the thought of a righteousness made available for us, and accessible to us, is preserved in this theory; not a righteousness infused into the soul by the operation of Divine Grace, as the Schoolmen taught, nor one set down to our account

[1] *Adv. Hær.*, Præf.   [2] *De Incarnatione*, 54, 3.

as popular Reformation teaching affirmed, but a righteousness attained through our faith-relationship to Christ and His sacrificial ministry.

Finally, the thought of *love revealed* 'by this singular grace shown to us, that His Son took our nature and persevered in instructing us both in word and deed even unto death', as emphasized in the great words of Abailard,[1] is the fundamental assumption of the sacrificial theory, with the added advantage that an objective expression for this love is affirmed, not alone because it comes to us in flesh and blood, but because in the ministry of Christ God provides all things necessary to our full reconciliation with Himself, 'so that kindled as we are by so great a benefit of the Divine Grace, true charity should henceforth fear nothing at all. . . .'[2]

When we survey these positive merits of the sacrificial theory of the Atonement, it would appear that our immediate task is not to replace it by some presentation, more congruous with modern thought, in which terms like 'blood', 'sacrifice', and 'offering' are quietly eliminated, but rather to put to the test its worth as a mode of intellectual apprehension and a basis for worship and service. The intellectual aspects of the theory have been our constant concern, and it will be well in conclusion to dwell more upon its religious and social merits. Especially important is the challenge this theory brings to us to give to the Eucharist a greater place in our worship. No less a Protestant than Karl Barth has recently reminded us that 'what we know to-day as the church service both in Roman Catholicism *and* in Protestantism is a torso'. 'The Roman Catholic Church', he affirms, 'has a sacramental service without preaching. . . . We have a service with a sermon but without sacraments. Both types of service are impossible.'[3] These words are worthy to be pondered, as well as his question: 'Would the sermon not be delivered and listened to quite differently and would we not offer thanks during the service quite differently, if everything outwardly and visibly began with baptism and moved towards the Lord's Supper?'[4] Such a development of worship as these words have in mind would inevitably follow if the sacrificial theory of the Atonement held the mind and thought of the Church.

---

[1] Cf. Migne edition of the works of Abailard, lib. ii, col. 836.

[2] *Ibid.*

[3] *The Knowledge of God and the Service of God*, p. 211.

[4] *Ibid.*

And what must be said of its devotional and social implications? The two must be considered together, because the one without the other cannot be healthy and strong. Every theory of the Atonement which gives prominence to the idea of reconciliation must have social implications, but in the sacrificial theory these are especially strong. In the first place, in seeking reconciliation through the work of Christ, the believer relies on One whose relationship, as the Son of Man, is with all men. The religious attitude of the believer is: 'Behold, the Lamb of God, which taketh away the sin *of the world*!' Again, he appropriates the blessings of that ministry by means of a faith, and a faith-union, which are interpreted to him by the Church as well as the Scriptures, and by a sacramental communion which in its nature is a communal experience. Further, he enters as a perfectly natural consequence into the fellowship of a Society which is the expression and the prophecy of the Kingdom of God. Finally, his relationship to his Lord, who presents to the Father the offering of His obedience, sorrow, and suffering, schools him in parallel experiences in his life in the world of men. In the fellowship of the sufferings of Christ, he also learns something of the bearing of sins, bows his head beneath the judgments of God upon a thoughtless and disobedient world, yearns after its reconciliation with God, and even voices the penitence it is powerless to utter. In all this he has no thought of doing or matching the work of Christ. Such a thought would be intolerable and even blasphemous to him. His activity is the inevitable expression of a life based on the truth of the One Sacrifice.

In a world hag-ridden by suspicion, hatred, and fear, torn by the ravages of war, and mocked by the dreams of peace, how great a mission is opened to the individual and to the Church by a presentation of the Cross steeped from beginning to end in the idea of sacrifice! As the Church of the Lamb, the New Israel must needs consist of 'men of every tribe, and tongue, and nation, and people'. As the writer of the Epistle to the Hebrews saw, we 'are come unto mount Zion, and unto the city of the living God, the heavenly Jerusalem, and to innumerable hosts of angels, to the general assembly and church of the firstborn who are enrolled in heaven, and to God the Judge of all, and to the spirits of just men made perfect, and to Jesus the mediator of a new covenant, and to the blood of sprinkling that speaketh better than Abel'.[1] This

---

[1] xii. 22–4.

communal emphasis in an Epistle which presents the work of Christ in terms of sacrifice is characteristic. The sacrificial theory of the Atonement meets the deepest spiritual needs of the individual, but always in the closest relation to a conception of reconciliation which stops at nothing short of the ideal of the world in fellowship with God.

(d) The Purpose of God and the Problem of History

Of the ultimate problems raised by the New Testament teaching which were mentioned at the end of the preceding chapter, the representative and the sacrificial aspects of the Atonement have been treated, and it now remains to consider the two remaining issues, the purpose of God as fulfilled in the ministry of Jesus and the significance of the Atonement as it is related to events in history and in time. We might claim to be absolved from the consideration of these questions, since they present difficulties which confront all theories of the Atonement, except those which are manifestly inadequate in treatment. All the way through our investigation, however, we have had these problems in mind, as, indeed, is inevitable in any detailed examination of New Testament teaching, not because the New Testament is concerned with philosophical problems as such, but because it is so deeply rooted in religious experiences which cannot be separated from theological and philosophical questions.

The first problem is that of showing how the Atonement, as the purpose of God, is fulfilled in the work of Christ, without accepting an immanental view of His Person which is not that of the New Testament, and without dividing the unity of the Godhead by setting the representative ministry of the Son of God over against the love, justice, and mercy of the Father. Something was said in answer to this question when the teaching of St. Paul was under consideration, because it is especially in Pauline teaching that the problem arises, but it must now be faced in the light of the New Testament teaching as a whole.

We have seen how decisively the New Testament describes the Atonement as the purpose of God. This truth is assumed in the sayings of Jesus and in the earliest preaching; it is the doctrinal assumption of the Epistle to the Hebrews, and it receives emphatic statement in the writings of St. Paul and St. John. Theology is compelled to work with the belief that God is active to redeem

o

in the Cross of Christ as the *sine qua non* of the doctrine of the Atonement.

No difficulty appears to arise if we accept, as an adequate explanation of the Person of Christ, the view that God, who is immanent in His universe and in man, expresses Himself fully and completely in the human personality of Jesus, who is divine only in the sense that in Him the process of revelation reaches its climax. Such an estimate of the Person of Christ, however, while not without its worth as a preliminary stage in the apprehension of the significance of His Incarnation, is manifestly far short of the New Testament witness and of the teaching of the Church in her creeds and confessions. We believe also that it utterly fails to do justice to the religious experience of multitudes of Christian believers who are not deeply interested in theological questions. In an immanental theology the difficulty we have specially in mind does not arise because within the human personality of Jesus the will of God to redeem humanity comes clearly to light. The relationship of the doctrine of the Atonement becomes mainly manward. There is no Godward relationship at all, except in the human response which the fulfilment of the divine purpose is intended to evoke.

It is just at this point that the inadequacy of such a doctrinal scheme emerges. The claim that a full manifestation of the divine love is assured is mere assertion. If we could entirely divest ourselves of the religious influences of theories of the Atonement which, as intellectual constructions, we have discarded, we should find that we have received a revelation of the divine love greater only in degree than that which comes to us in the death of Socrates. Moreover, the purpose of God, which the theology in question appears to safeguard, is not fulfilled, since it does not meet the problem of sin or provide a sufficient means of reconciliation. Man is left to respond, certainly with the aid of divine grace, to an indication of love which provides him with nothing in which he can rest, and on which in his frailty he can rely, save an unconfirmed telegram from heaven that all is well. Immunity from philosophical problems on the basis of such a theology is too dearly purchased. We merely escape them by reason of its poverty. It is far better to accept a theology which leaves us puzzled than to buy clarity at the cost of inadequacy.

Happily, the dilemma described is not the actual situation. A theology which includes the recognition of a representative and sacrificial ministry of Jesus gives power and meaning to the purpose of God. God Himself provides this ministry and in it gives decisive effect to the burning of His love. All that man needs to find himself in the Father's home is provided. God not only declares His love; He embodies it; He goes out to seek men, raises them in their despair, and supports them in their journey from the far country. This He does in Christ, but in His Work as well as in the revelation which shines in His Person. Indeed, the revelation in His Person becomes incandescent in His Work.

The basis for this theology can be nothing less than the doctrine of the Trinity in unity. This doctrine supplies the only philosophical basis which is adequate to a complete doctrine of the Atonement, because it excludes any activity on the part of the Son, or the Spirit, which is not equally the work of the Father. For those who accept this doctrine there can be no question of division within the Godhead in consequence of the Atonement. On the contrary, the way is entirely open to speak of the purpose of the Father, the work of the Son, and the inspiration of the Holy Spirit, without surrendering the unity of the Godhead.[1]

Admittedly, our argument depends upon the acceptance of the doctrine of the Trinity. On this question all that we can say here is that a reverent acceptance of this holy mystery is possible because it provides the only satisfactory basis to the witness of New Testament teaching and belief, because it comes to us under the aegis of the Creeds of the Undivided Church, and because any alternative presentation of the nature of the Godhead fails to provide a sufficient explanation of the relation of the revelation of God to the universe, to history, and to man. We affirm its truth, not as a matter of intellectual demonstration, but as the ultimate assumption without which we can give no rational account of God, man, and the world.

Against this background of belief, it does not seem to us that our account of the representative and sacrificial ministry of Christ raises serious difficulties. This claim cannot be made for all 'satisfaction' theories. The theory of Anselm, for example, with its emphasis upon the work of Christ as a satisfaction of the wounded honour of God, threatens the unity of the Persons of the Godhead; but it does this, not because it is an attempt to meet con-

---

[1] This possibility exists because, within the unity of the Godhead, the term 'person' is used with a richness of meaning to which personality as we know it in man furnishes only a faint analogue.

ditions grounded in the Being of God which are necessary to the attainment of reconciliation, but by reason of its fundamental assumption that the conditions are those of wounded honour. The sole conditions necessary to reconciliation are those of love; they are not legal or governmental, but ethical and spiritual.

If our theory of the Atonement presupposed the over-coming of the Father's hostility by the compassionate work of Christ; if it entailed the satisfaction of legal obligations; we could not resist the objection that, thereby, the unity of the Godhead would be broken. The attitude of the Father would be one; that of the Son another; and the Atonement would be the doctrine of how the Son succeeded in changing the Father's judgment of sinful men.

Our account of the work of Christ is entirely different from this. That which Christ expresses for men is obedience, penitence, and submission. What is there in any of these aspects of His self-offering which in the slightest degree stands in opposition to the mind and will of the Father? Every one of them is a necessary characteristic of the mind of men seeking to enter into fellowship with God. Without them fellowship is impossible. Every one of them, moreover, represents a state of mind which the Father longs to welcome. Nay, on our submission, they are all expressions of a relationship which He Himself makes possible by the gift of His Son. So far, therefore, from the work of the Son implying any division within the Godhead, it is the expression of its unity in action. God is supremely Himself in that He reconciled men to Himself through the representative and sacrificial ministry of His Son.

We now turn to the second of the two questions under consideration. How can the death of Christ, as an event in history and in time, be related to the eternal reconciling purpose of God for all men, in all ages, and in all circumstances?

This question also we have had in mind at several points in the inquiry, and it is fitting that it should come before us again as the final problem of our investigation. To the present writer it seems the most difficult question of all, and without presuming to be able to solve it completely, he will offer suggestions prompted by the sacrificial theory which contribute to the solution.

Let us put to ourselves this problem in its most naked and challenging form.

As near as we can compute, Jesus died upon the Cross at about three o'clock on the afternoon of the fourteenth day of the Jewish month of Nisan, A.D. 29. If, as we have maintained, His ministry of representative suffering and obedience is the means by which God reconciles men to Himself, what are we to say of those who lived before that date, and of all since who, for one reason or another, have not been able to accept His claims, and, in consequence, have not made that response to His ministry which leads to reconciliation with God? This putting of the question, as we shall claim later, unduly narrows the work of Christ by concentrating the issue upon the fact of His death; but it has the merit of throwing the problem into its most pressing form.

In answering this question, there are various tentative replies which we have no option but to dismiss. We cannot argue, for example, that the self-offering of Christ avails in itself, irrespective of man's response, since this argument is excluded by the nature of the theory we have advanced, in which the offering together with the response are the sacrifice.

Again, it is not satisfactory to argue that those who lived before the time of Christ are judged prospectively in the light of the ministry of Christ subsequently to be fulfilled. This claim would imply two standards in the conditions of reconciliation, a lower and provisional standard and a higher and more perfect standard. Moreover, to the degree that the former is acceptable to God, the latter is seen to be unnecessary, or at most only supplementary. Again, the personal relationship between the believer and the work of Christ disappears, and the essential character of the One Sacrifice is altered. Equally is this conclusion valid with respect to all who have not yet heard of Christ, or, having heard of Him, have not accepted Him as the mediator in things pertaining to God.

If, however, we dismiss these answers, as we must, we cannot ease the problem by admitting that, apart from Christ, men can know reconciliation in the full sense of the word. This admission would not be true. We cannot agree that the Old Testament saints enjoyed that depth and intimacy of fellowship with God open to men in New Testament times. Courtesy, moreover, and easy tolerance must not allow us to admit that men to-day who do not know the power of Christ have, or can have, a knowledge of reconciliation comparable to that known by the simplest believer. The claim that the reverent agnostic is nearer God than the theologian supposes is a delusion. Such men may attain a high standard of morality, though much more rarely than is often supposed, but, in any case, until they are conscious of their sin and of their dependence upon God, they are not even in a position to approach the ideal of fellowship with Him.

In order to deal satisfactorily with the problem under discussion, we must expand the statement of the work of Christ with which we began. As we have fully shown, it is not alone by His death that Christ brings us to God; it is also by His life, resurrection and present mediatorial ministry on high. Calvary is the focal point of that ministry in terms of history; it is the place where we see God in the plenitude of His reconciling love. This fact forces upon us the recognition that the Atonement is richer and fuller than anything we can observe in history and in time. It must be eternal in character, however impossible it may be for us, as the creatures of time, to describe what this statement implies. Wherever and whenever sin has existed, the Son of God has borne its consequences upon His heart, voicing the penitence of the impenitent and the submission of the rebellious. He is in truth the very Lamb of God slain from the foundation of the world.

If the Atonement is viewed in this light, it is possible to maintain that, whenever men have trusted in God, without knowing or accepting the claims of Christ, they have implicitly rested in that which He has done on their behalf. Like the woman who touched the hem of Christ's garment, they have relied on One whose greatness exceeds their comprehension and whose ministry of redeeming love transcends their wildest dreams. This view cannot be so easily dismissed as that mentioned earlier, in which forgiveness and reconciliation rests upon a prospective work of Christ, accomplished first in the fulness of time. Here faith rests on a work which is eternal, operative always and before the Son of God takes flesh and dies upon the tree. The Incarnation, culminating in death, is the expression in time of the Eternal Sacrifice within the heart of God.

It is difficult to resist the fascination of this doctrine, and for my own part I should be slow to deny its truth. Nevertheless, it needs to be supplemented by another solution of the mystery, which accepts the truth of the Eternal Sacrifice, but gives a greater place to the exercise of faith in Christ and reliance upon His redemptive ministry in time and in eternity.

Have we, in the statement of Christian doctrine, given sufficient importance to the revealing hour of death and to immortality? Must not many a delusion, due to ignorance and the limitations of our earthly existence, fall away in the fuller life that lies beyond? There is reason to hope that the ministry of Christ avails there as here, since He ever liveth to make intercession for us, and that it is open to men of ancient times and to those who have not proved its power upon earth. Who to-day will claim that the hour for reconciliation is sped when we pass from the house of our mortality?

These are reflections which rightly arise within the mind as we contemplate the divine drama of reconciliation. We cannot demonstrate their truth or proclaim them with the urgency of a Gospel. The Christian revelation concentrates on the present, upon this world of time and space as the scene of choice and of entrance into fellowship with God; and only as a protest against the unwarranted limitation of the range of the divine purpose can we cherish the larger hope. This concentration of interest is for our good, since it spares us from the perils of a false otherworldliness, in that we are called to decision here and now both for ourselves and the world in which we live.

Of the immediate duty which confronts us, as individuals and as members of Christ's Church, there can be no doubt. We are called, first, to seek reconciliation for ourselves through the power of Christ's ministry for men; secondly, to proclaim reconciliation to men as a present opportunity for them, and as the only solution for the sorrows of our troubled war-ridden world; thirdly, so to order our worship that through it men may find the path which leads to abiding fellowship with God; fourthly, to end the divisions which tear the Body of Christ, which is His Church, that more fully it may be the symbol and home of reconciliation in the world; and lastly, at all times to lift up our eyes to God, who alone brings good out of evil, peace out of confusion, and who will yet bring His universe into full harmony with His perfect love.

INDEX OF NEW TESTAMENT PASSAGES

INDEX OF PROPER NAMES